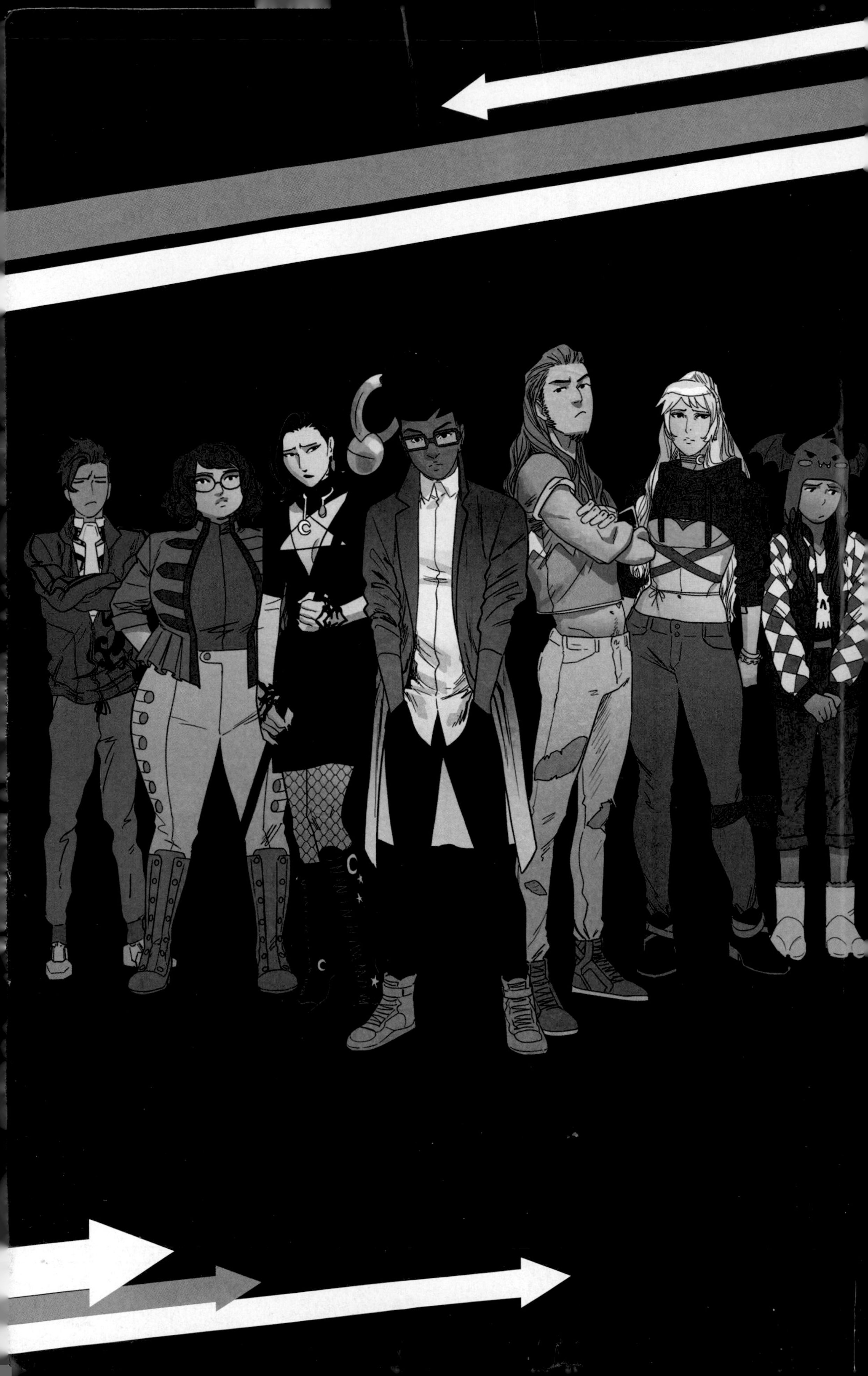

THE RUNAWAYS FINALLY GOT A BREAK FROM DISASTERS — BUT NOT FROM REVELATIONS. ON A DAY TRIP THROUGH TIME TO WITNESS THE MIGRATION OF THE CALIFORNIA BLUE BUTTERFLY, VICTOR SHARED HIS MOST PAINFUL SECRET WITH GERT. AND THEN THEY KISSED EACH OTHER FOR THE FIRST TIME. MEANWHILE, AFTER A BLACK-TIE GALA FOR KAROLINA'S PARENTS' LEGITIMATE CHARITY, NICO FINALLY KISSED KAROLINA. BEFORE ANY OF THE OTHERS COULD LEARN OF THESE TECTONIC SHIFTS IN THEIR FAMILY'S FOUNDATIONAL DYNAMICS, A FOUNDING FAMILY MEMBER REAPPEARED ON THEIR UNDERGROUND DOORSTEP.

RUNAWAYS

That was Yesterday

WRITER **RAINBOW ROWELL**

#13-14

ARTISTS **DAVID LAFUENTE**
WITH **TAKESHI MIYAZAWA** (#14)
COLOR ARTISTS **JIM CAMPBELL**
WITH **MICHAEL GARLAND** (#14)

#15-18

ARTIST **KRIS ANKA**
COLOR ARTIST **MATTHEW WILSON**

LETTERER **VC'S JOE CARAMAGNA**
COVER ART **KRIS ANKA**
ASSISTANT EDITOR **KATHLEEN WISNESKI**
EDITOR **NICK LOWE**

RUNAWAYS CREATED BY **BRIAN K. VAUGHAN** & **ADRIAN ALPHONA**

ASSOCIATE MANAGING EDITOR **KATERI WOODY**
COLLECTION EDITOR **JENNIFER GRÜNWALD** | ASSISTANT EDITOR **CAITLIN O'CONNELL** | ASSOCIATE MANAGING EDITOR **KATERI WOODY**
EDITOR, SPECIAL PROJECTS **MARK D. BEAZLEY** | VP PRODUCTION & SPECIAL PROJECTS **JEFF YOUNGQUIST**
SVP PRINT, SALES & MARKETING **DAVID GABRIEL** | BOOK DESIGNER **JAY BOWEN**
EDITOR IN CHIEF **C.B. CEBULSKI** | CHIEF CREATIVE OFFICER **JOE QUESADA**
PRESIDENT **DAN BUCKLEY** | EXECUTIVE PRODUCER **ALAN FINE**

RUNAWAYS BY RAINBOW ROWELL & KRIS ANKA VOL. 3: THAT WAS YESTERDAY. Contains material originally published in magazine form as RUNAWAYS #13-18. First printing 2019. ISBN 978-1-302-91413-4. Published by MARVEL WORLDWIDE, INC., a subsidiary of MARVEL ENTERTAINMENT, LLC. OFFICE OF PUBLICATION: 135 West 50th Street, New York, NY 10020. © 2019 MARVEL No similarity between any of the names, characters, persons, and/or institutions in this magazine with those of any living or dead person or institution is intended, and any such similarity which may exist is purely coincidental. **Printed in Canada.** DAN BUCKLEY, President, Marvel Entertainment; JOHN NEE, Publisher; JOE QUESADA, Chief Creative Officer; TOM BREVOORT, SVP of Publishing; DAVID BOGART, Associate Publisher & SVP of Talent Affairs; DAVID GABRIEL, SVP of Sales & Marketing, Publishing; JEFF YOUNGQUIST, VP of Production & Special Projects; DAN CARR, Executive Director of Publishing Technology; ALEX MORALES, Director of Publishing Operations; DAN EDINGTON, Managing Editor; SUSAN CRESPI, Production Manager; STAN LEE, Chairman Emeritus. For information regarding advertising in Marvel Comics or on Marvel.com, please contact Vit DeBellis, Custom Solutions & Integrated Advertising Manager, at vdebellis@marvel.com. For Marvel subscription inquiries, please call 888-511-5480. **Manufactured between 2/15/2019 and 3/19/2019 by SOLISCO PRINTERS, SCOTT, QC, CANADA.**

10 9 8 7 6 5 4 3 2 1

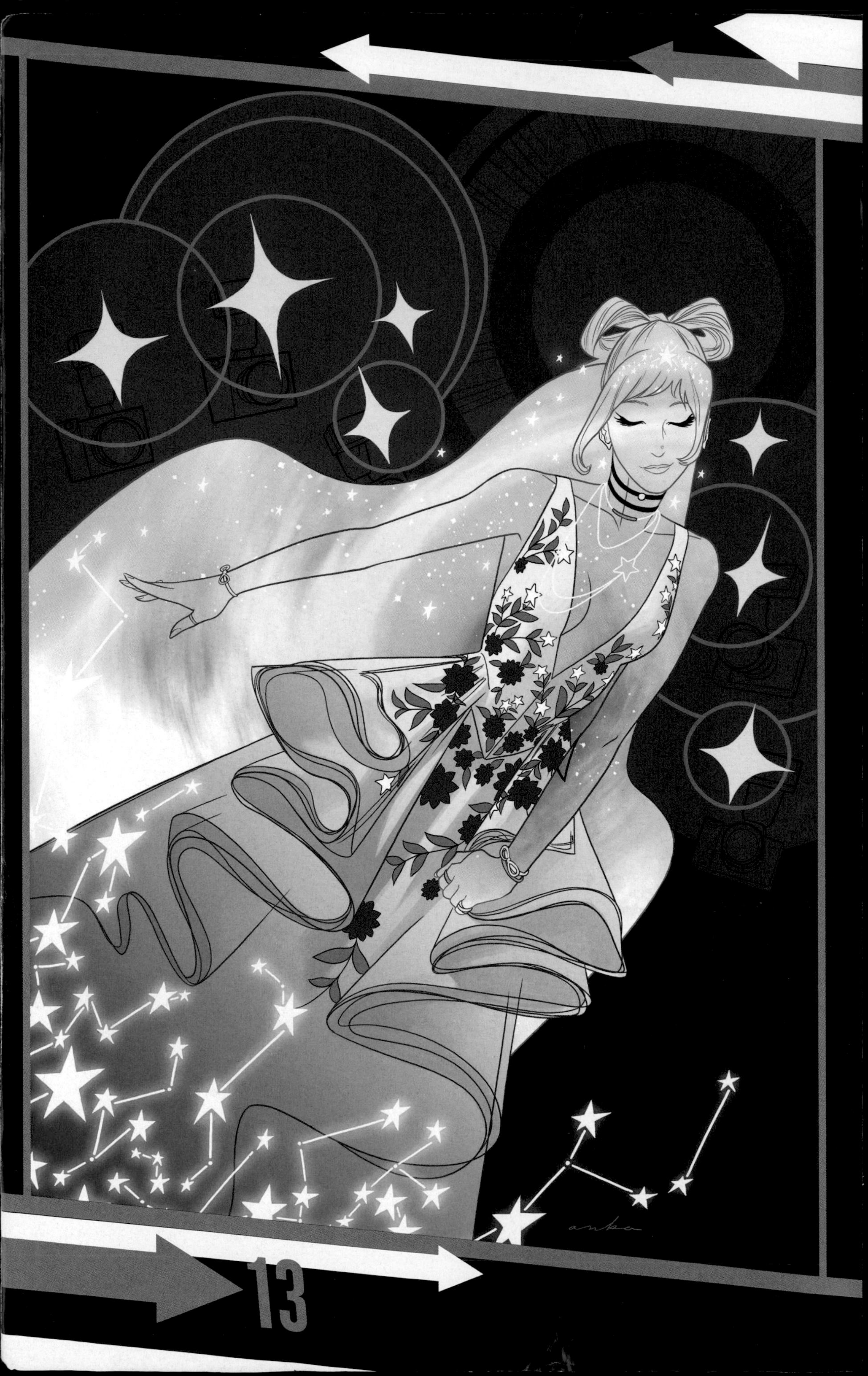
13

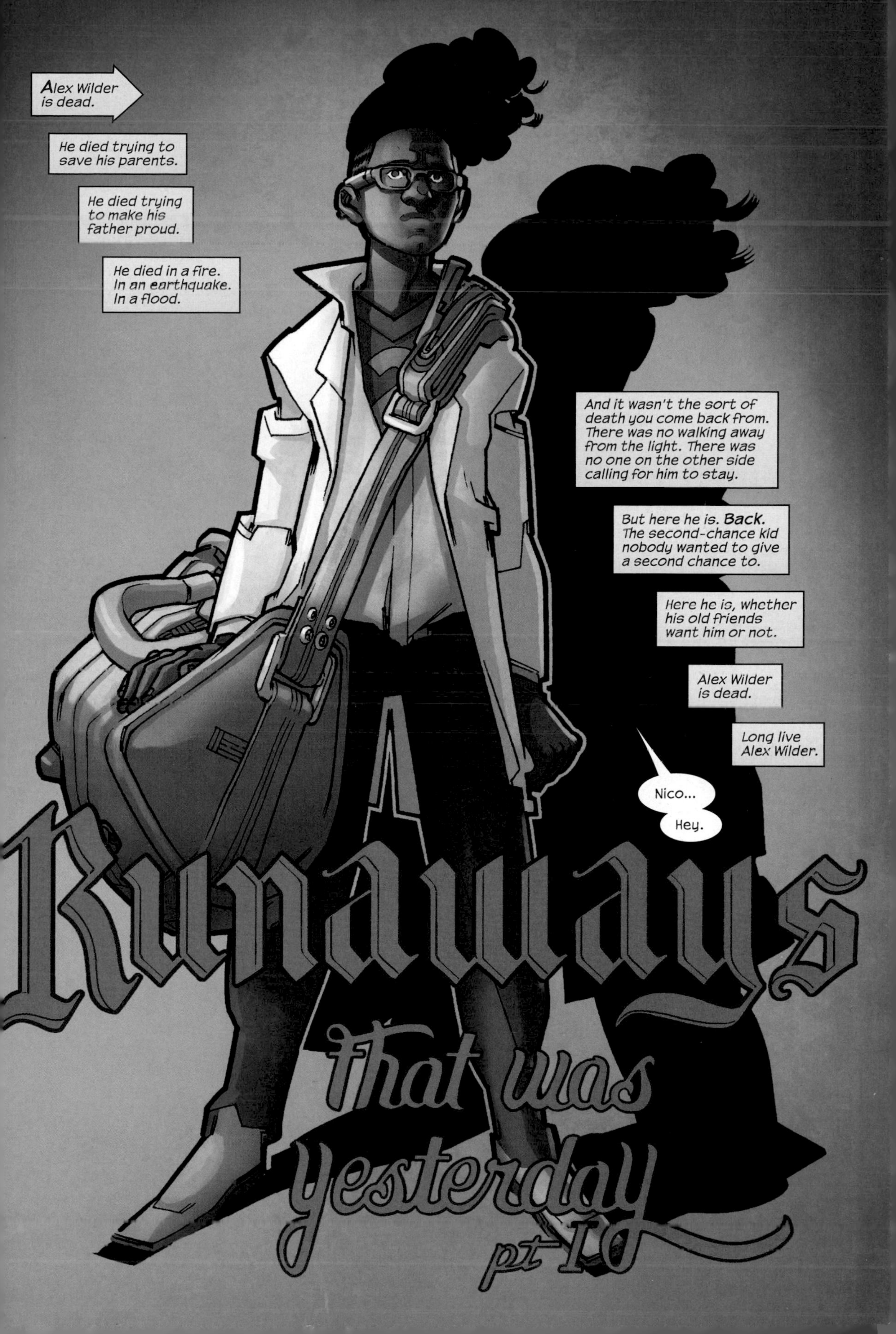
Alex Wilder is dead.
He died trying to save his parents.
He died trying to make his father proud.
He died in a fire. In an earthquake. In a flood.
And it wasn't the sort of death you come back from. There was no walking away from the light. There was no one on the other side calling for him to stay.
But here he is. Back. The second-chance kid nobody wanted to give a second chance to.
Here he is, whether his old friends want him or not.
Alex Wilder is dead.
Long live Alex Wilder.
Nico...
Hey.
Runaways
that was yesterday
pt I

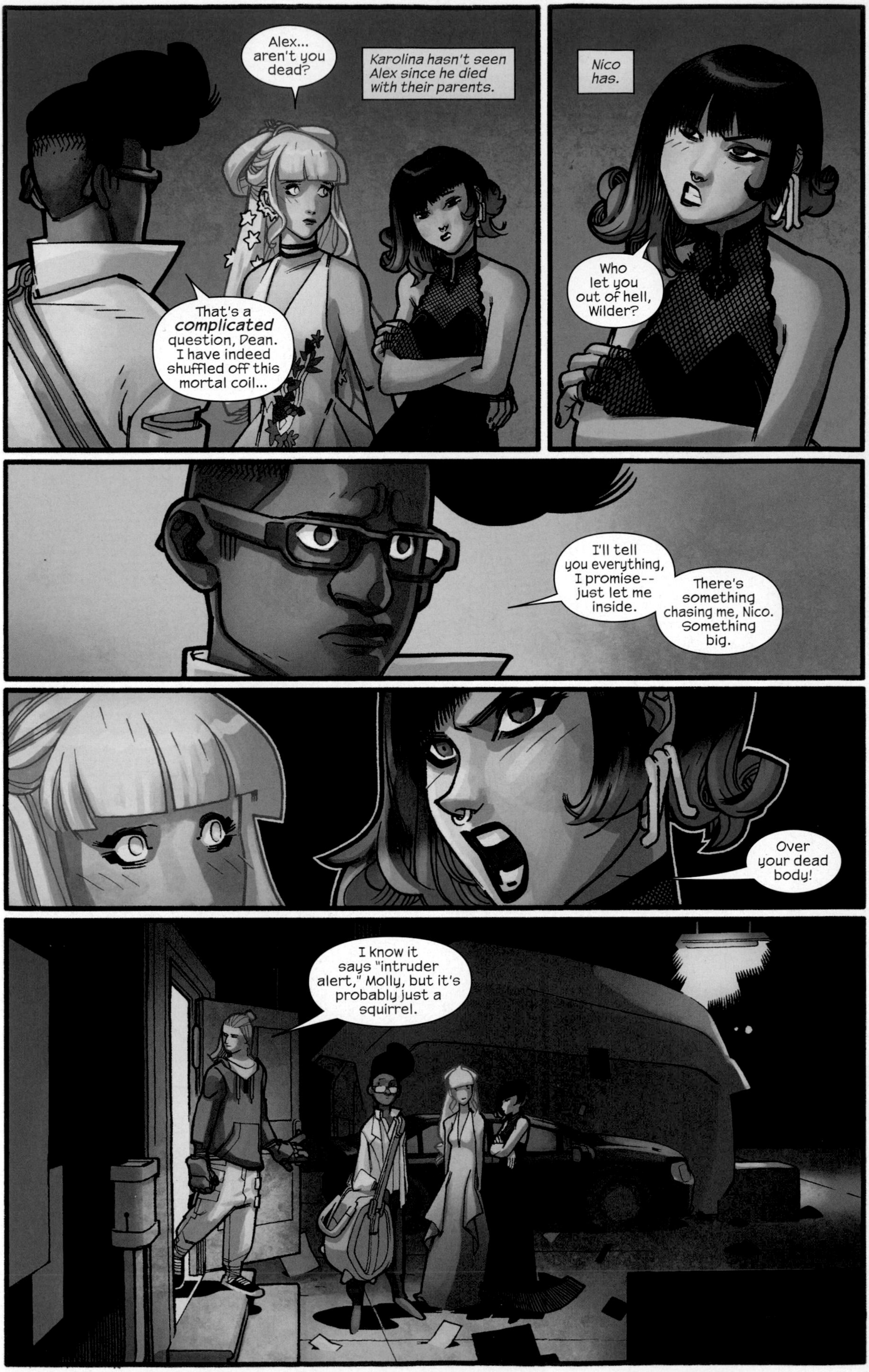
Alex... aren't you dead?
Karolina hasn't seen Alex since he died with their parents.
That's a complicated question, Dean. I have indeed shuffled off this mortal coil...
Nico has.
Who let you out of hell, Wilder?
I'll tell you everything, I promise-- just let me inside.
There's something chasing me, Nico. Something big.
Over your dead body!
I know it says "intruder alert," Molly, but it's probably just a squirrel.

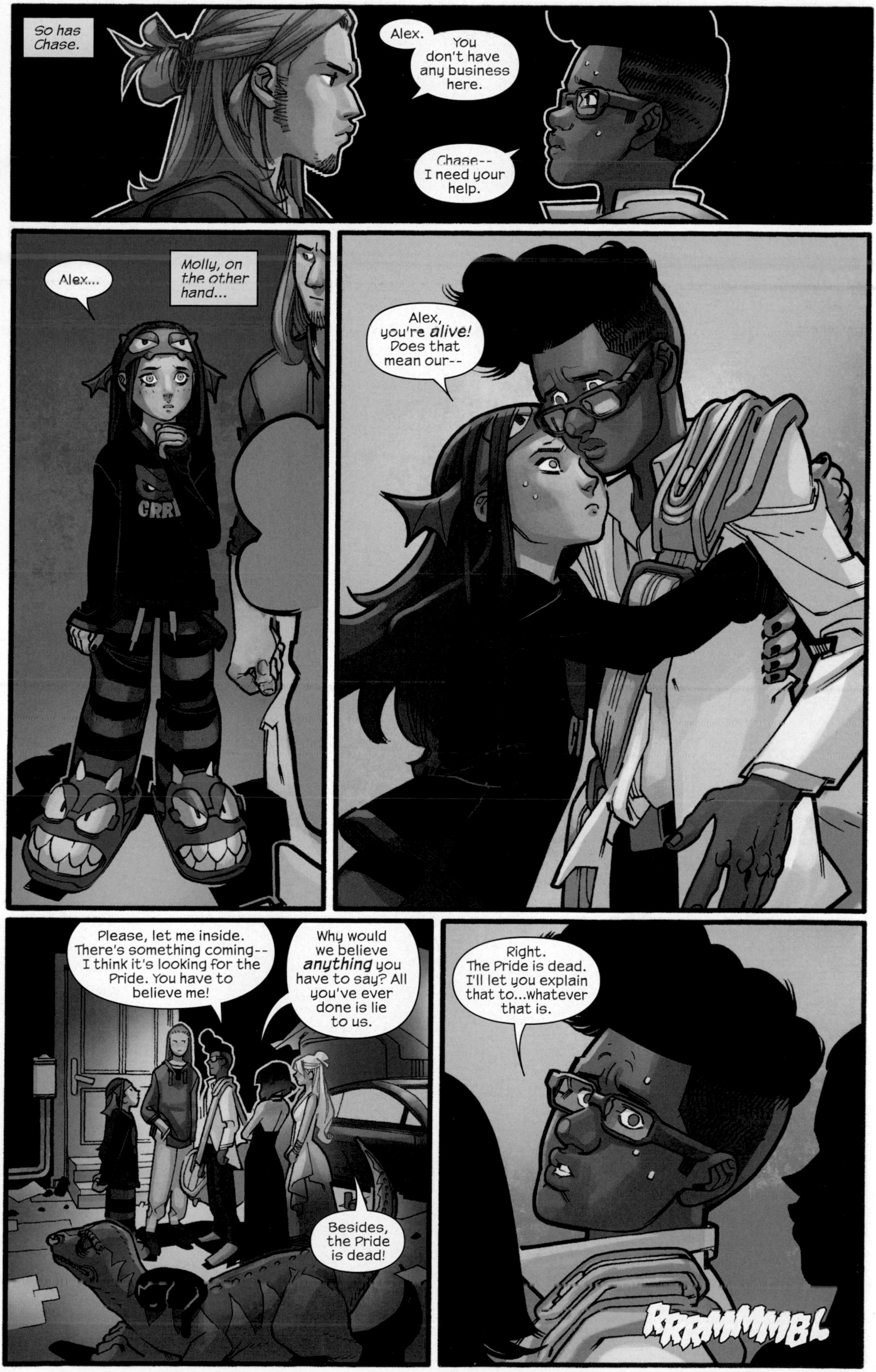

So has Chase.
Alex.
You don't have any business here.
Chase-- I need your help.
Alex...
Molly, on the other hand...
Alex, you're *alive!* Does that mean our--
Please, let me inside. There's something coming-- I think it's looking for the Pride. You have to believe me!
Why would we believe *anything* you have to say? All you've ever done is lie to us.
Besides, the Pride is dead!
Right. The Pride is dead. I'll let you explain that to...whatever that is.
RRRMMMMBL

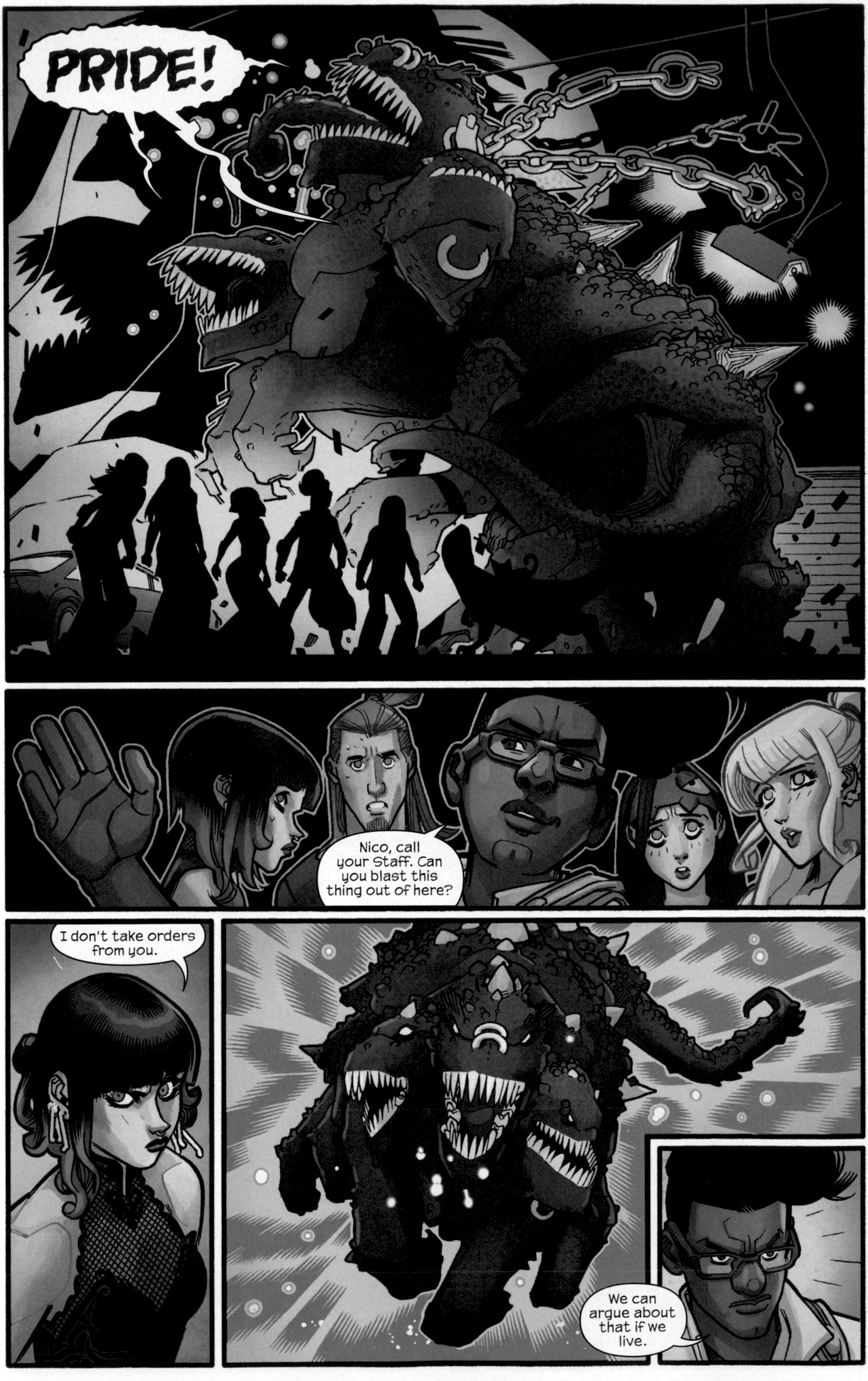

PRIDE!
Nico, call your Staff. Can you blast this thing out of here?
I don't take orders from you.
We can argue about that if we live.

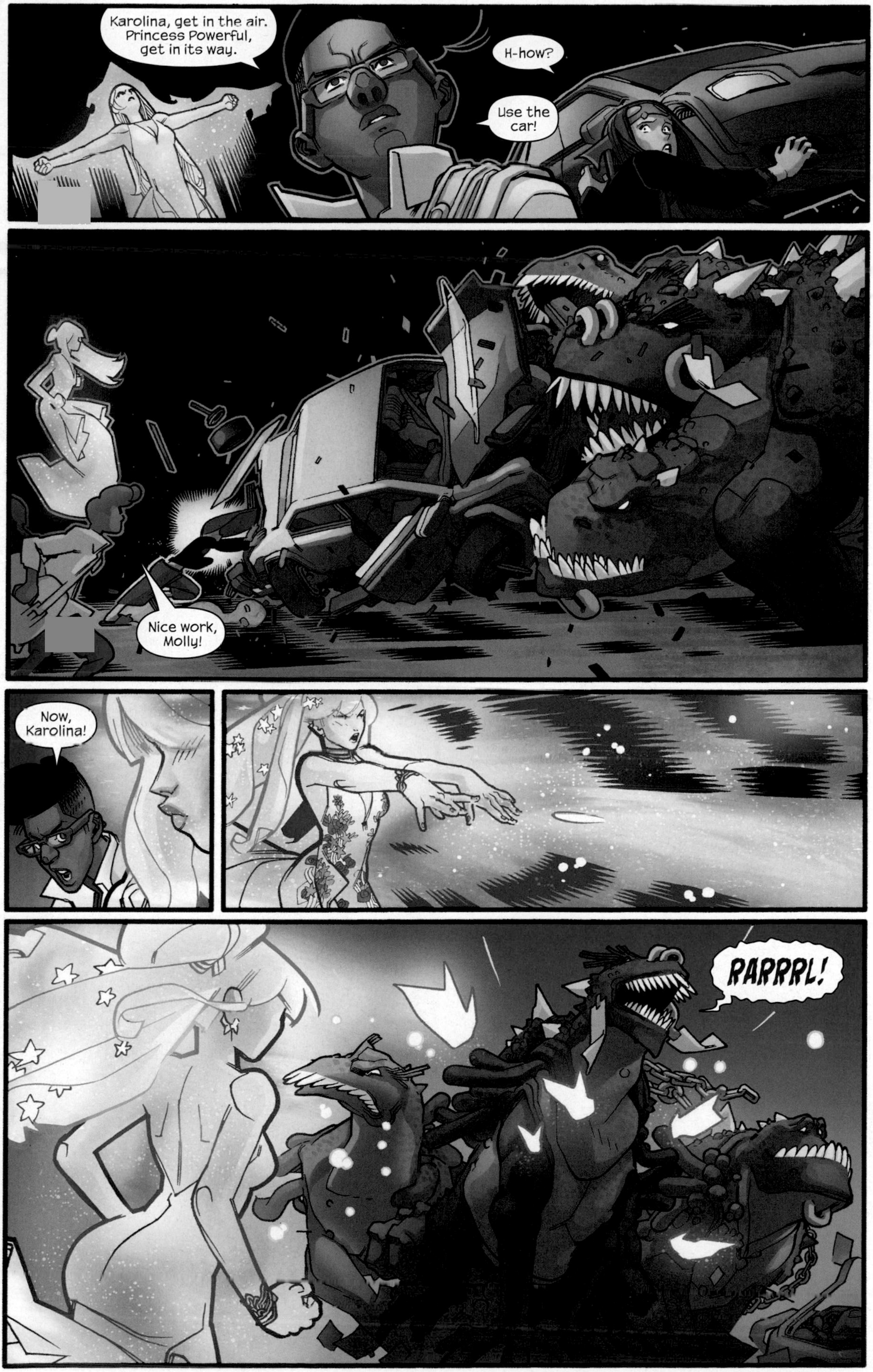
Karolina, get in the air. Princess Powerful, get in its way.
H-how?
Use the car!
Nice work, Molly!
Now, Karolina!
RARRRL!

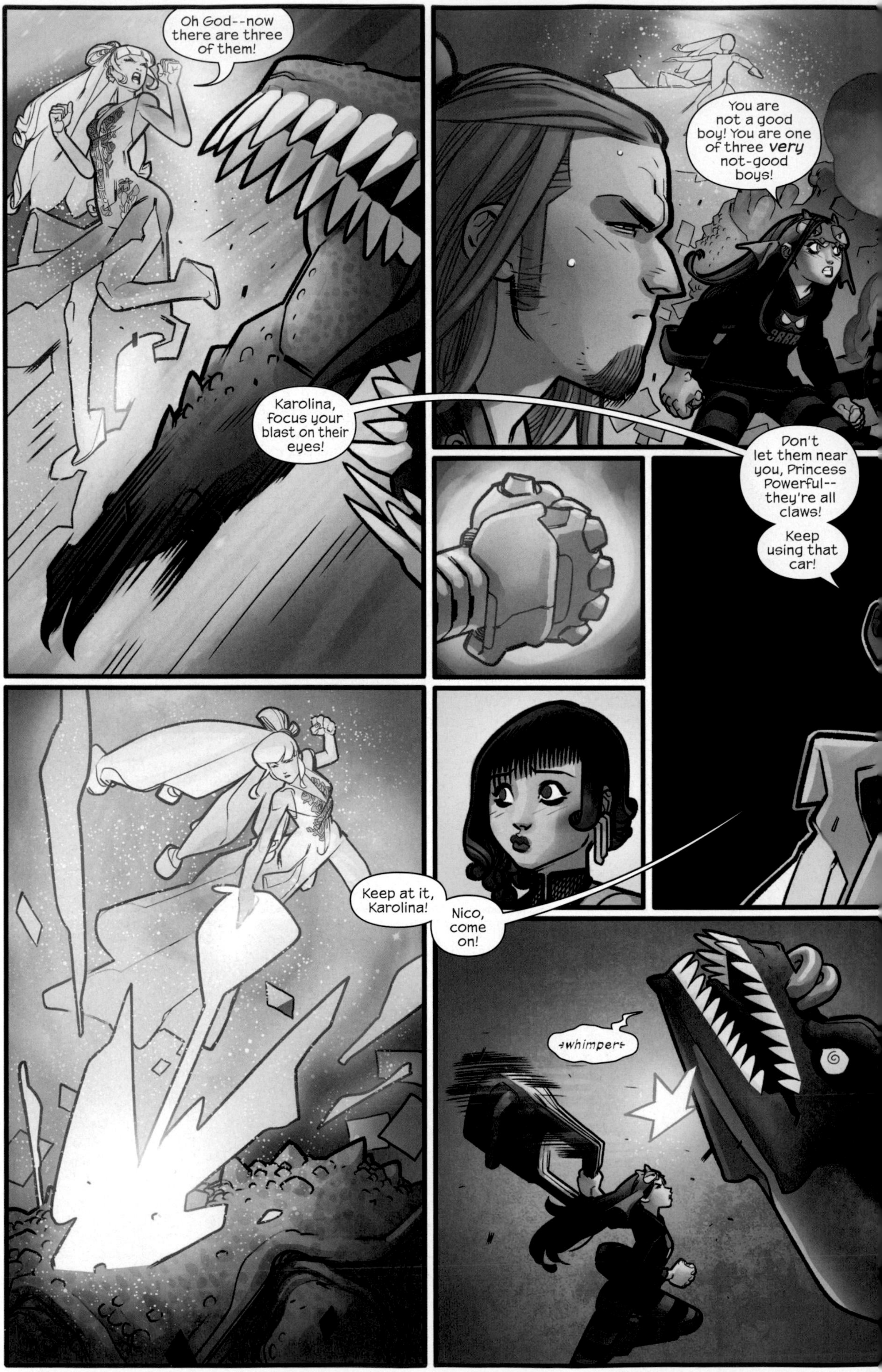
Oh God--now there are three of them!
You are not a good boy! You are one of three *very* not-good boys!
Karolina, focus your blast on their eyes!
Don't let them near you, Princess Powerful--they're all claws!
Keep using that car!
Keep at it, Karolina!
Nico, come on!
whimper

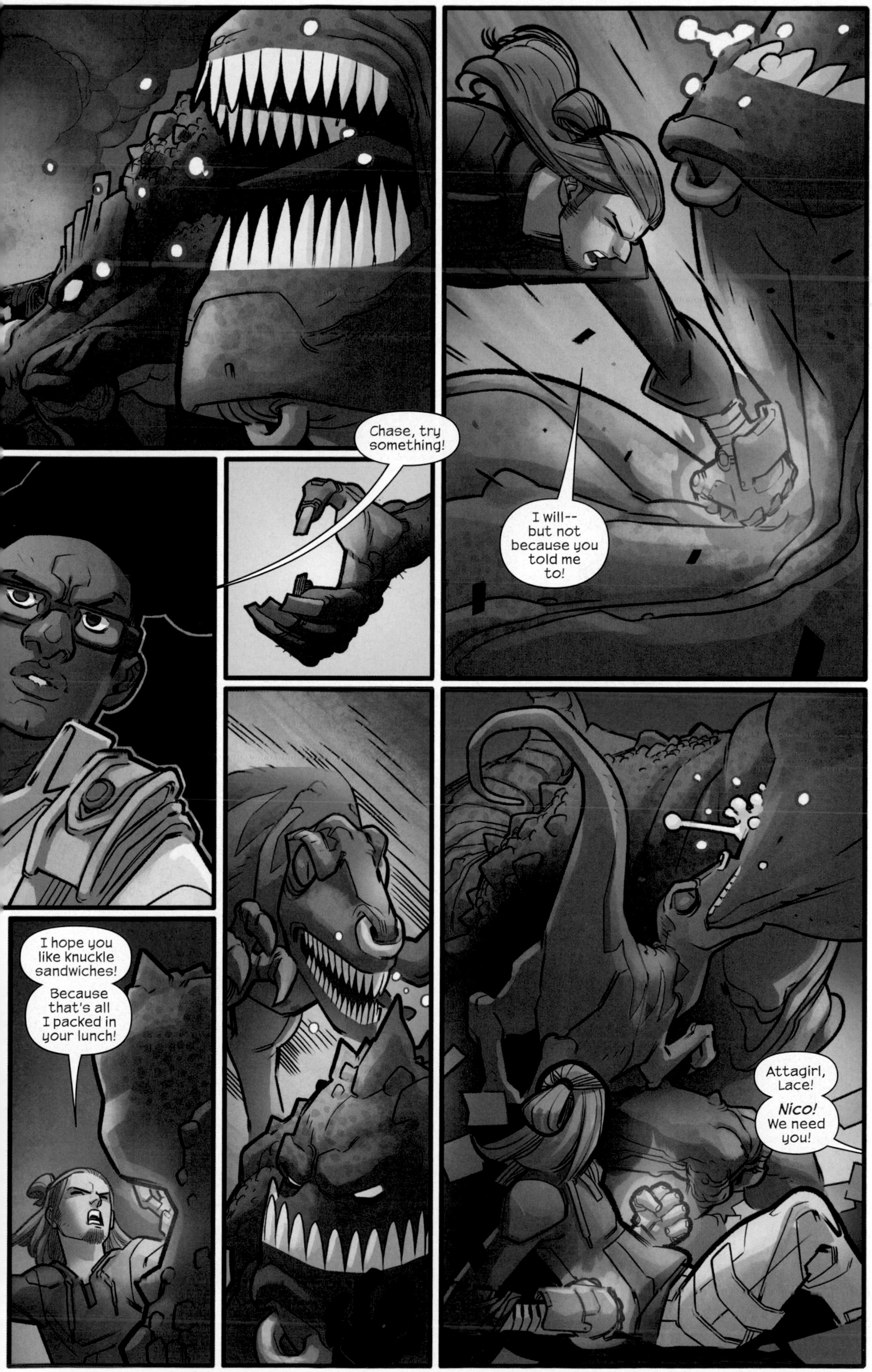

Chase, try something!
I will-- but not because you told me to!
I hope you like knuckle sandwiches!
Because that's all I packed in your lunch!
Attagirl, Lace!
Nico! We need you!

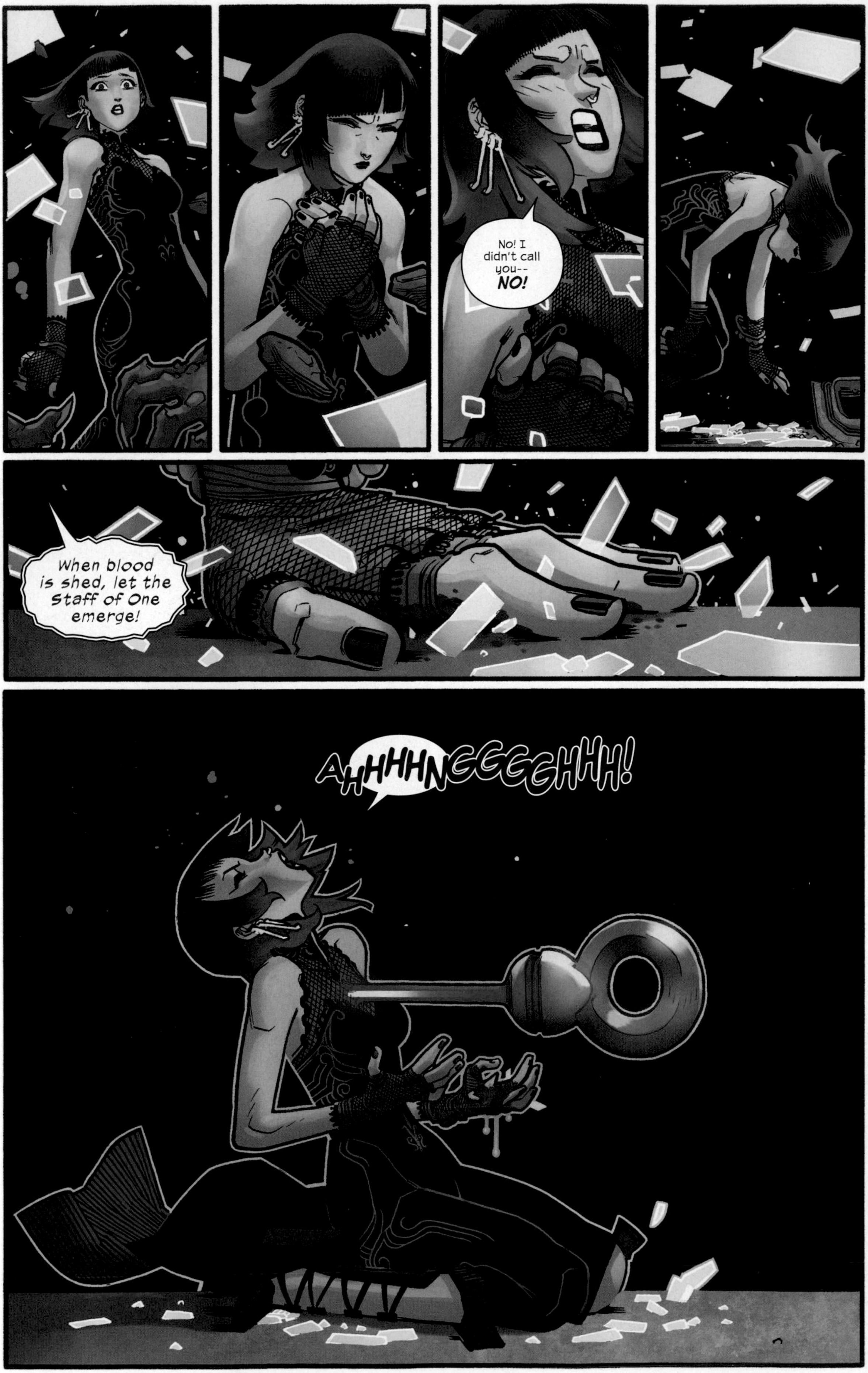
No! I didn't call you-- NO!
When blood is shed, let the Staff of One emerge!
AHHHHNGGGGHHHH!

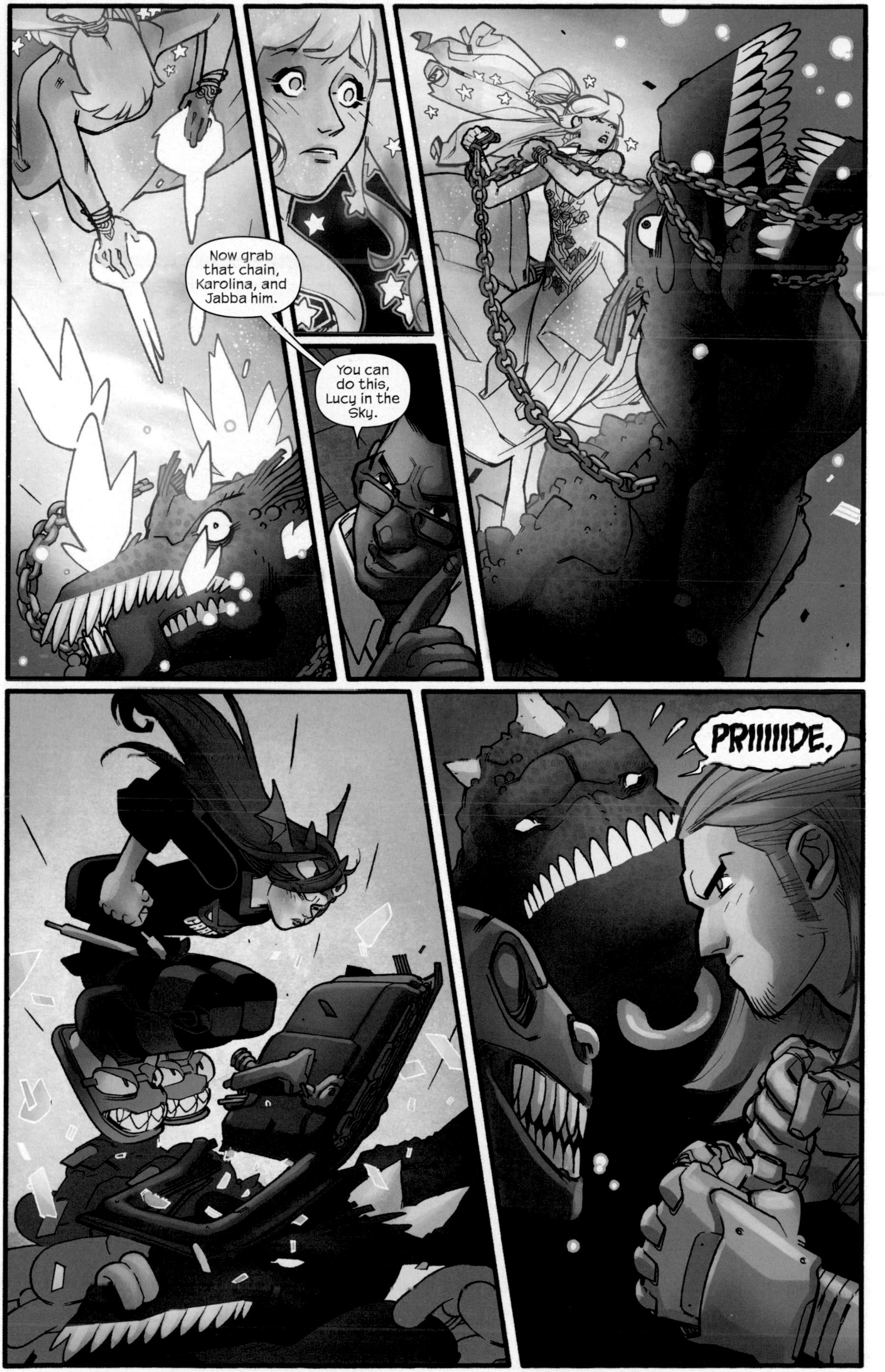
Now grab that chain, Karolina, and Jabba him.
You can do this, Lucy in the Sky.
PRIIIIIDE.

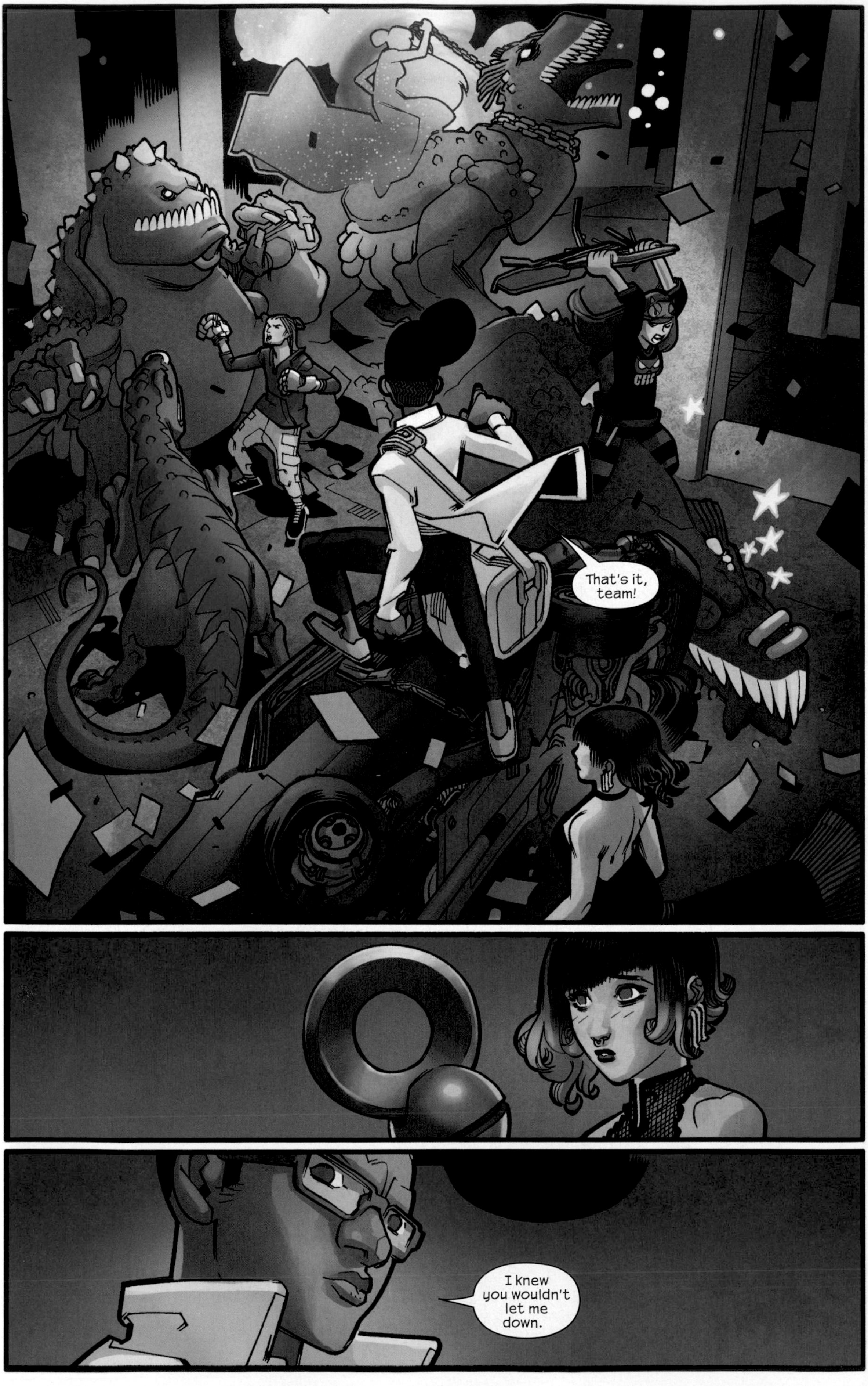
That's it, team!
I knew you wouldn't let me down.

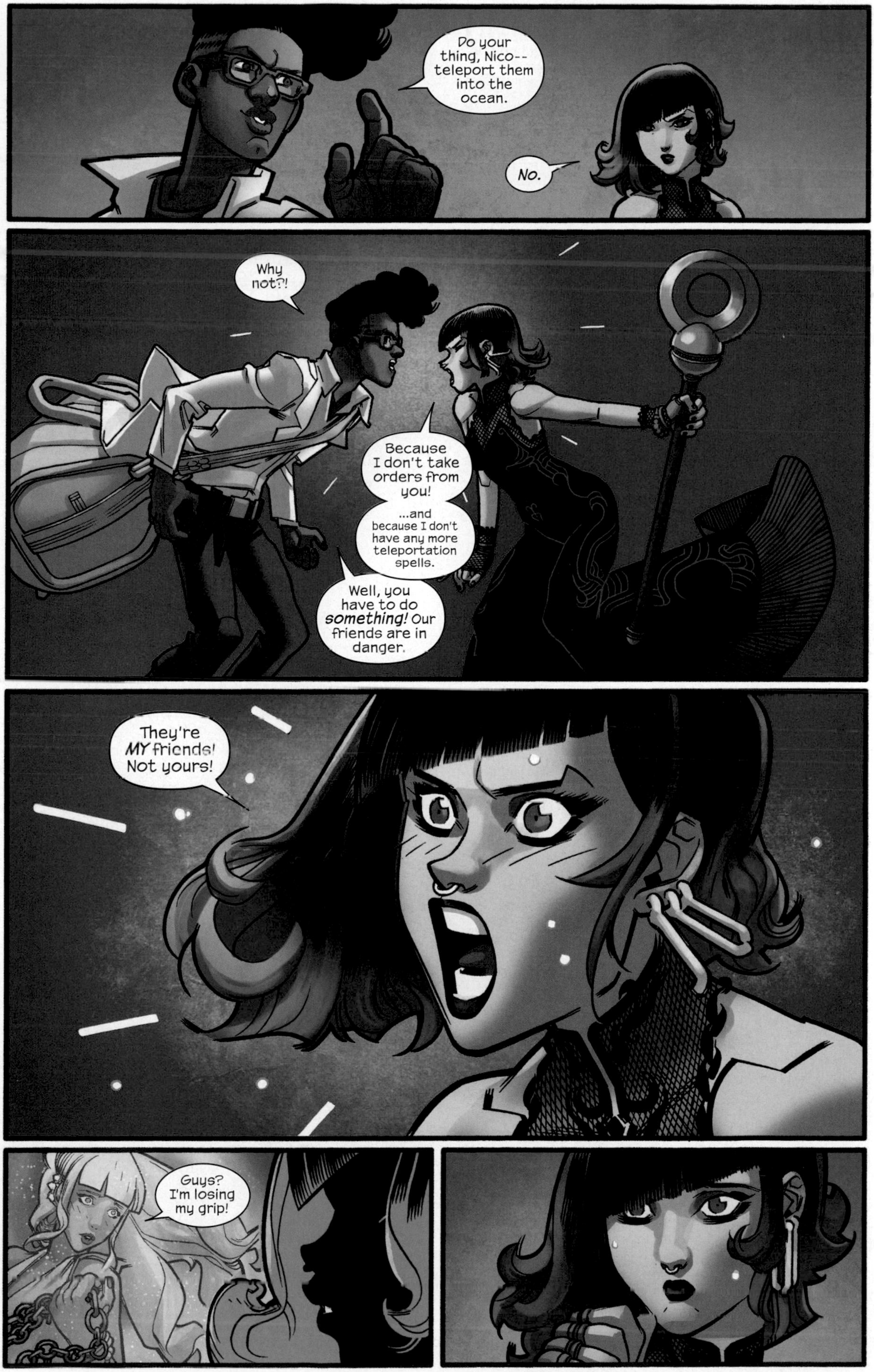
Do your thing, Nico-- teleport them into the ocean.
No.
Why not?!
Because I don't take orders from you!
...and because I don't have any more teleportation spells.
Well, you have to do *something!* Our friends are in danger.
They're *MY* friends! Not yours!
Guys? I'm losing my grip!

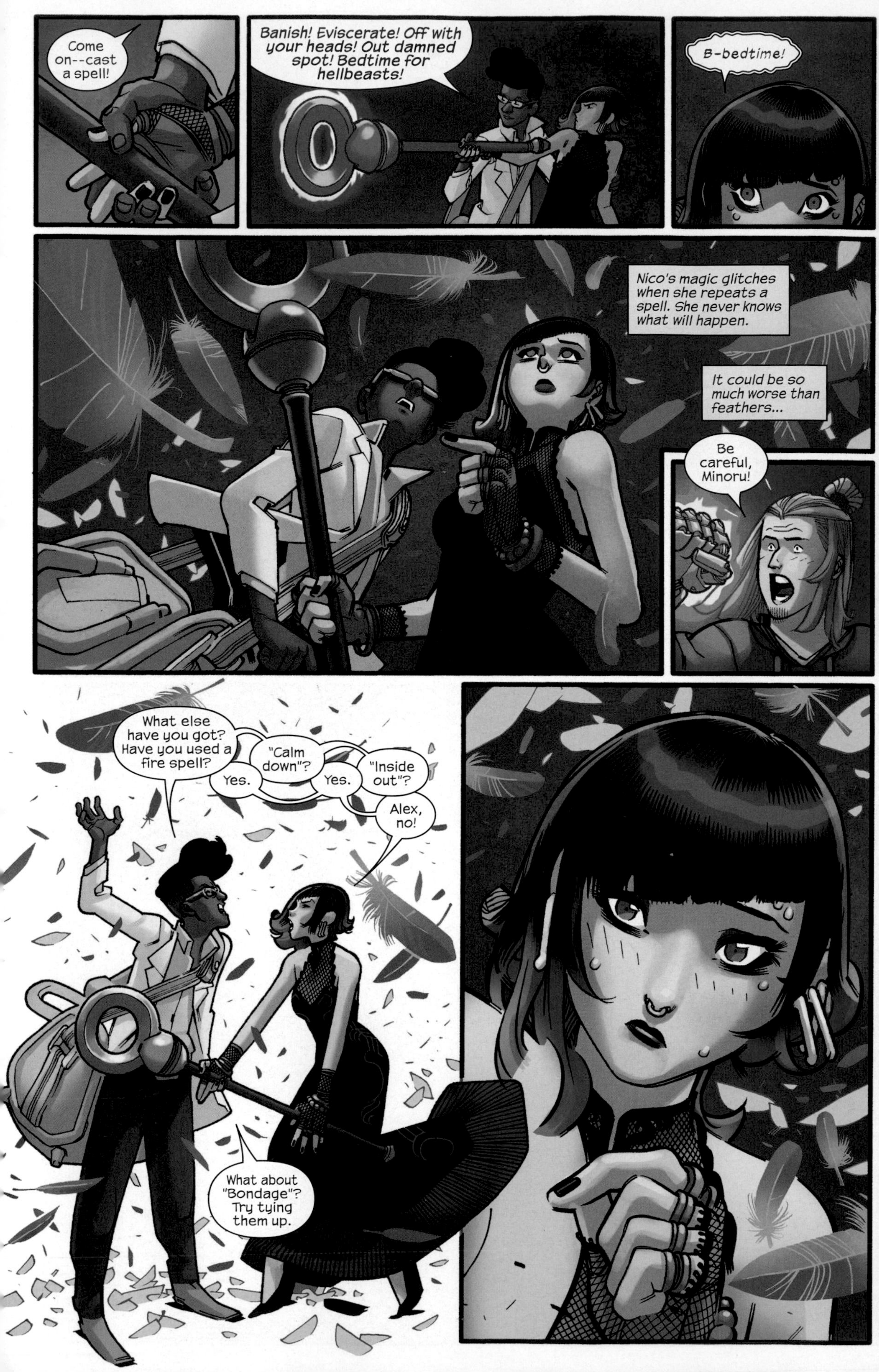
Come on--cast a spell!
Banish! Eviscerate! Off with your heads! Out damned spot! Bedtime for hellbeasts!
B-bedtime!
Nico's magic glitches when she repeats a spell. She never knows what will happen.
It could be so much worse than feathers...
Be careful, Minoru!
What else have you got? Have you used a fire spell?
Yes.
"Calm down"?
Yes.
"Inside out"?
Alex, no!
What about "Bondage"? Try tying them up.

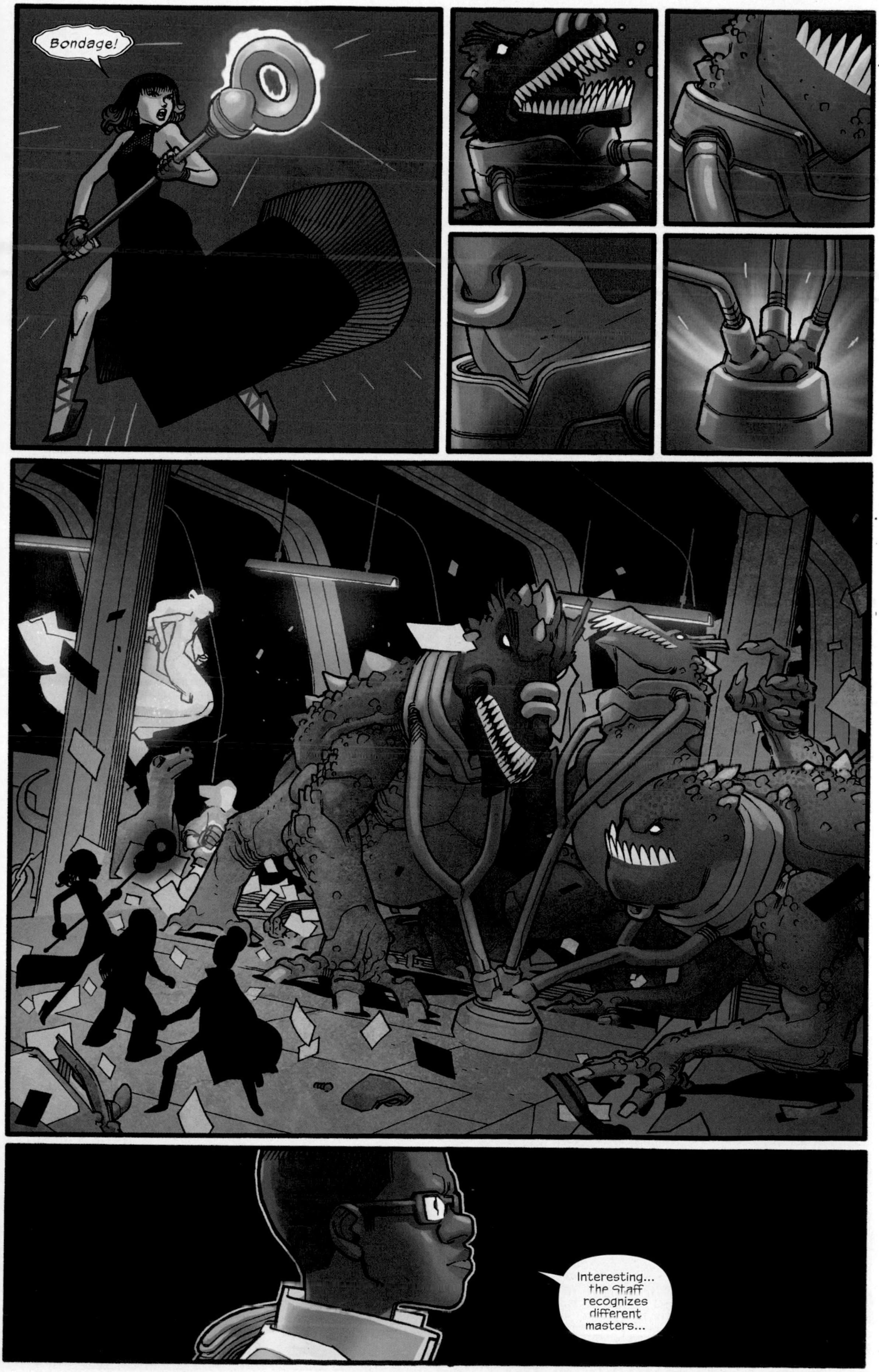
Bondage!
Interesting... the Staff recognizes different masters...

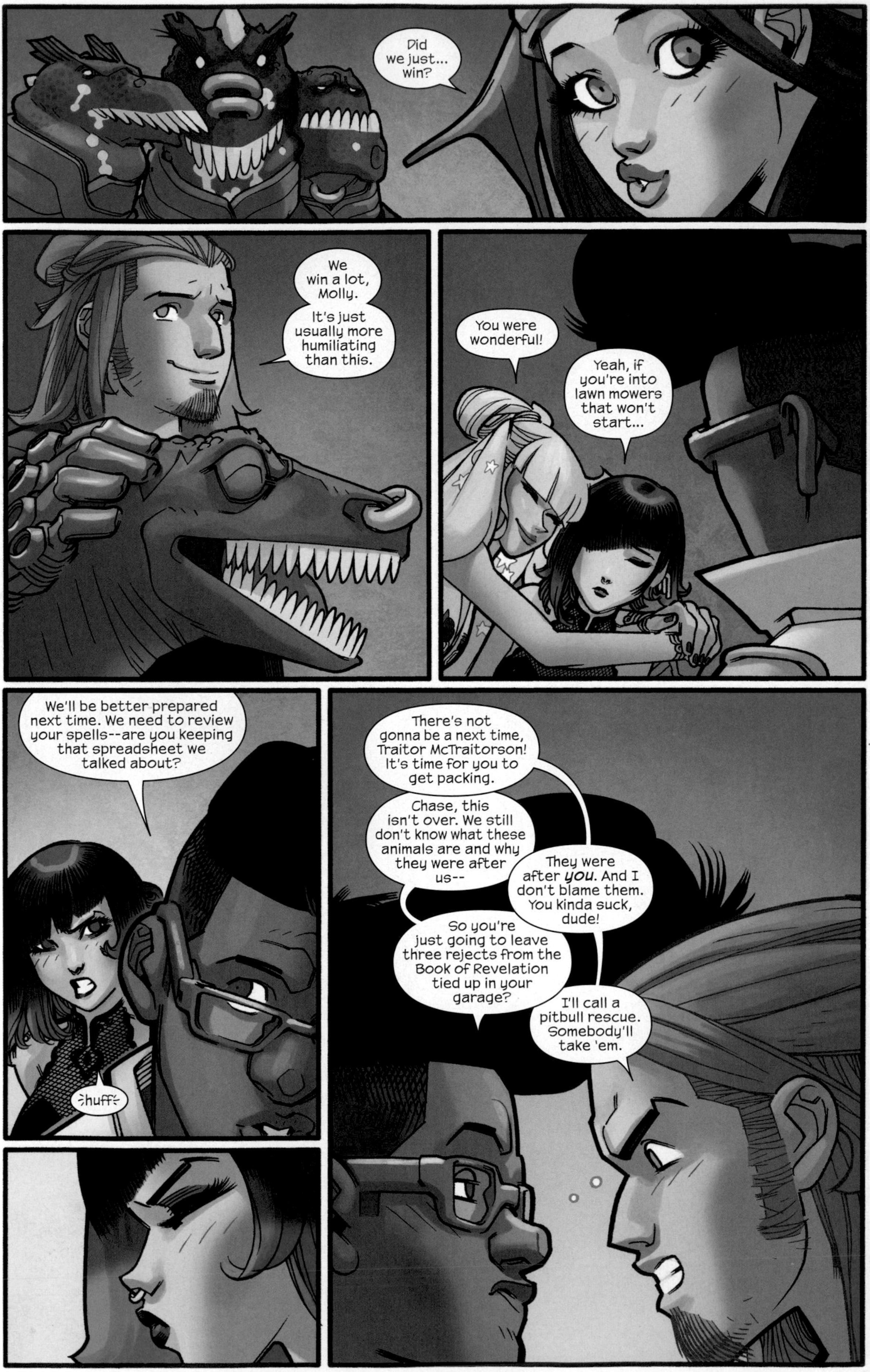
Did we just... win?
We win a lot, Molly.
It's just usually more humiliating than this.
You were wonderful!
Yeah, if you're into lawn mowers that won't start...
We'll be better prepared next time. We need to review your spells--are you keeping that spreadsheet we talked about?
huff
There's not gonna be a next time, Traitor McTraitorson! It's time for you to get packing.
Chase, this isn't over. We still don't know what these animals are and why they were after us--
They were after *you*. And I don't blame them. You kinda suck, dude!
So you're just going to leave three rejects from the Book of Revelation tied up in your garage?
I'll call a pitbull rescue. Somebody'll take 'em.

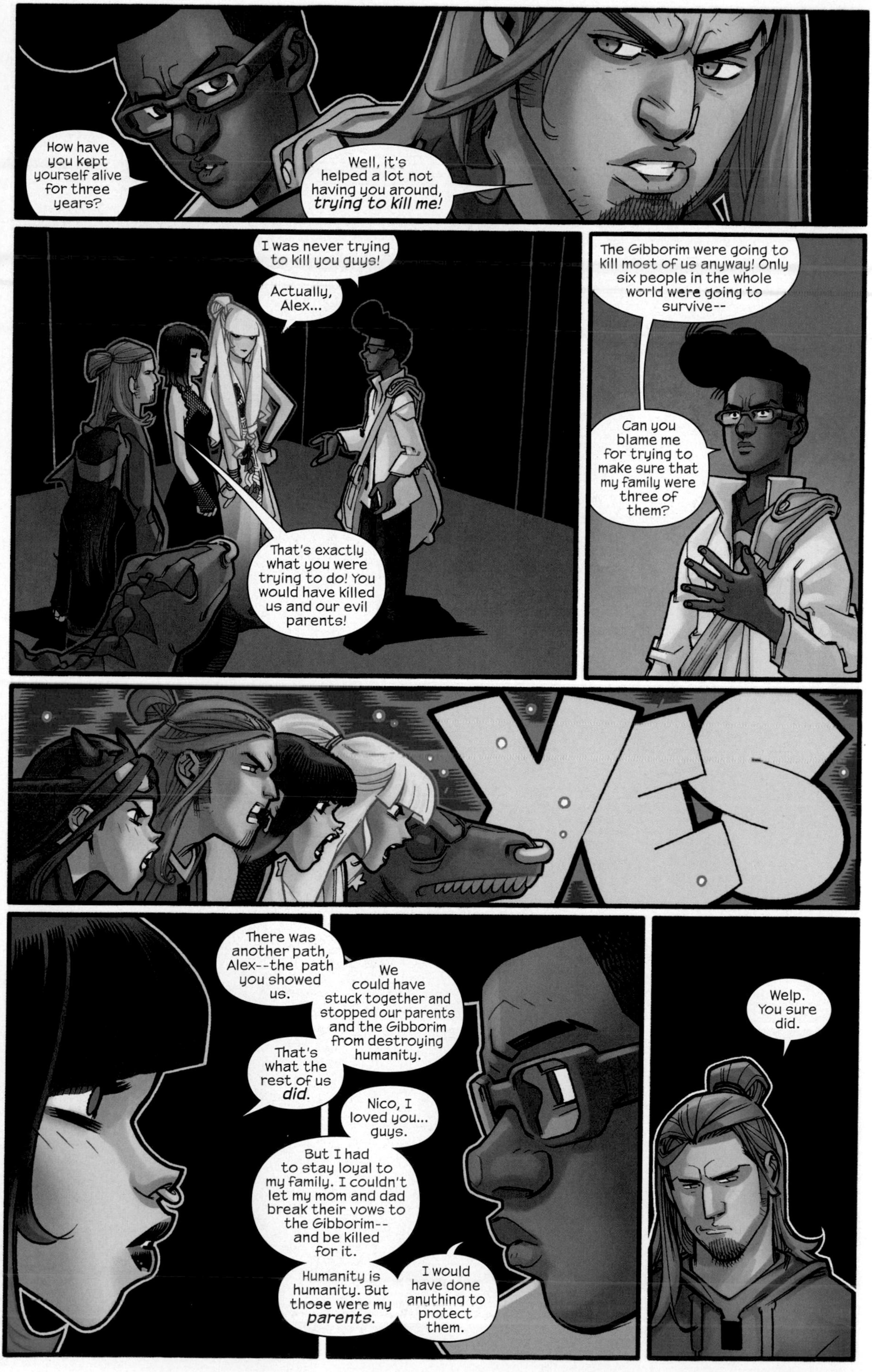
How have you kept yourself alive for three years?
Well, it's helped a lot not having you around, *trying to kill me!*
I was never trying to kill you guys!
Actually, Alex...
That's exactly what you were trying to do! You would have killed us and our evil parents!
The Gibborim were going to kill most of us anyway! Only six people in the whole world were going to survive--
Can you blame me for trying to make sure that my family were three of them?
YES
There was another path, Alex--the path you showed us.
We could have stuck together and stopped our parents and the Gibborim from destroying humanity.
That's what the rest of us *did*.
Nico, I loved you... guys.
But I had to stay loyal to my family. I couldn't let my mom and dad break their vows to the Gibborim-- and be killed for it.
Humanity is humanity. But those were my *parents*.
I would have done anything to protect them.
Welp. You sure did.

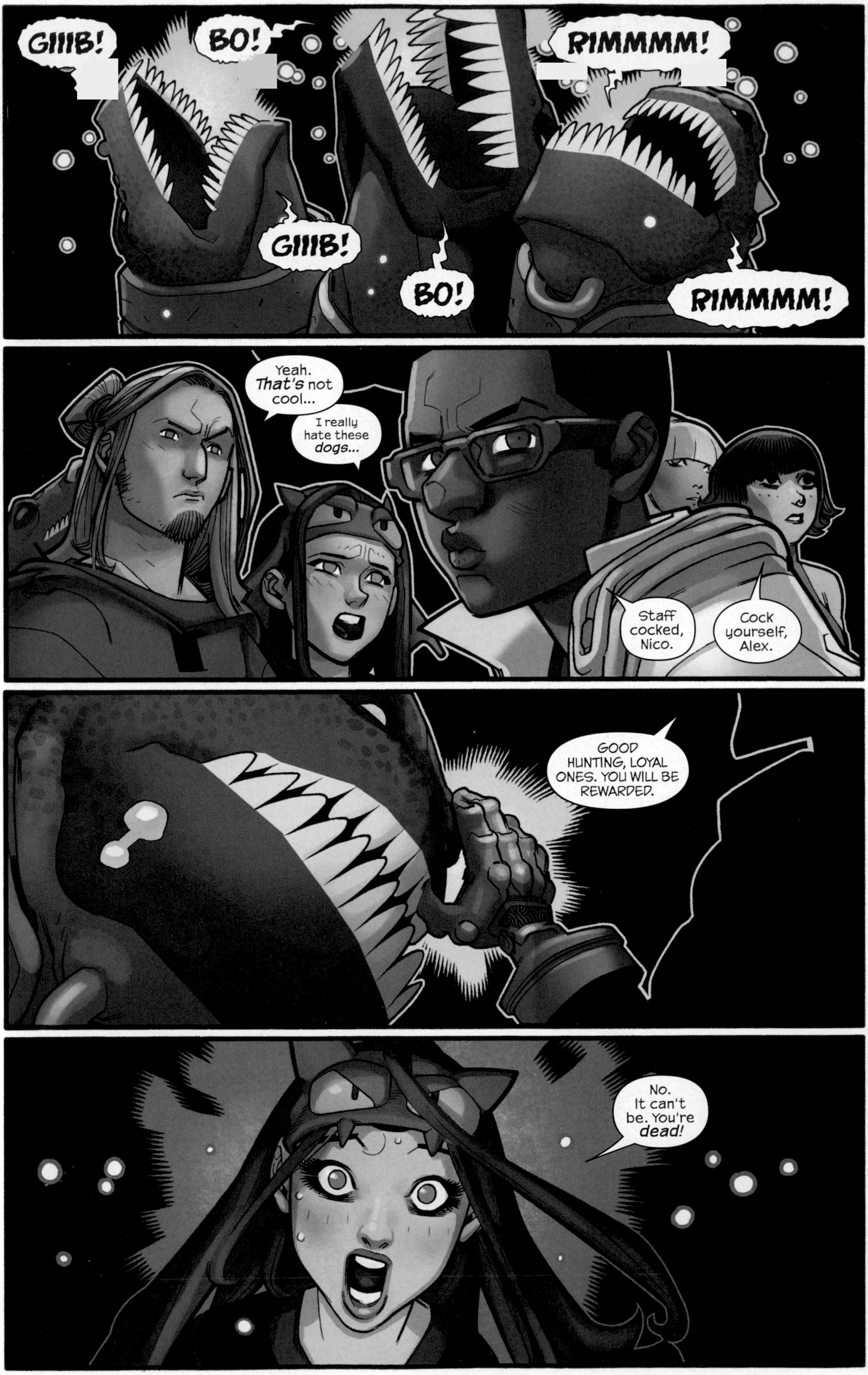
GIIIB!
BO!
RIMMMM!
GIIIB!
BO!
RIMMMM!
Yeah. *That's* not cool...
I really hate these *dogs*...
Staff cocked, Nico.
Cock yourself, Alex.
GOOD HUNTING, LOYAL ONES. YOU WILL BE REWARDED.
No. It can't be. You're *dead!*

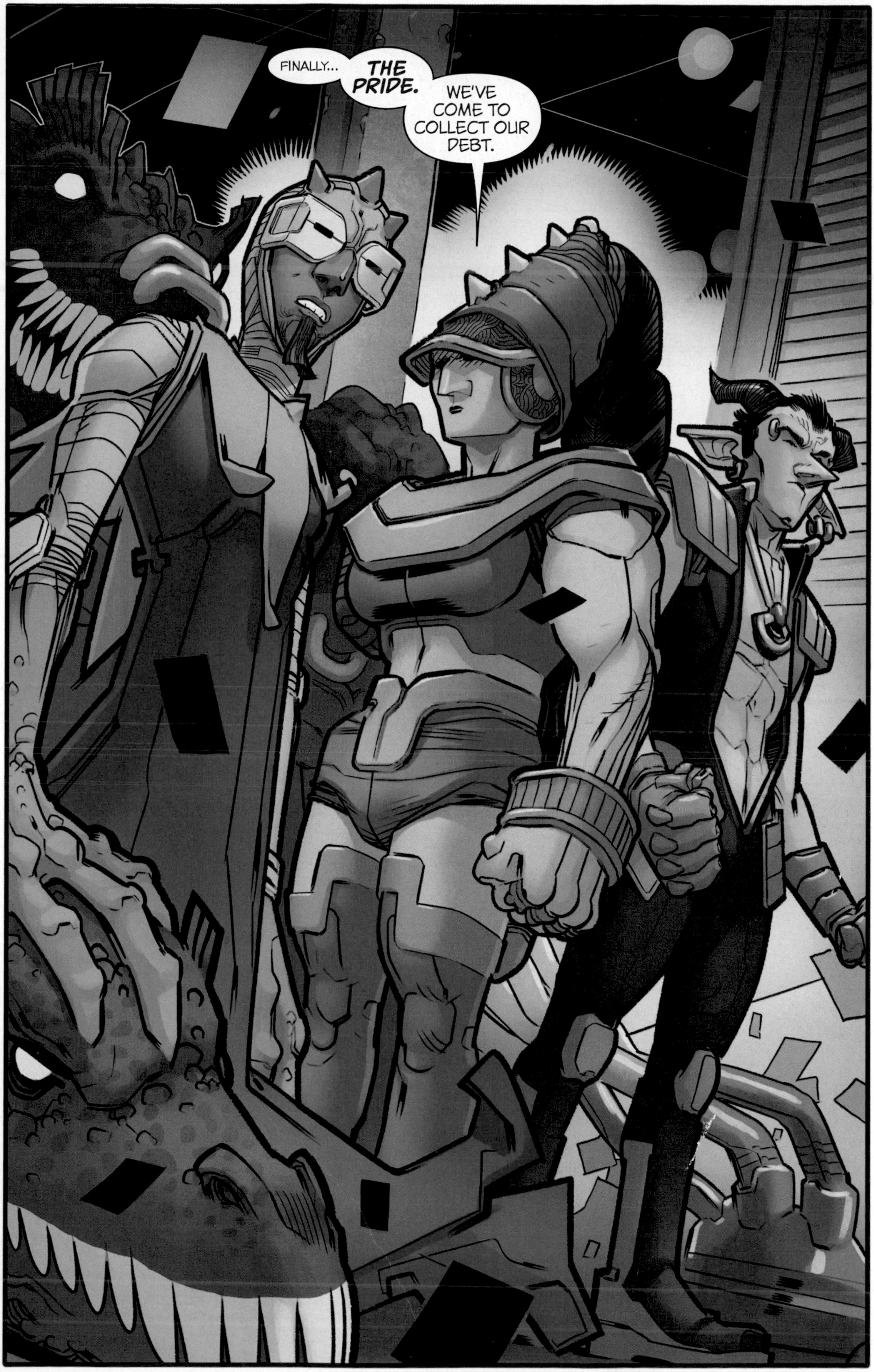
FINALLY... THE PRIDE.
WE'VE COME TO COLLECT OUR DEBT.

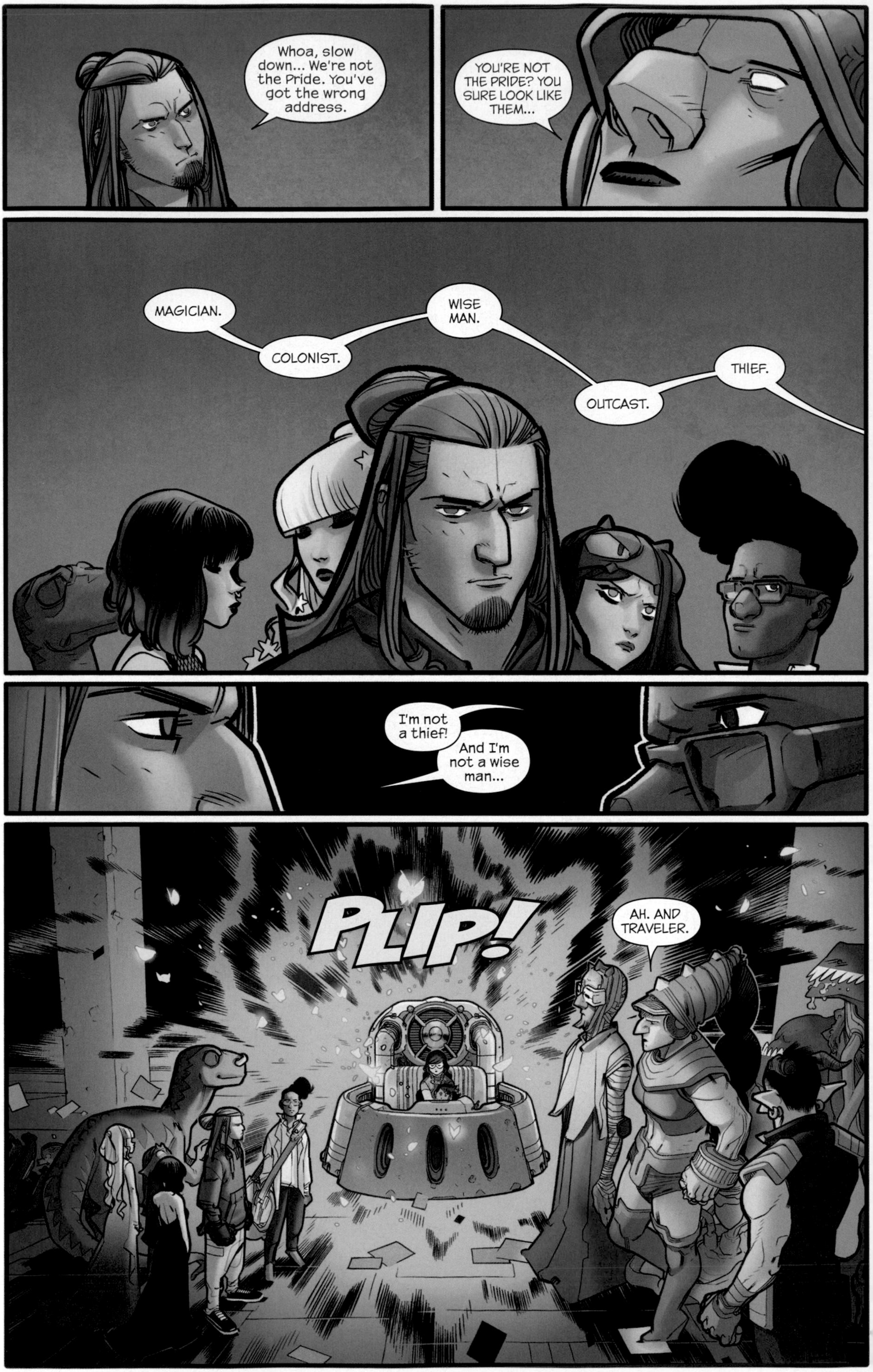
Whoa, slow down... We're not the Pride. You've got the wrong address.
YOU'RE NOT THE PRIDE? YOU SURE LOOK LIKE THEM...
MAGICIAN.
COLONIST.
WISE MAN.
OUTCAST.
THIEF.
I'm not a thief!
And I'm not a wise man...
PLIP!
AH. AND TRAVELER.

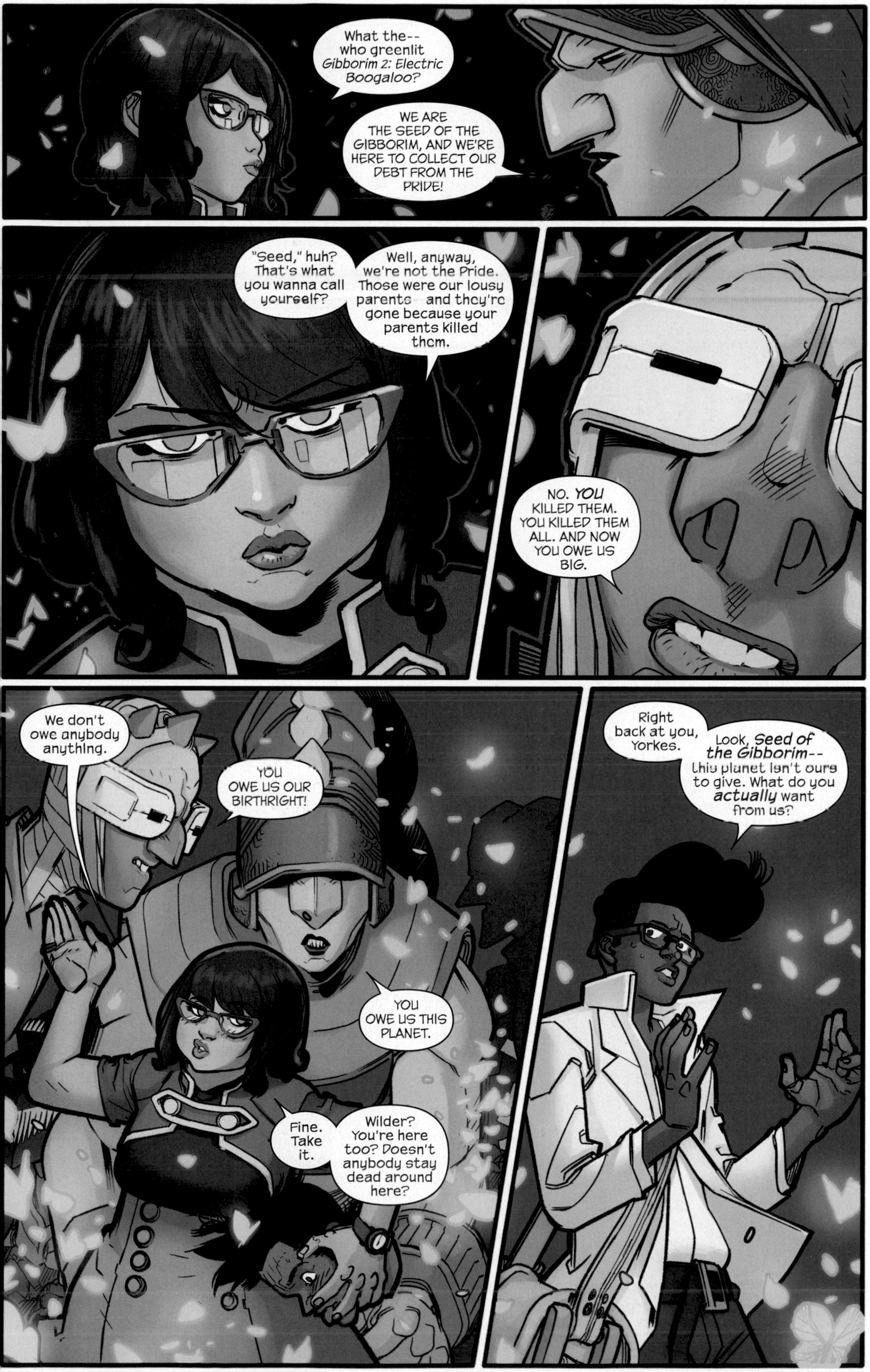
What the-- who greenlit *Gibborim 2: Electric Boogaloo?*
WE ARE THE SEED OF THE GIBBORIM, AND WE'RE HERE TO COLLECT OUR DEBT FROM THE PRIDE!
"Seed," huh? That's what you wanna call yourself?
Well, anyway, we're not the Pride. Those were our lousy parents-- and they're gone because your parents killed them.
NO. *YOU* KILLED THEM. YOU KILLED THEM ALL. AND NOW YOU OWE US BIG.
We don't owe anybody anything.
YOU OWE US OUR BIRTHRIGHT!
YOU OWE US THIS PLANET.
Fine. Take it.
Wilder? You're here too? Doesn't anybody stay dead around here?
Right back at you, Yorkes.
Look, *Seed of the Gibborim*-- this planet isn't ours to give. What do you *actually* want from us?

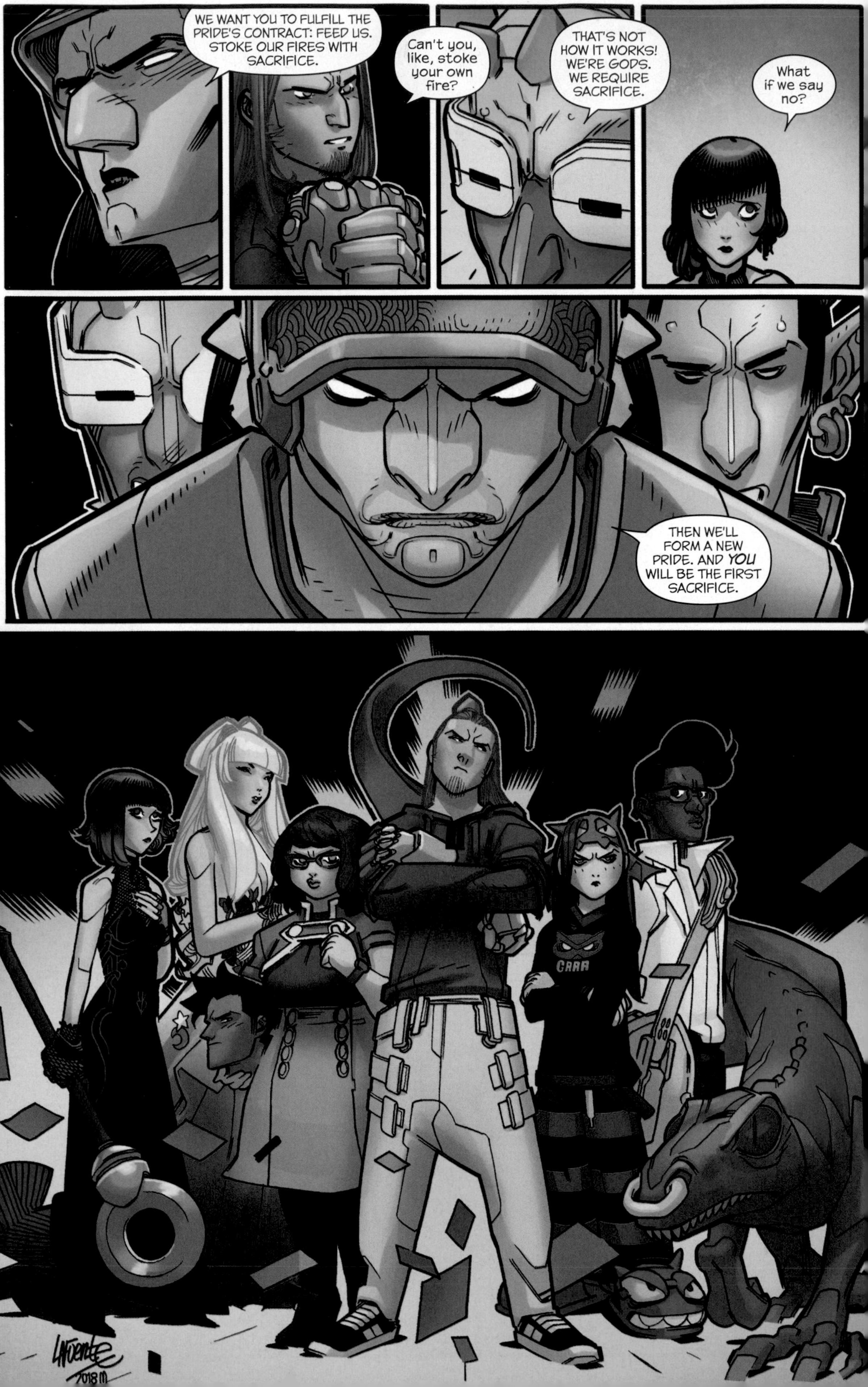
WE WANT YOU TO FULFILL THE PRIDE'S CONTRACT: FEED US. STOKE OUR FIRES WITH SACRIFICE.
Can't you, like, stoke your own fire?
THAT'S NOT HOW IT WORKS! WE'RE GODS. WE REQUIRE SACRIFICE.
What if we say no?
THEN WE'LL FORM A NEW PRIDE. AND YOU WILL BE THE FIRST SACRIFICE.
CRRR
LAFUENTE
2018

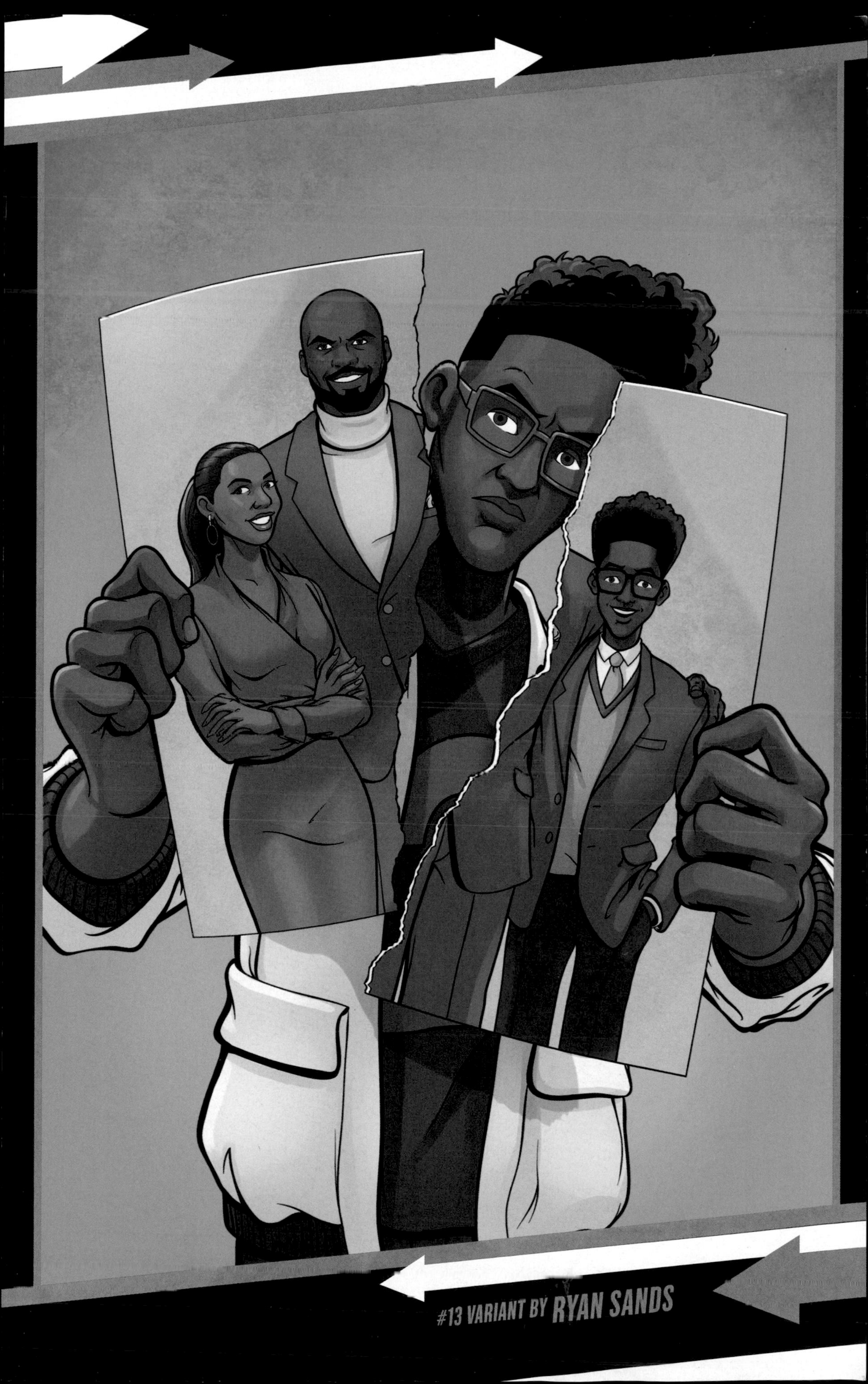

#13 VARIANT BY RYAN SANDS

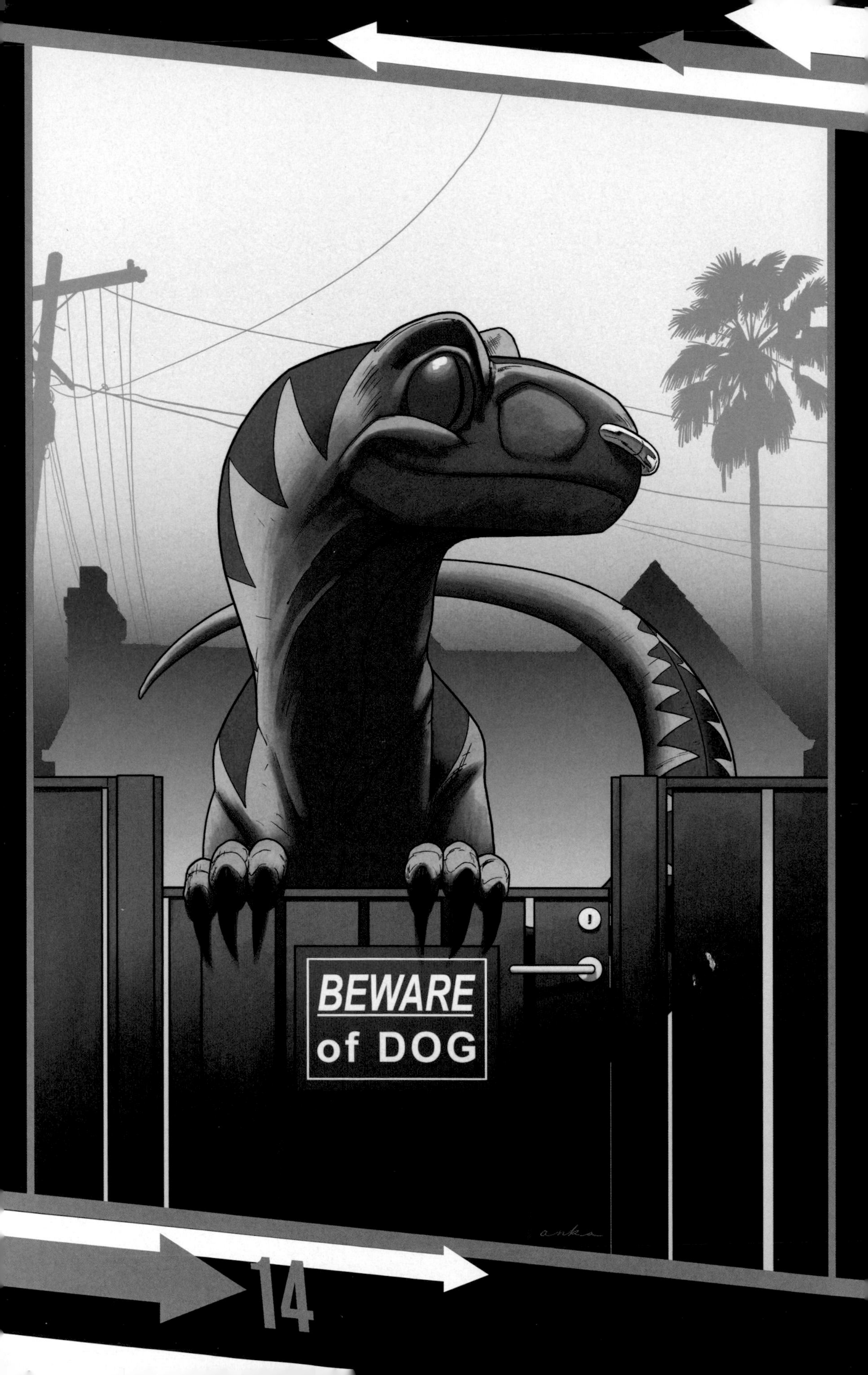
BEWARE
of DOG
anka

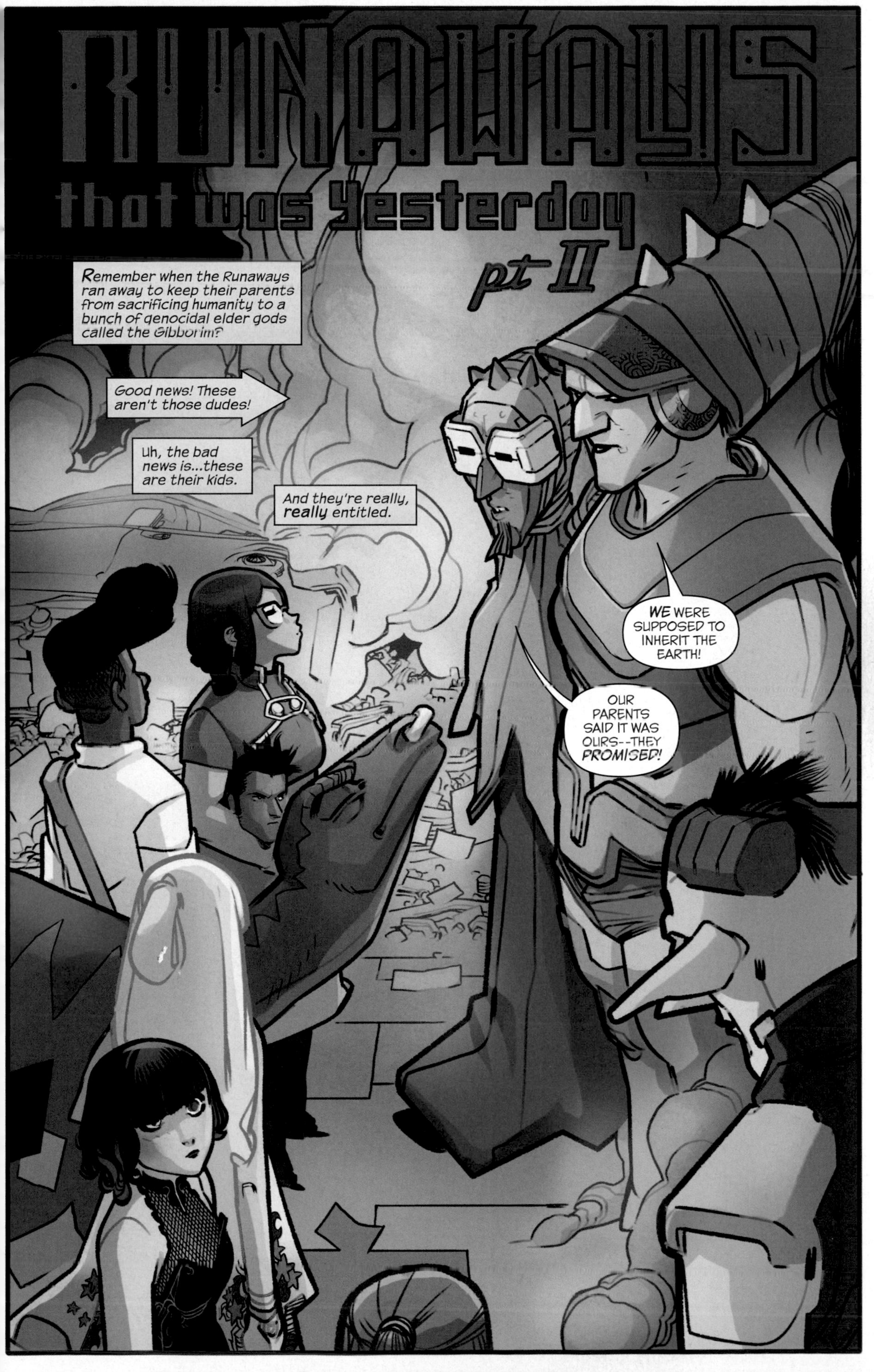
RUNAWAYS
that was Yesterday
pt II
Remember when the Runaways ran away to keep their parents from sacrificing humanity to a bunch of genocidal elder gods called the Gibborim?
Good news! These aren't those dudes!
Uh, the bad news is...these are their kids.
And they're really, really entitled.
WE WERE SUPPOSED TO INHERIT THE EARTH!
OUR PARENTS SAID IT WAS OURS--THEY PROMISED!

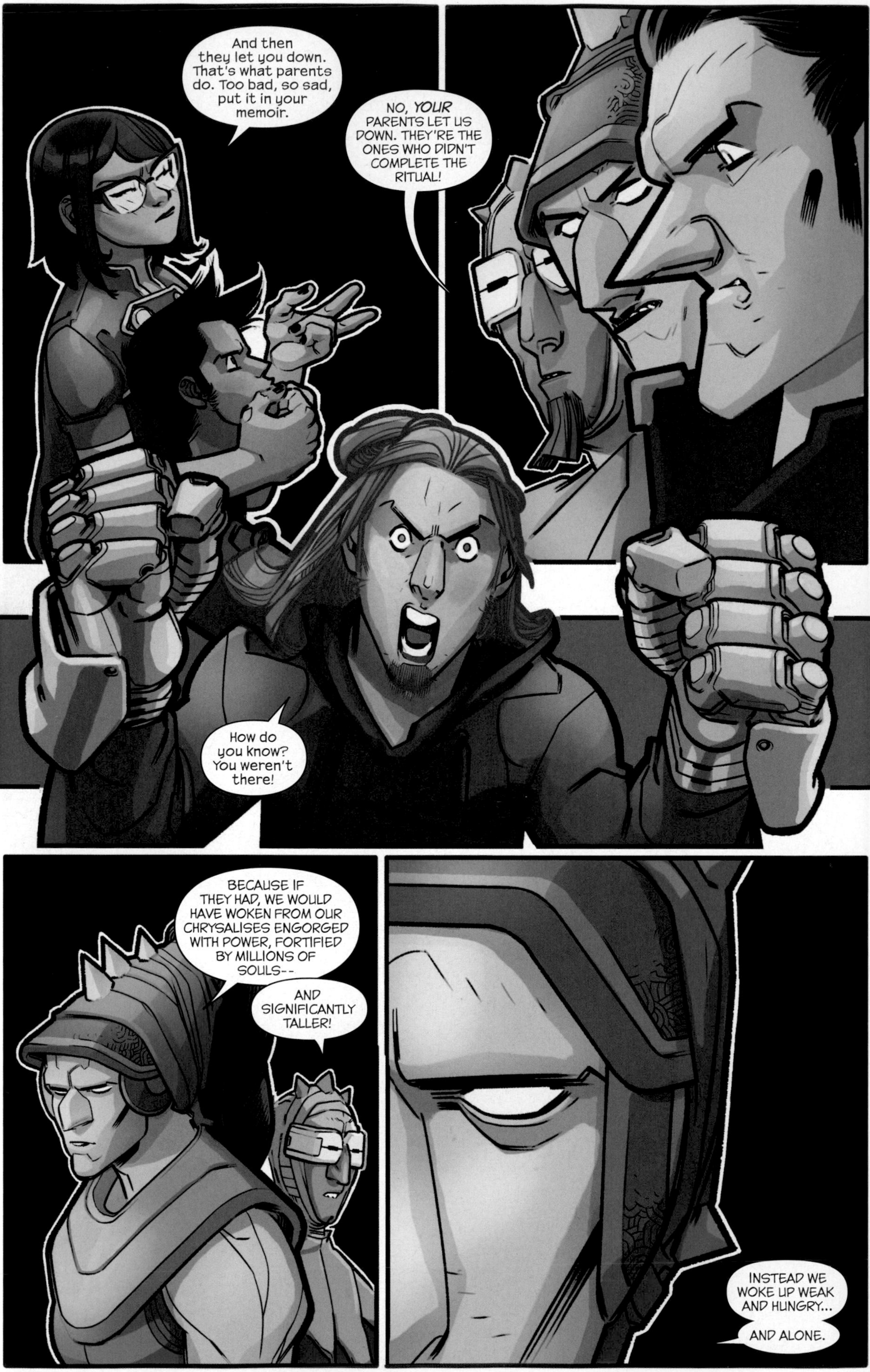
And then they let you down. That's what parents do. Too bad, so sad, put it in your memoir.
NO, YOUR PARENTS LET US DOWN. THEY'RE THE ONES WHO DIDN'T COMPLETE THE RITUAL!
How do you know? You weren't there!
BECAUSE IF THEY HAD, WE WOULD HAVE WOKEN FROM OUR CHRYSALISES ENGORGED WITH POWER, FORTIFIED BY MILLIONS OF SOULS--
AND SIGNIFICANTLY TALLER!
INSTEAD WE WOKE UP WEAK AND HUNGRY...
AND ALONE.

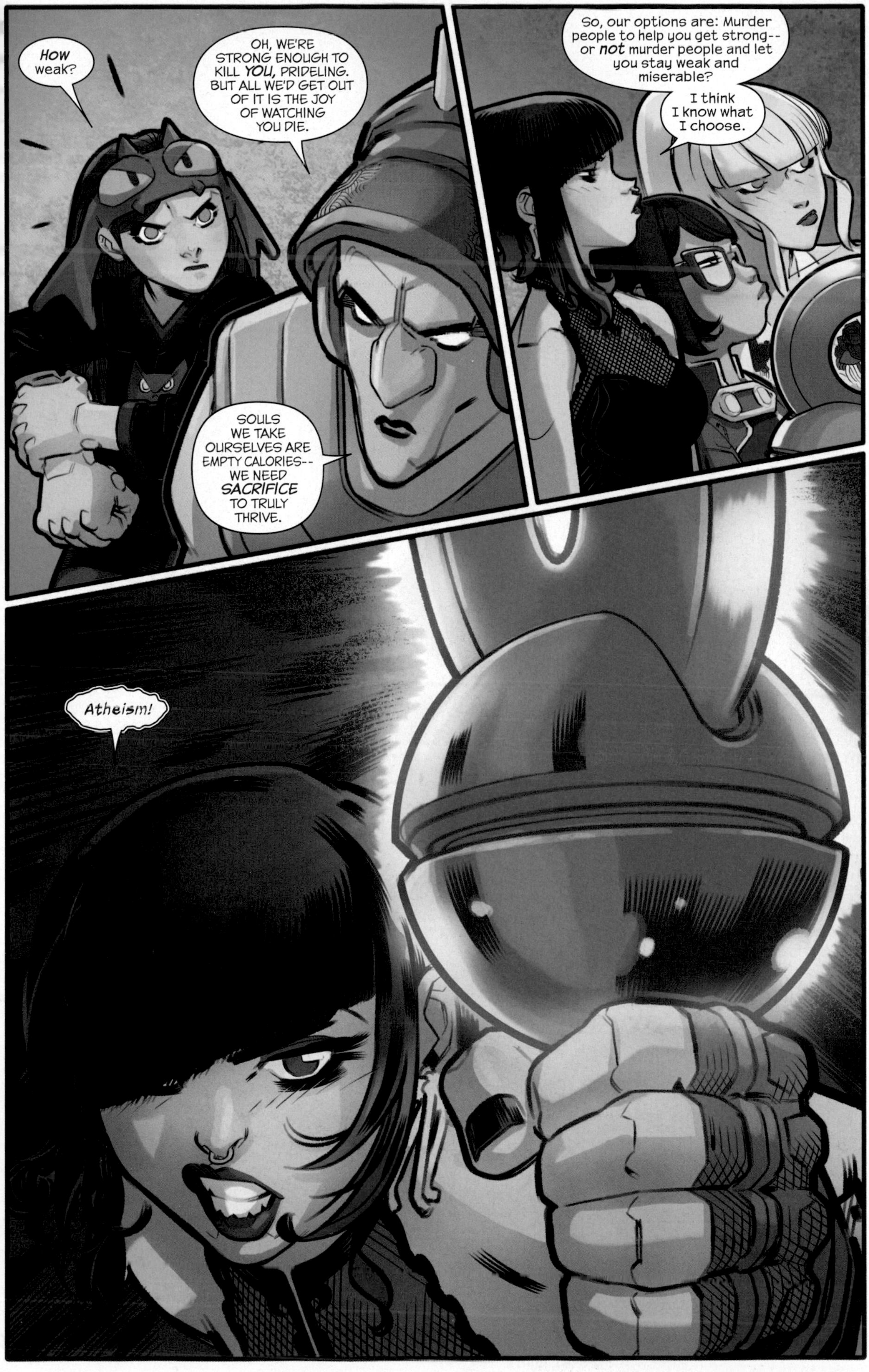

HOW weak?
OH, WE'RE STRONG ENOUGH TO KILL YOU, PRIDELING. BUT ALL WE'D GET OUT OF IT IS THE JOY OF WATCHING YOU DIE.
SOULS WE TAKE OURSELVES ARE EMPTY CALORIES-- WE NEED SACRIFICE TO TRULY THRIVE.
So, our options are: Murder people to help you get strong-- or not murder people and let you stay weak and miserable?
I think I know what I choose.
Atheism!

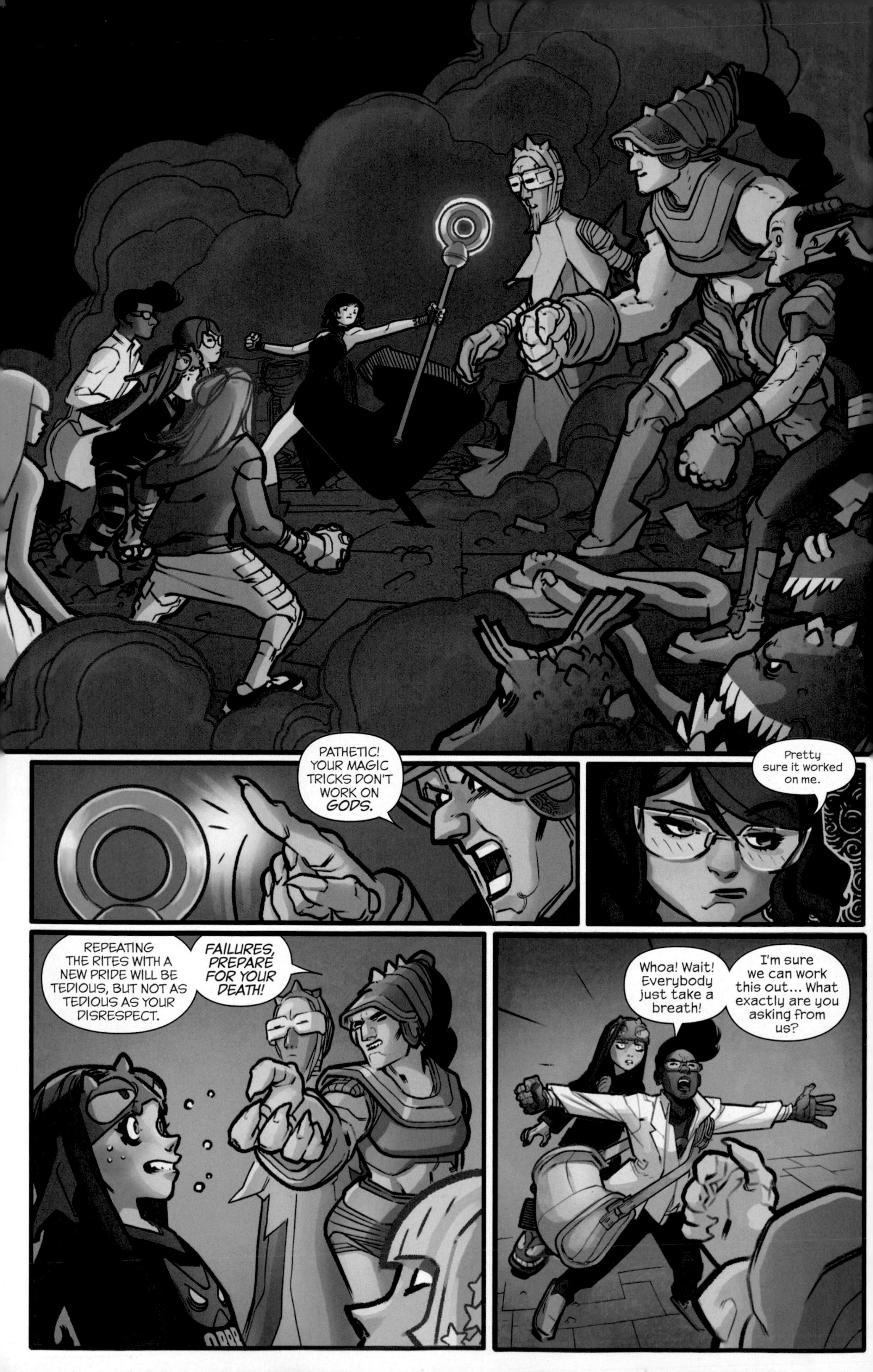
PATHETIC! YOUR MAGIC TRICKS DON'T WORK ON GODS.
Pretty sure it worked on me.
REPEATING THE RITES WITH A NEW PRIDE WILL BE TEDIOUS, BUT NOT AS TEDIOUS AS YOUR DISRESPECT.
FAILURES, PREPARE FOR YOUR DEATH!
Whoa! Wait! Everybody just take a breath!
I'm sure we can work this out... What exactly are you asking from us?

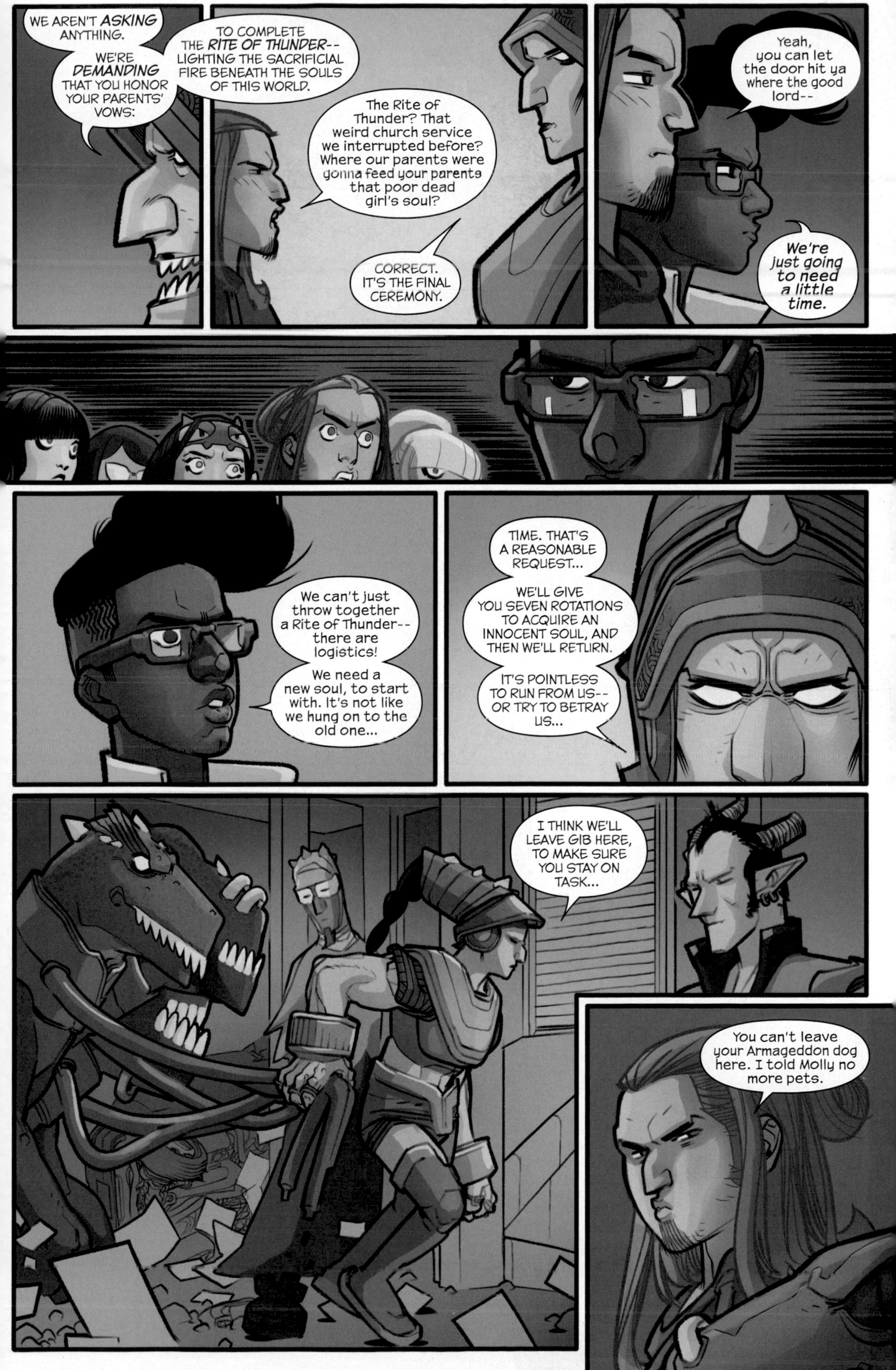

WE AREN'T ASKING ANYTHING.
WE'RE DEMANDING THAT YOU HONOR YOUR PARENTS' VOWS:
TO COMPLETE THE RITE OF THUNDER-- LIGHTING THE SACRIFICIAL FIRE BENEATH THE SOULS OF THIS WORLD.
The Rite of Thunder? That weird church service we interrupted before? Where our parents were gonna feed your parents that poor dead girl's soul?
CORRECT. IT'S THE FINAL CEREMONY.
Yeah, you can let the door hit ya where the good lord--
We're just going to need a little time.
We can't just throw together a Rite of Thunder-- there are logistics!
We need a new soul, to start with. It's not like we hung on to the old one...
TIME. THAT'S A REASONABLE REQUEST...
WE'LL GIVE YOU SEVEN ROTATIONS TO ACQUIRE AN INNOCENT SOUL, AND THEN WE'LL RETURN.
IT'S POINTLESS TO RUN FROM US-- OR TRY TO BETRAY US...
I THINK WE'LL LEAVE GIB HERE, TO MAKE SURE YOU STAY ON TASK...
You can't leave your Armageddon dog here. I told Molly no more pets.

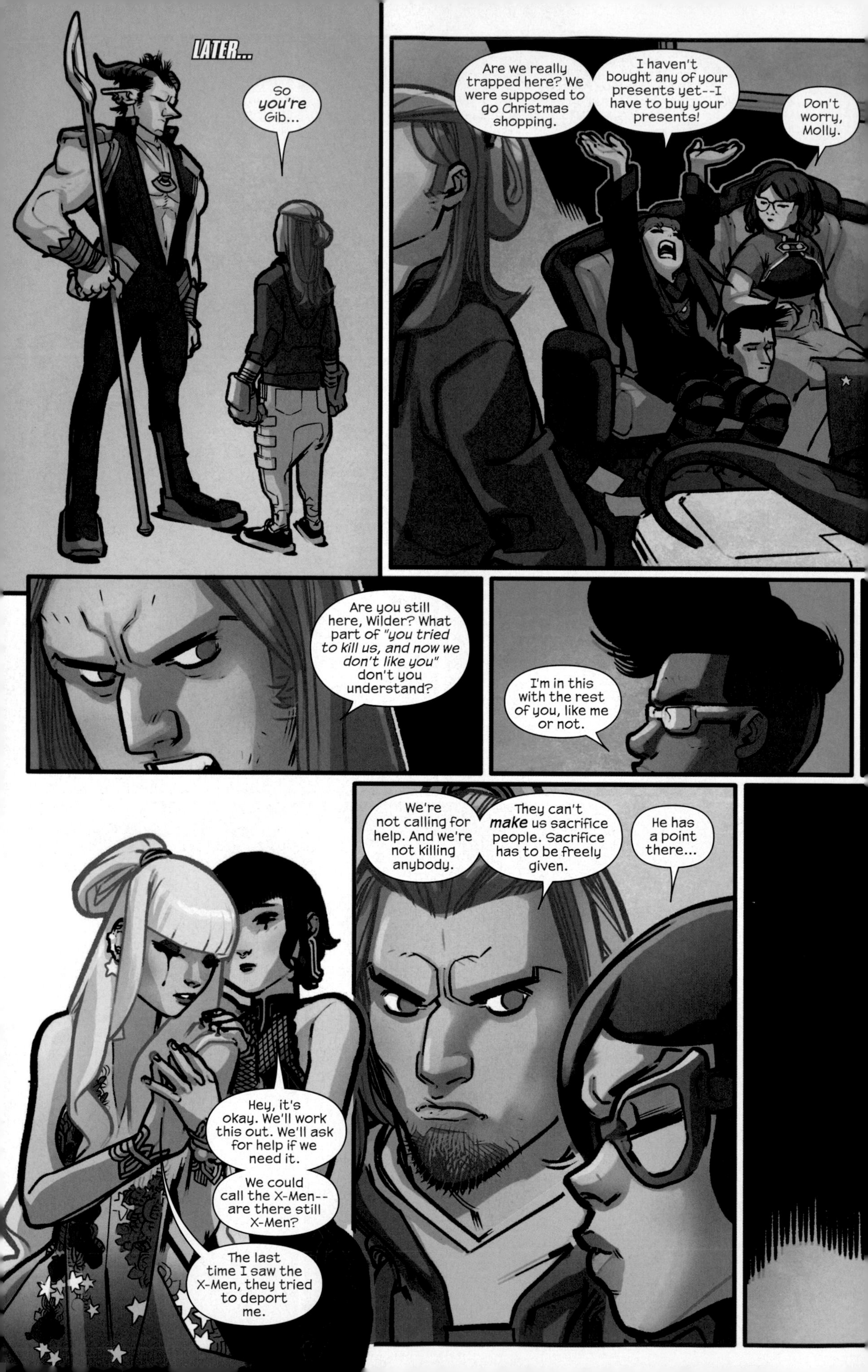
LATER...
So you're Gib...
Are we really trapped here? We were supposed to go Christmas shopping.
I haven't bought any of your presents yet--I have to buy your presents!
Don't worry, Molly.
Are you still here, Wilder? What part of "you tried to kill us, and now we don't like you" don't you understand?
I'm in this with the rest of you, like me or not.
Hey, it's okay. We'll work this out. We'll ask for help if we need it.
We could call the X-Men--are there still X-Men?
The last time I saw the X-Men, they tried to deport me.
We're not calling for help. And we're not killing anybody.
They can't make us sacrifice people. Sacrifice has to be freely given.
He has a point there...

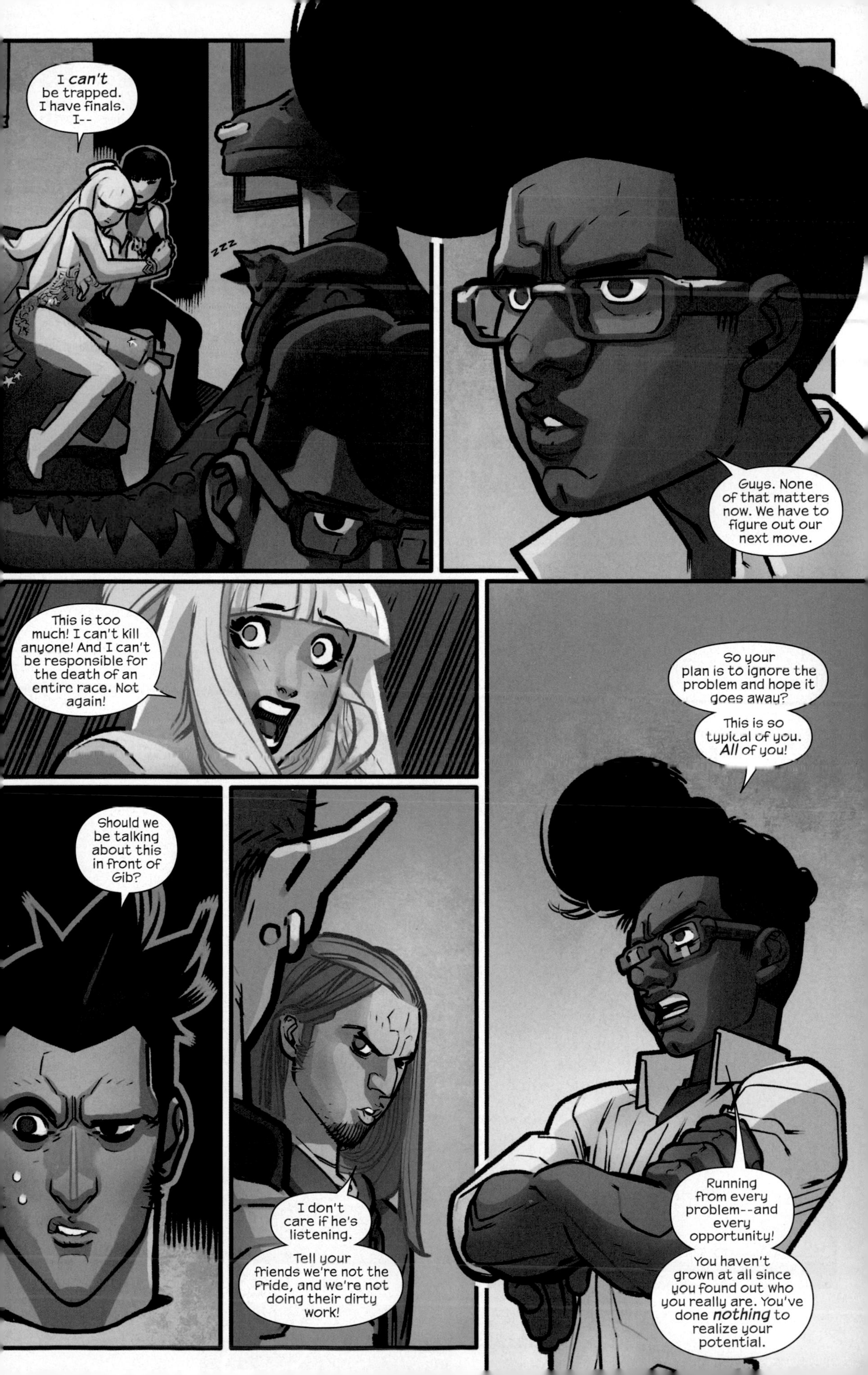
I *can't* be trapped. I have finals. I--
ZZZ
Guys. None of that matters now. We have to figure out our next move.
This is too much! I can't kill anyone! And I can't be responsible for the death of an entire race. Not again!
So your plan is to ignore the problem and hope it goes away?
This is so typical of you. *All* of you!
Should we be talking about this in front of Gib?
I don't care if he's listening.
Tell your friends we're not the Pride, and we're not doing their dirty work!
Running from every problem--and every opportunity!
You haven't grown at all since you found out who you really are. You've done *nothing* to realize your potential.

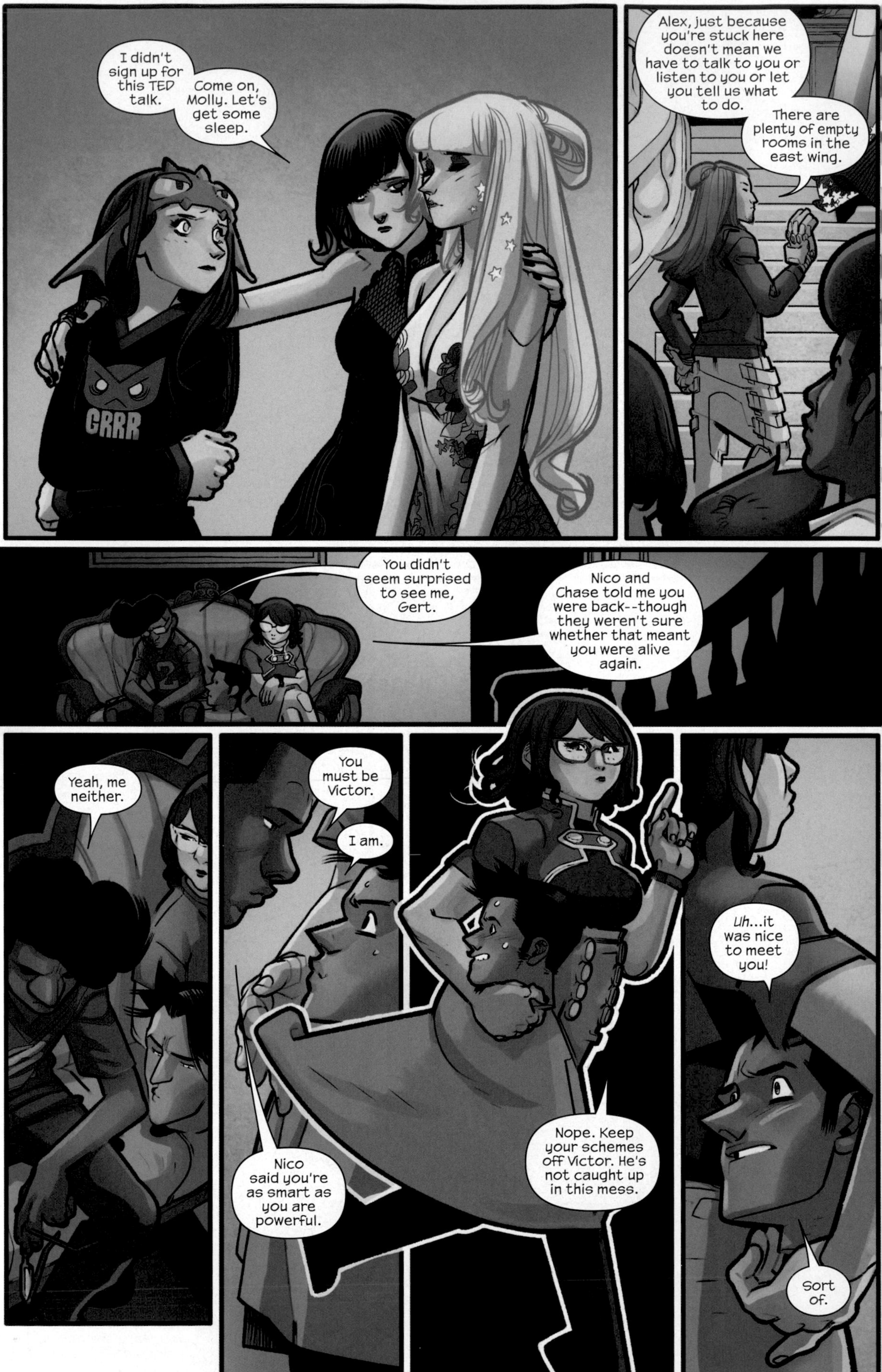
I didn't sign up for this TED talk.
Come on, Molly. Let's get some sleep.
GRRR
Alex, just because you're stuck here doesn't mean we have to talk to you or listen to you or let you tell us what to do.
There are plenty of empty rooms in the east wing.
You didn't seem surprised to see me, Gert.
Nico and Chase told me you were back--though they weren't sure whether that meant you were alive again.
Yeah, me neither.
You must be Victor.
I am.
Nico said you're as smart as you are powerful.
Nope. Keep your schemes off Victor. He's not caught up in this mess.
Uh...it was nice to meet you!
Sort of.

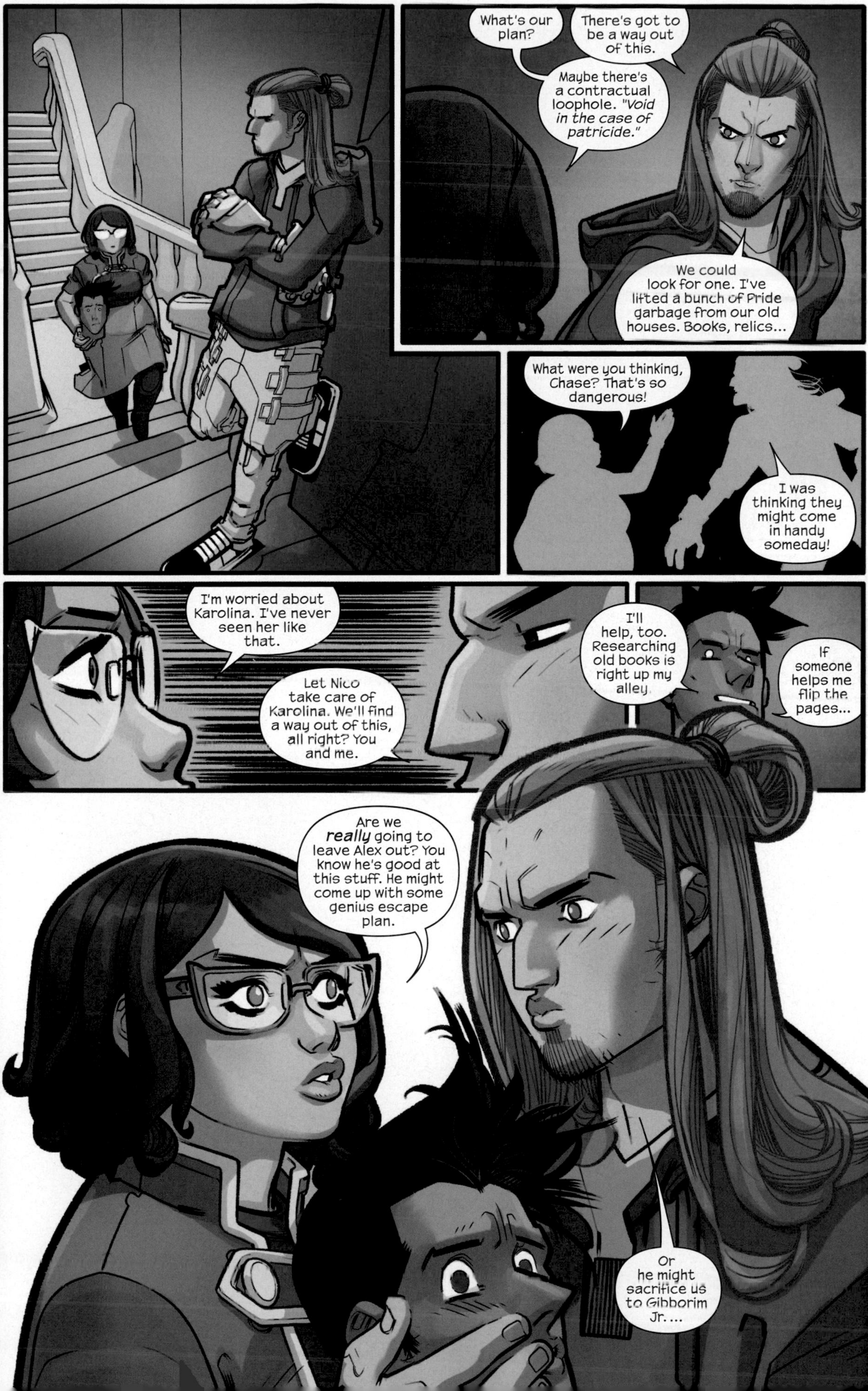
What's our plan?
There's got to be a way out of this.
Maybe there's a contractual loophole. "Void in the case of patricide."
We could look for one. I've lifted a bunch of Pride garbage from our old houses. Books, relics...
What were you thinking, Chase? That's so dangerous!
I was thinking they might come in handy someday!
I'm worried about Karolina. I've never seen her like that.
Let Nico take care of Karolina. We'll find a way out of this, all right? You and me.
I'll help, too. Researching old books is right up my alley.
If someone helps me flip the pages...
Are we *really* going to leave Alex out? You know he's good at this stuff. He might come up with some genius escape plan.
Or he might sacrifice us to Gibborim Jr. ...

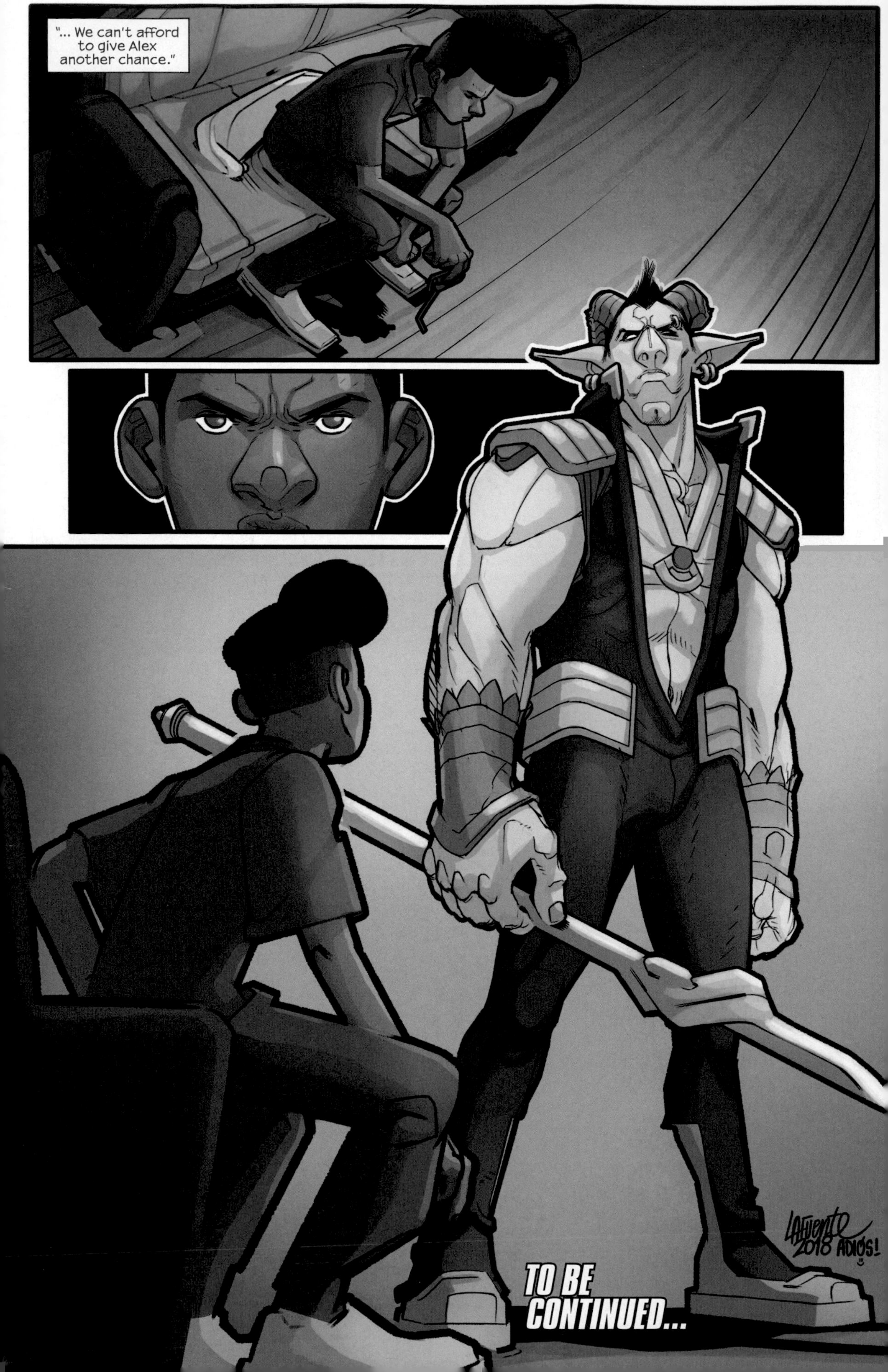
"... We can't afford to give Alex another chance."
LAFUENTE 2018 ADIÓS!
TO BE CONTINUED...

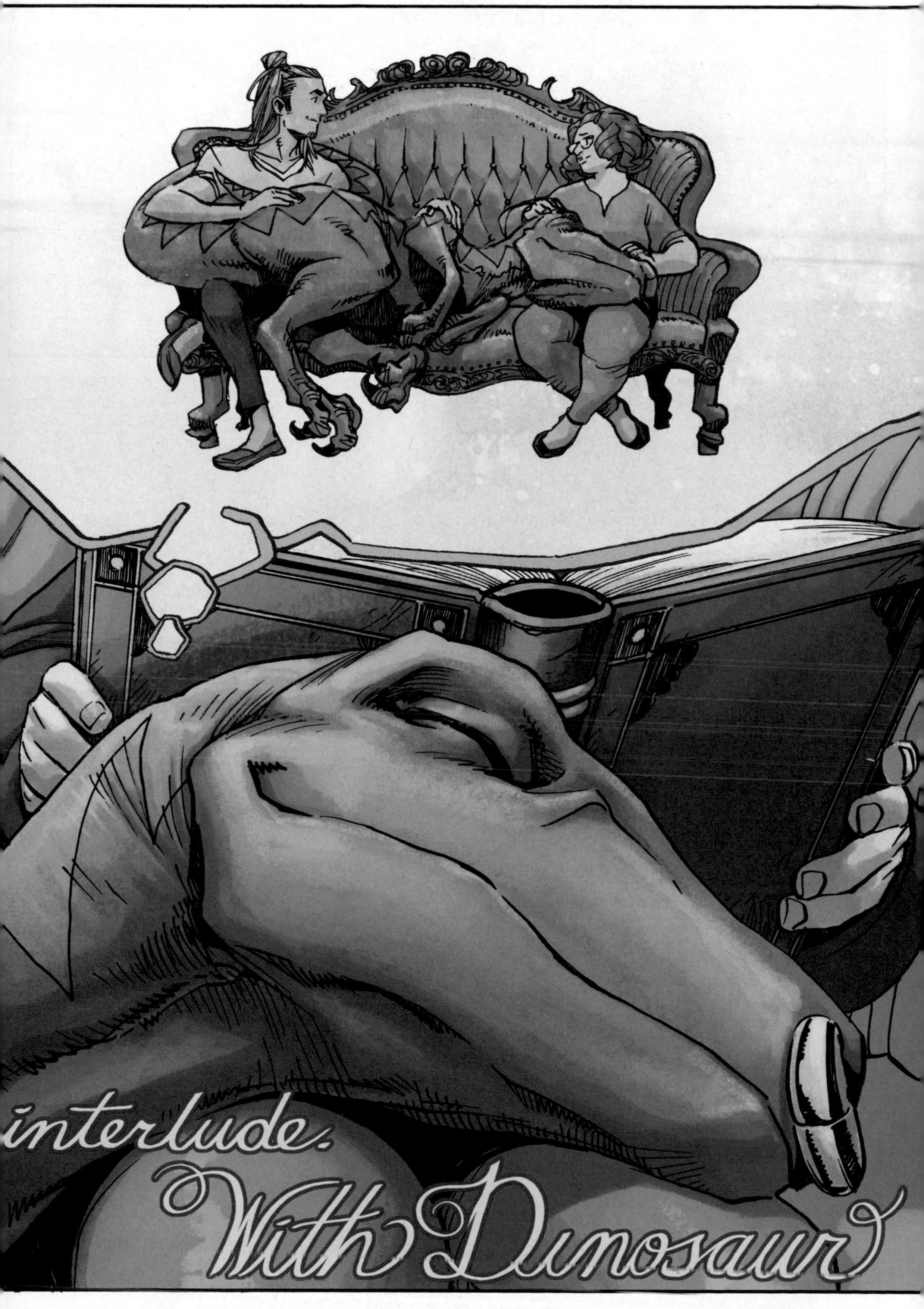
interlude.
With Dinosaur

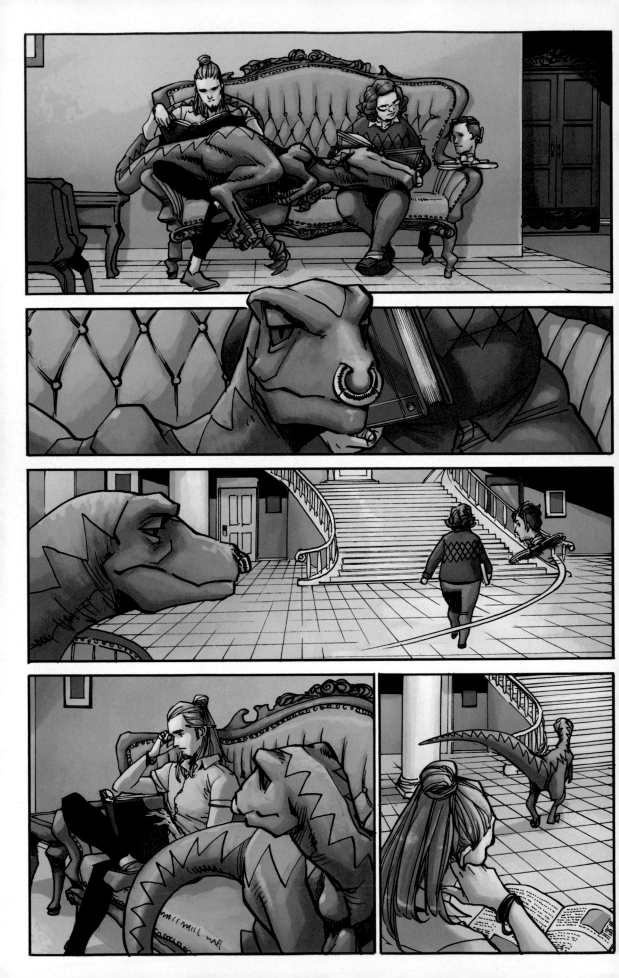

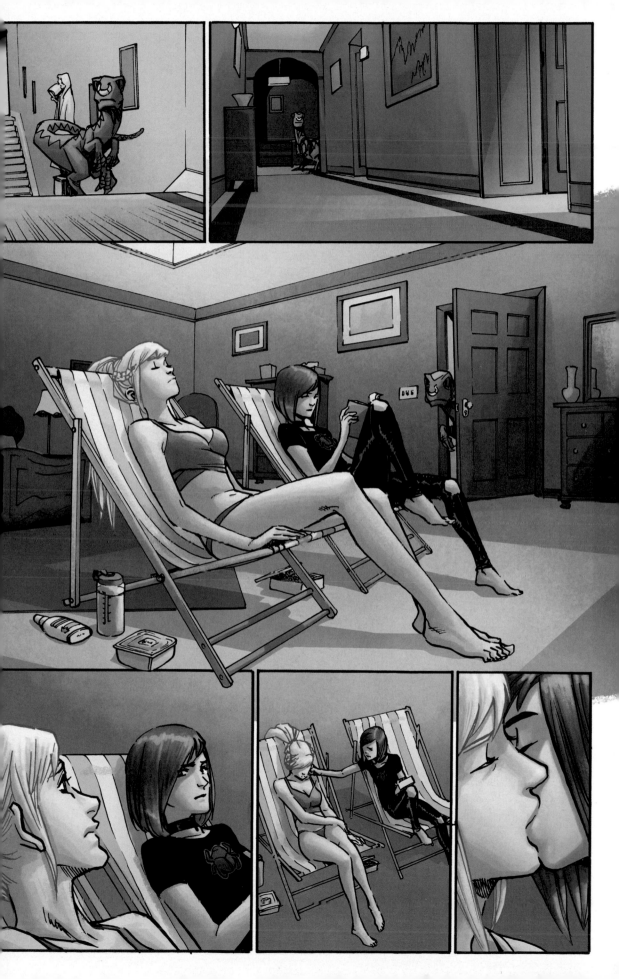

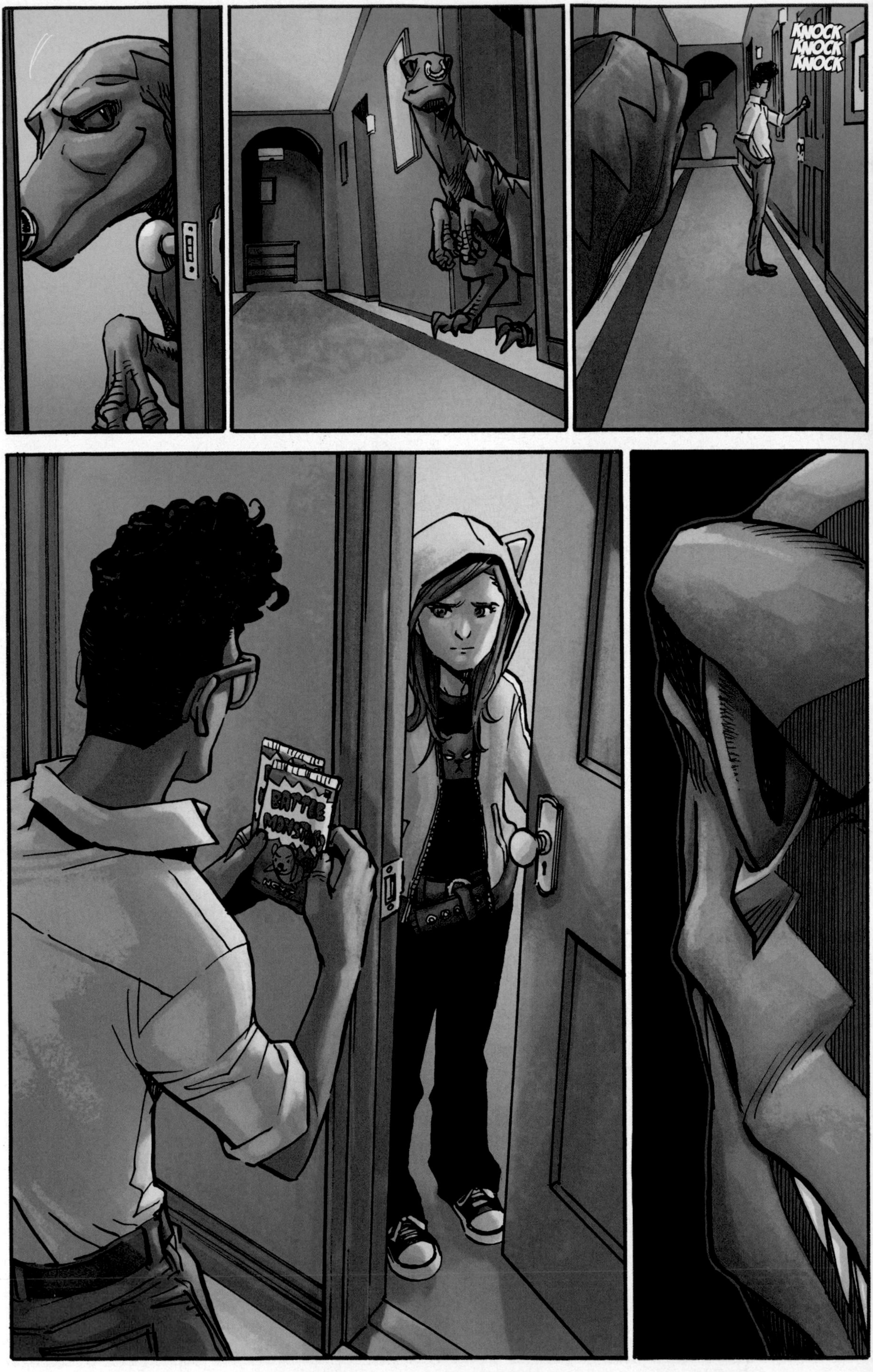
KNOCK KNOCK KNOCK
BATTLE MONSTERS

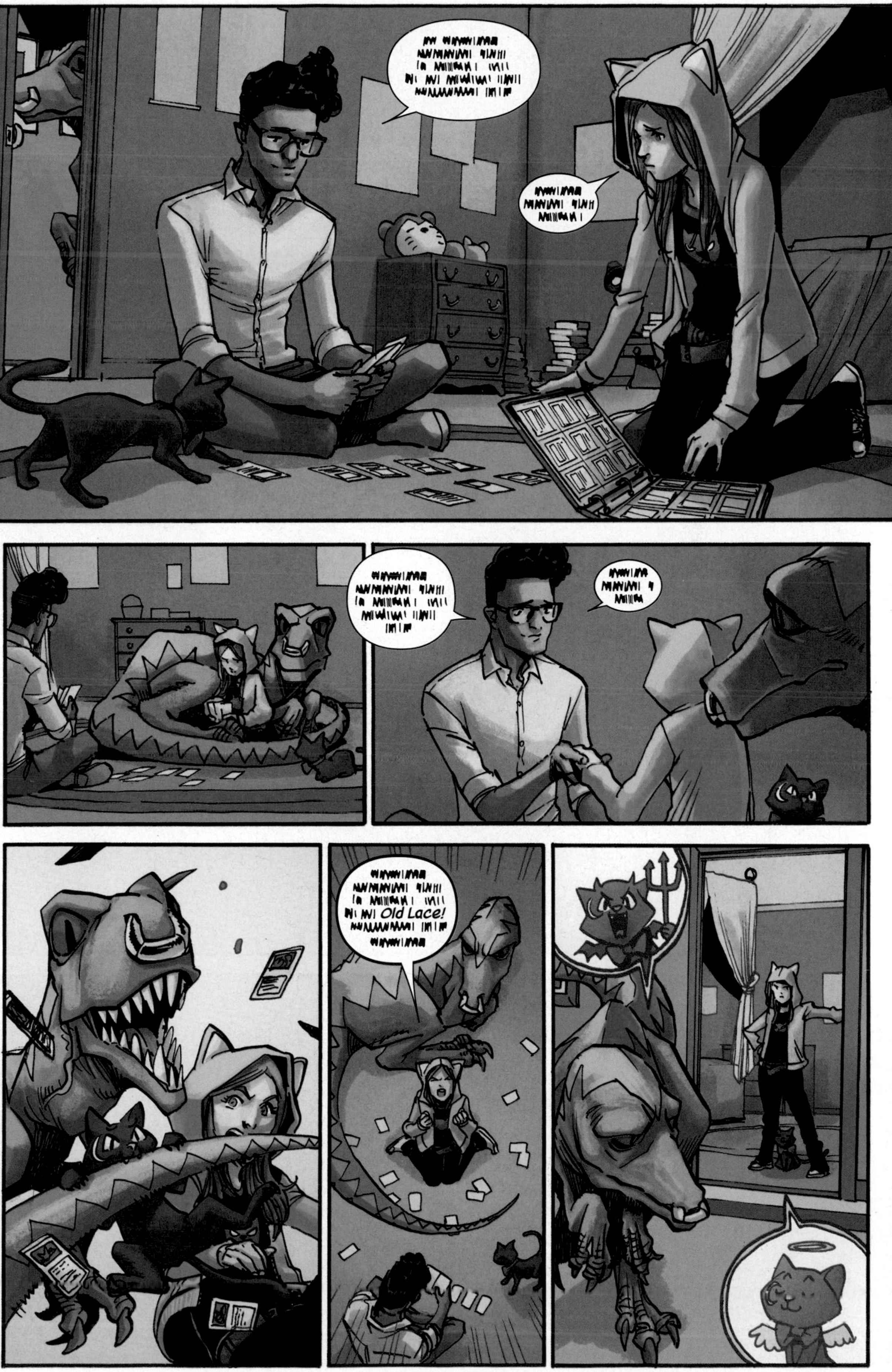
Old Lace!

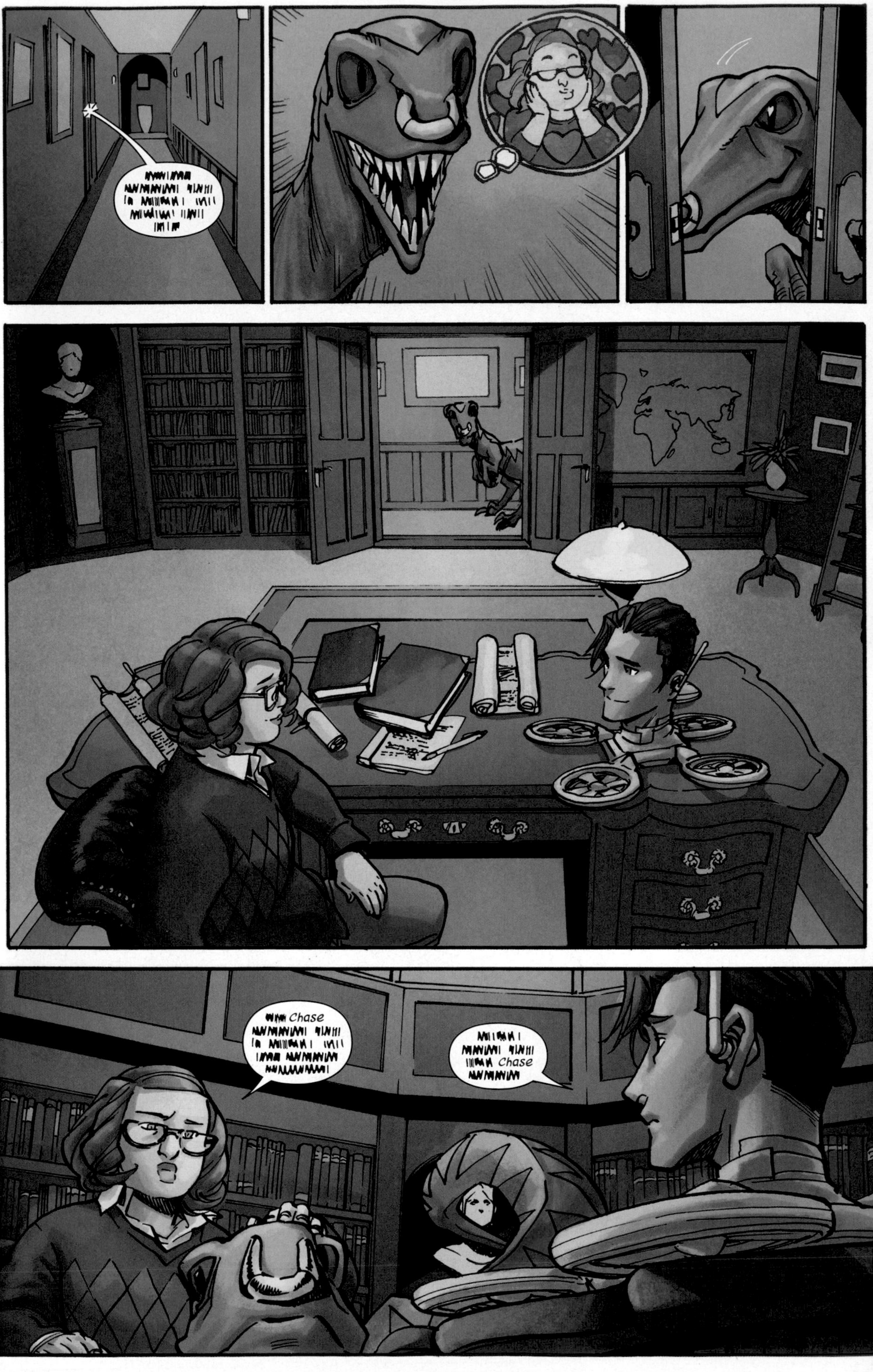
Chase
Chase

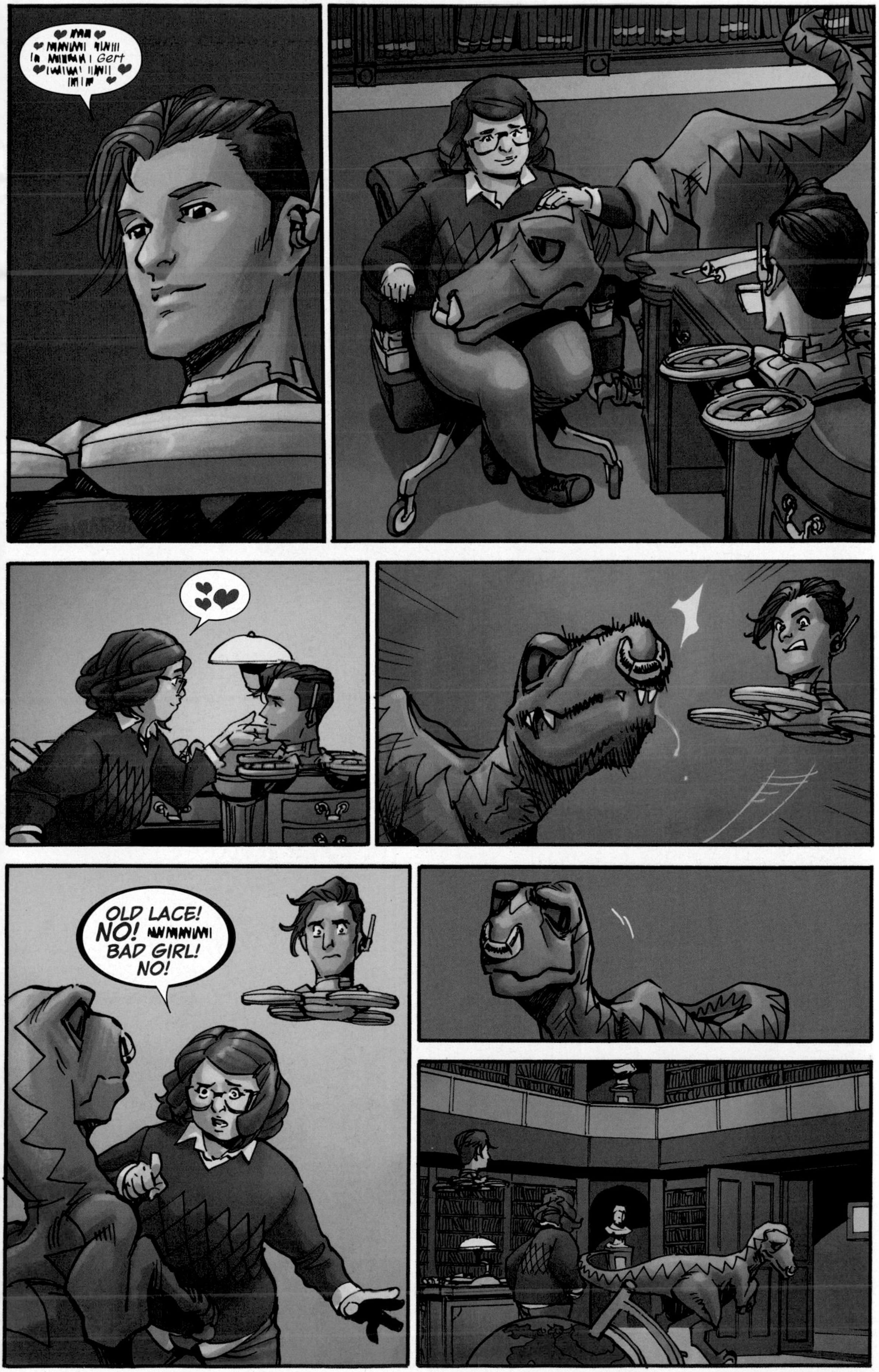
Gert
OLD LACE! NO! BAD GIRL! NO!

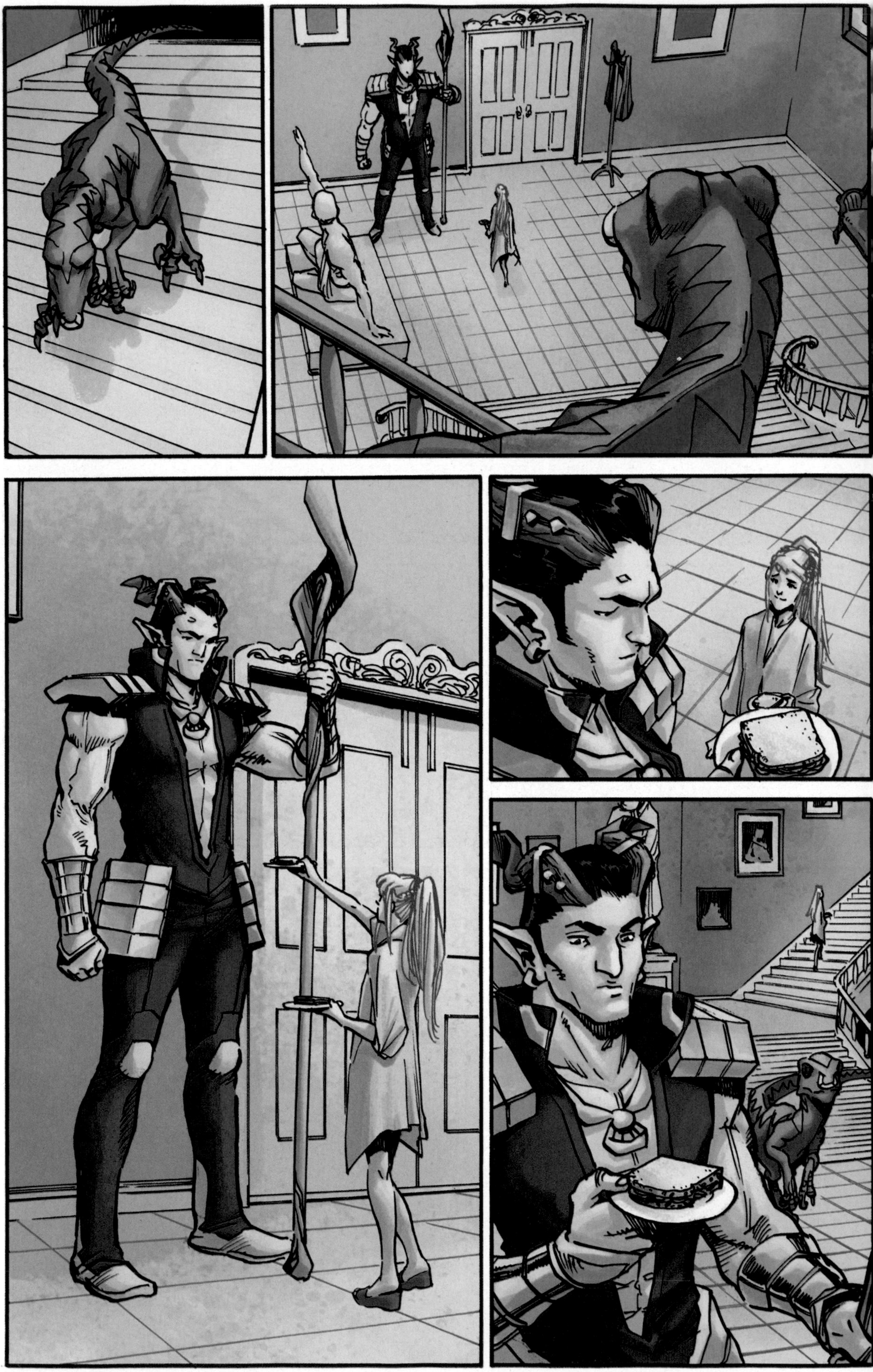

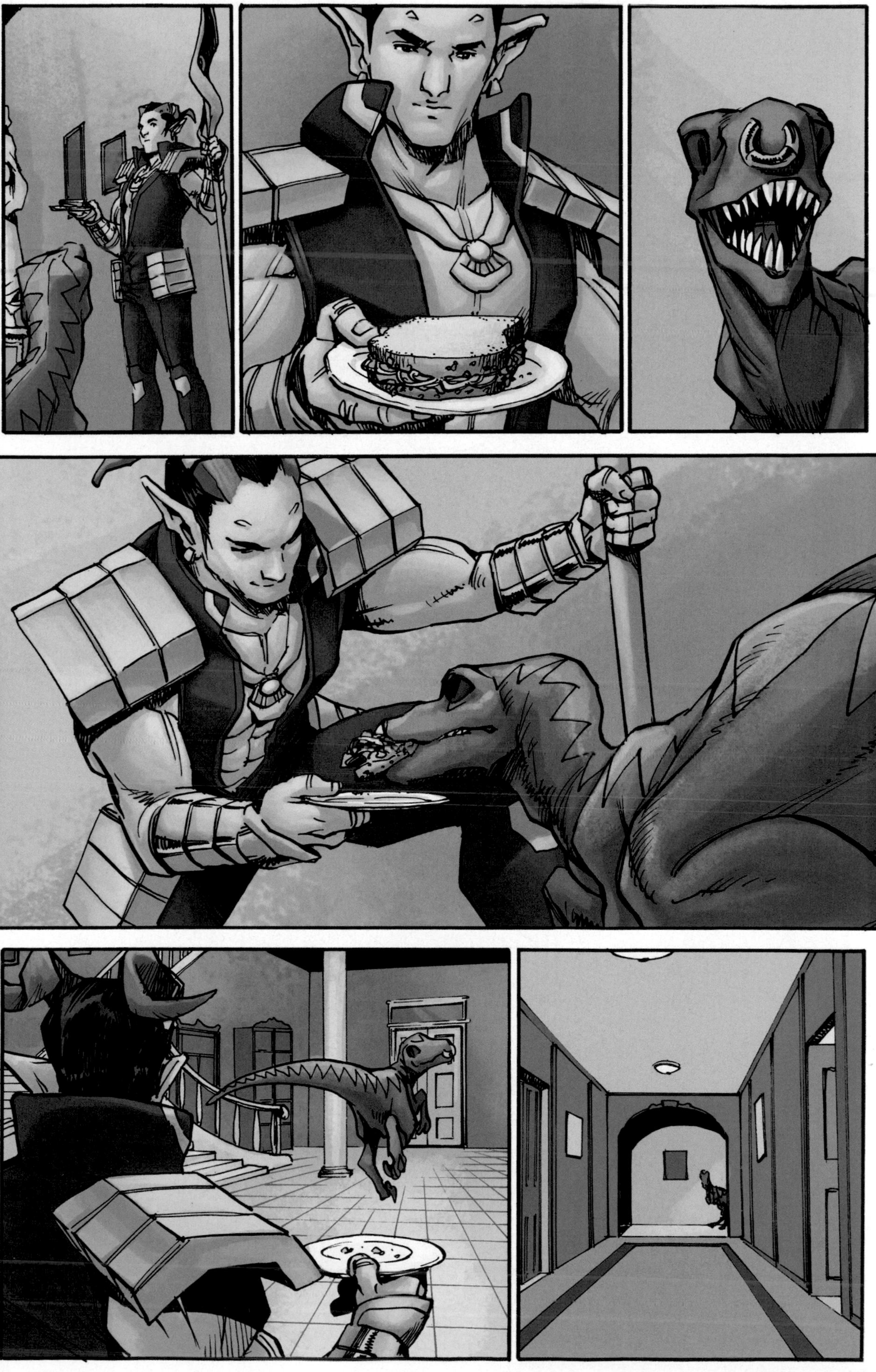

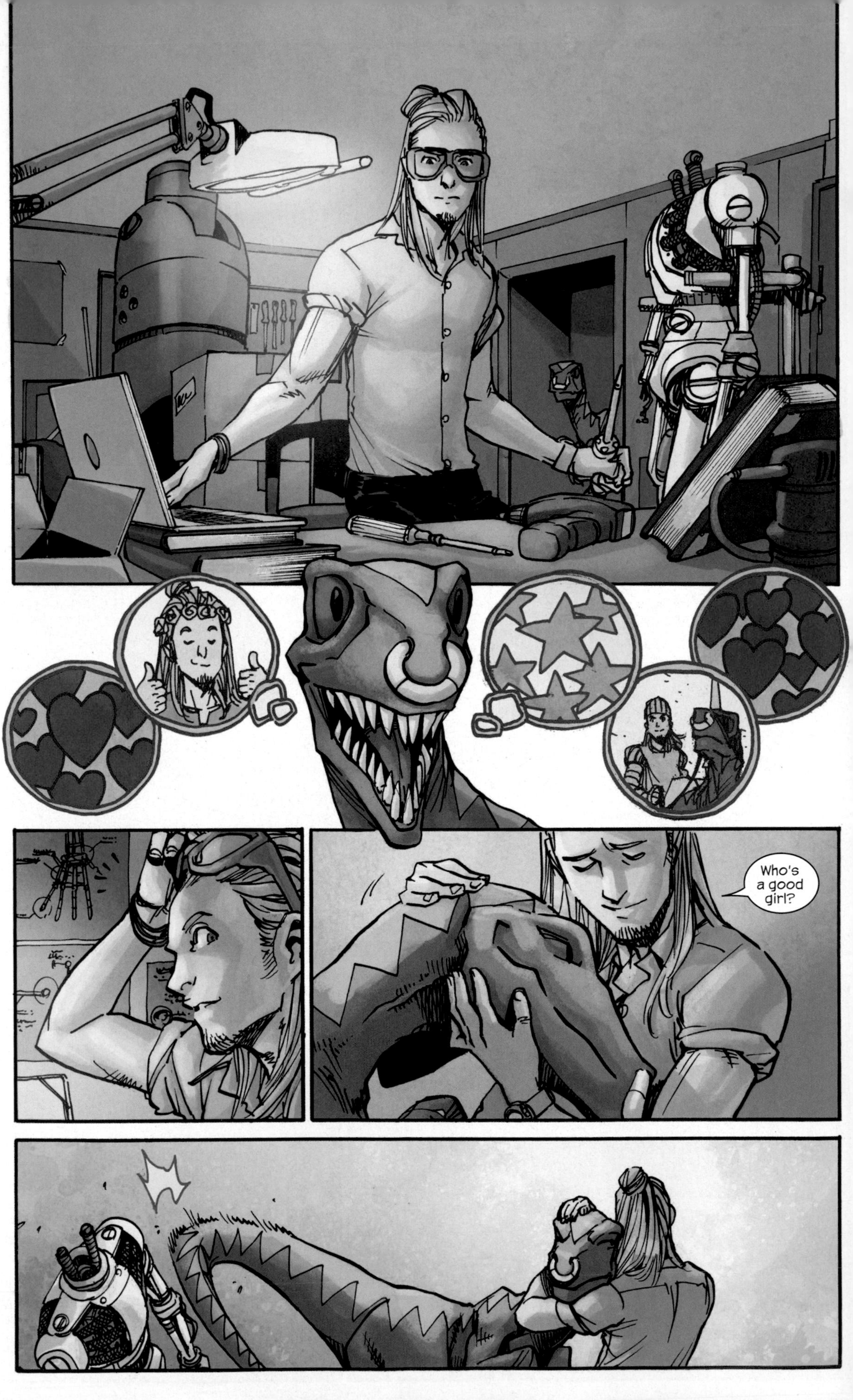
Who's a good girl?

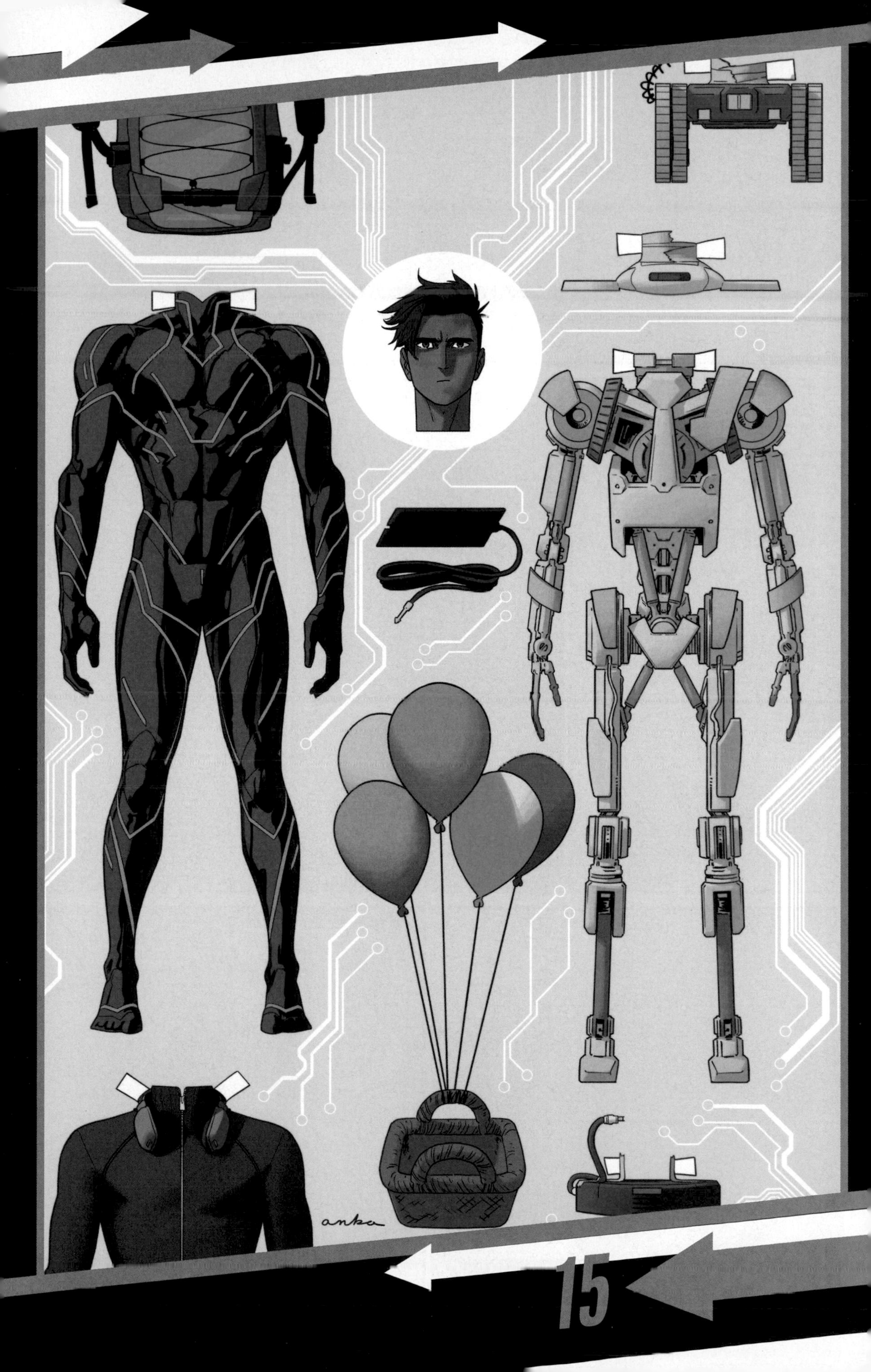
anka

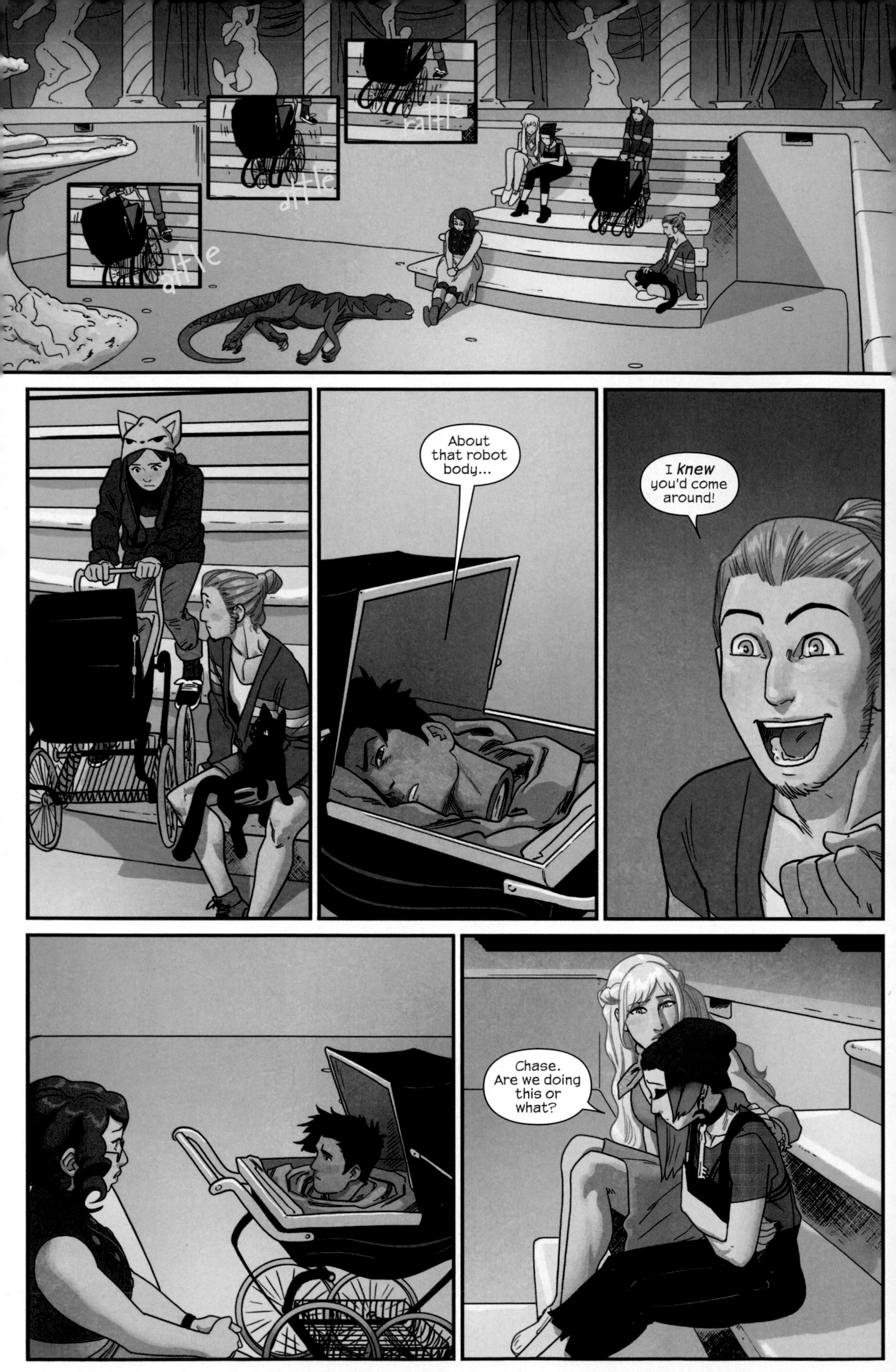
rattle
rattle
rattle
rattle
About that robot body...
I knew you'd come around!
Chase. Are we doing this or what?

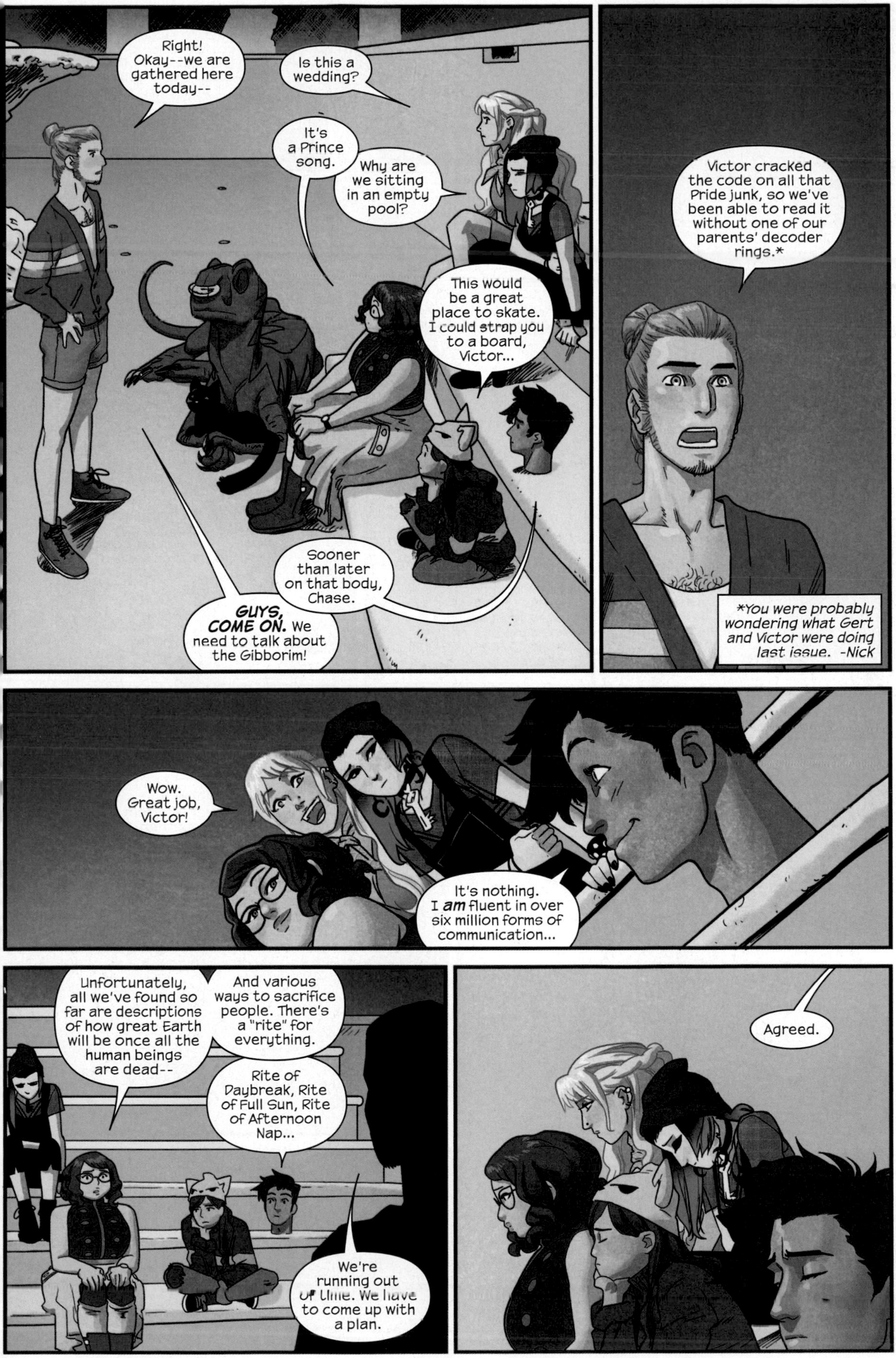
Right! Okay--we are gathered here today--
Is this a wedding?
It's a Prince song.
Why are we sitting in an empty pool?
This would be a great place to skate. I could strap you to a board, Victor...
Sooner than later on that body, Chase.
GUYS, COME ON. We need to talk about the Gibborim!
Victor cracked the code on all that Pride junk, so we've been able to read it without one of our parents' decoder rings.*
*You were probably wondering what Gert and Victor were doing last issue. -Nick
Wow. Great job, Victor!
It's nothing. I am fluent in over six million forms of communication...
Unfortunately, all we've found so far are descriptions of how great Earth will be once all the human beings are dead--
And various ways to sacrifice people. There's a "rite" for everything.
Rite of Daybreak, Rite of Full Sun, Rite of Afternoon Nap...
We're running out of time. We have to come up with a plan.
Agreed.

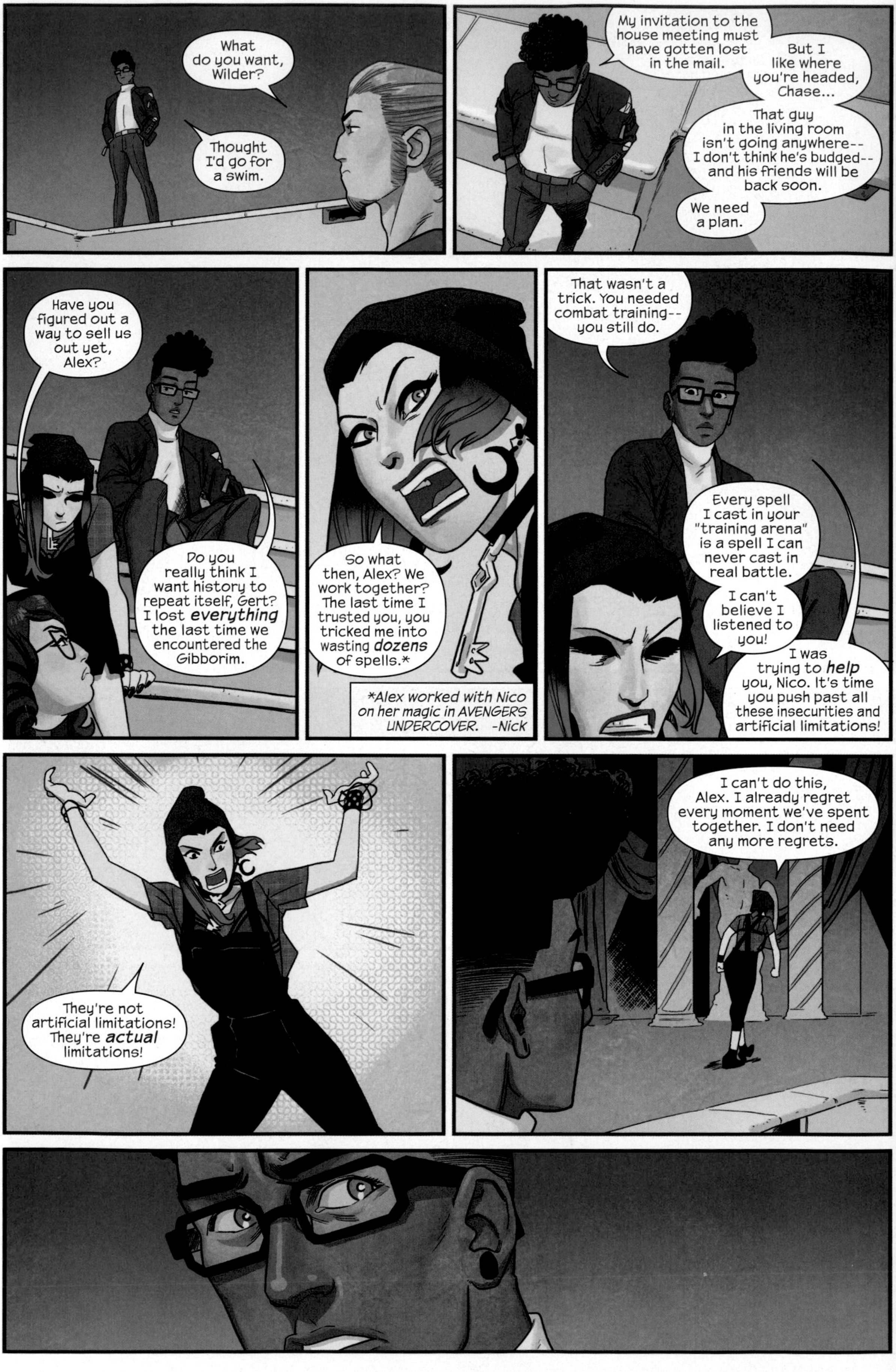
What do you want, Wilder?
Thought I'd go for a swim.
My invitation to the house meeting must have gotten lost in the mail.
But I like where you're headed, Chase...
That guy in the living room isn't going anywhere-- I don't think he's budged-- and his friends will be back soon.
We need a plan.
Have you figured out a way to sell us out yet, Alex?
Do you really think I want history to repeat itself, Gert? I lost *everything* the last time we encountered the Gibborim.
So what then, Alex? We work together? The last time I trusted you, you tricked me into wasting *dozens* of spells.*
*Alex worked with Nico on her magic in AVENGERS UNDERCOVER. -Nick
That wasn't a trick. You needed combat training-- you still do.
Every spell I cast in your "training arena" is a spell I can never cast in real battle.
I can't believe I listened to you!
I was trying to *help* you, Nico. It's time you push past all these insecurities and artificial limitations!
They're not artificial limitations! They're *actual* limitations!
I can't do this, Alex. I already regret every moment we've spent together. I don't need any more regrets.

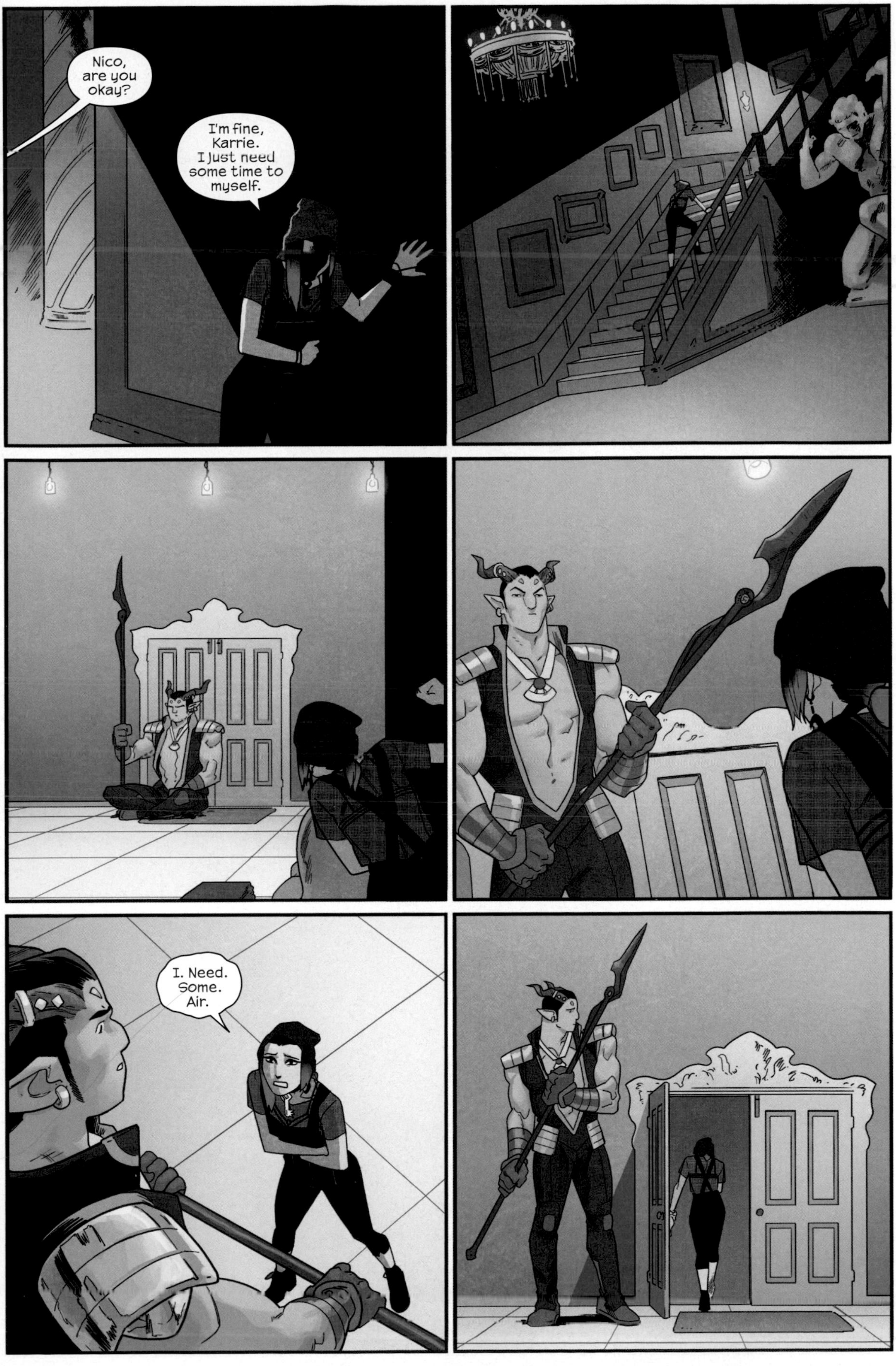
Nico, are you okay?
I'm fine, Karrie. I just need some time to myself.
I. Need. Some. Air.

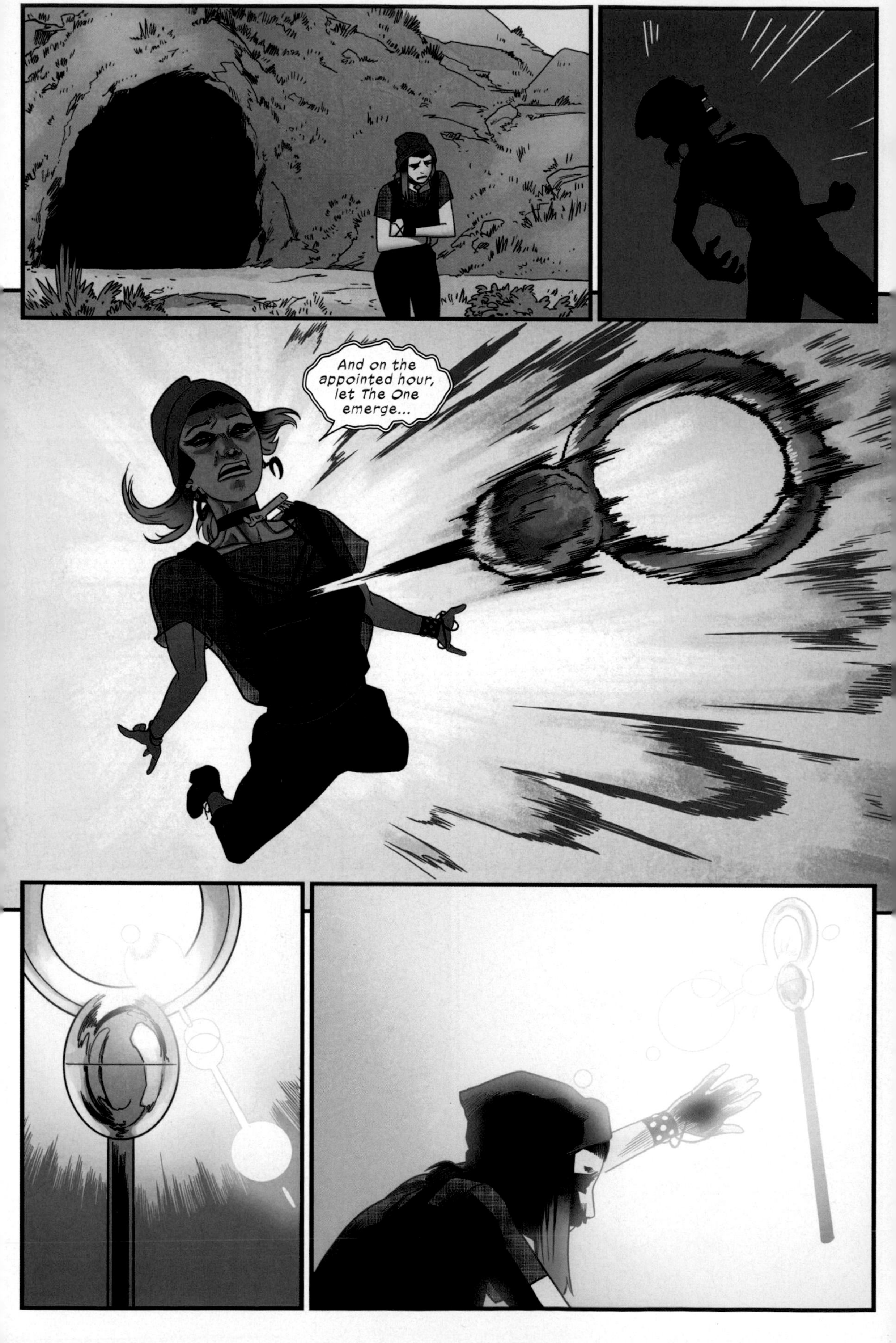
And on the appointed hour, let The One emerge...

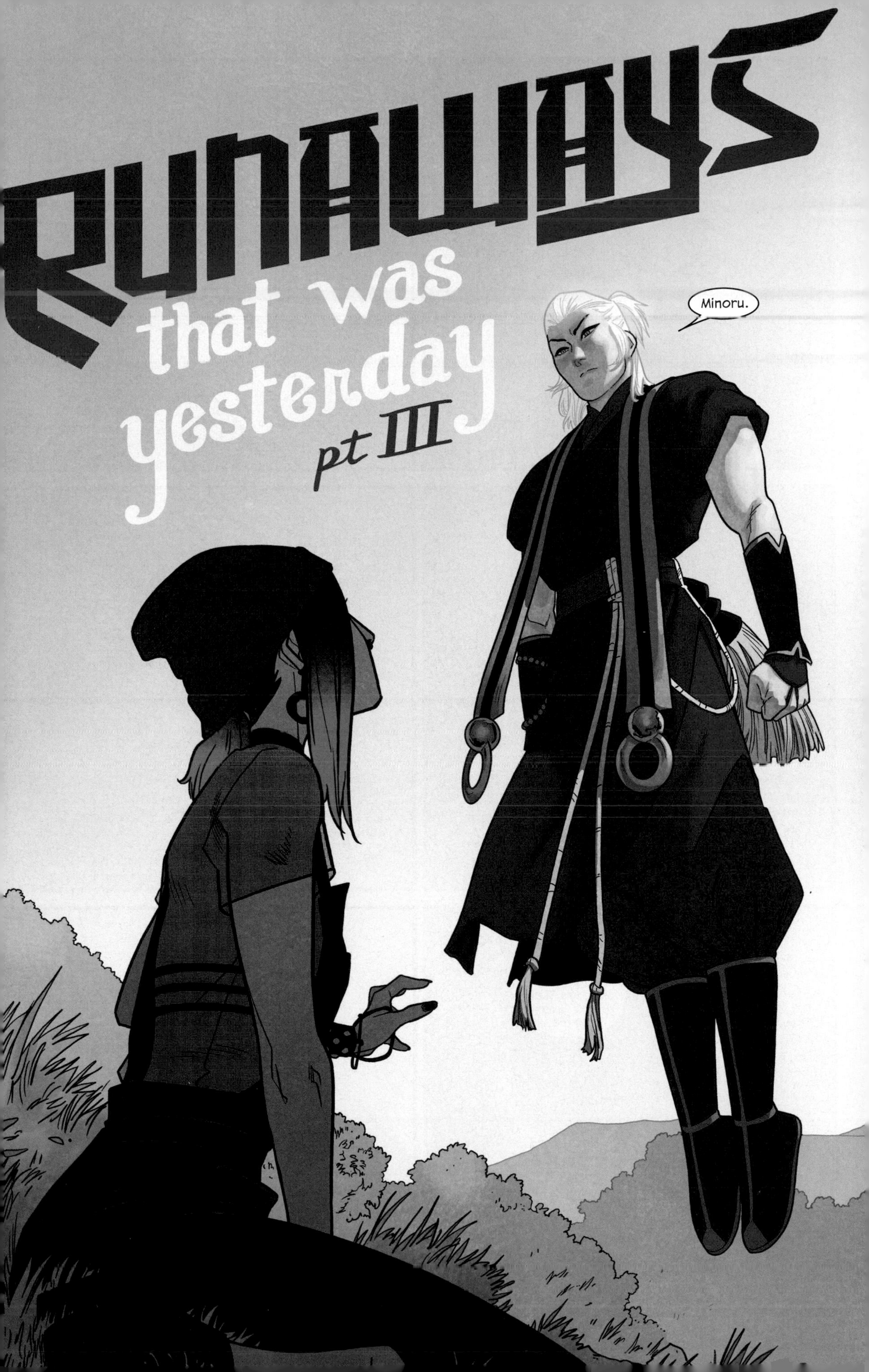
RUNAWAYS
that was yesterday pt III
Minoru.

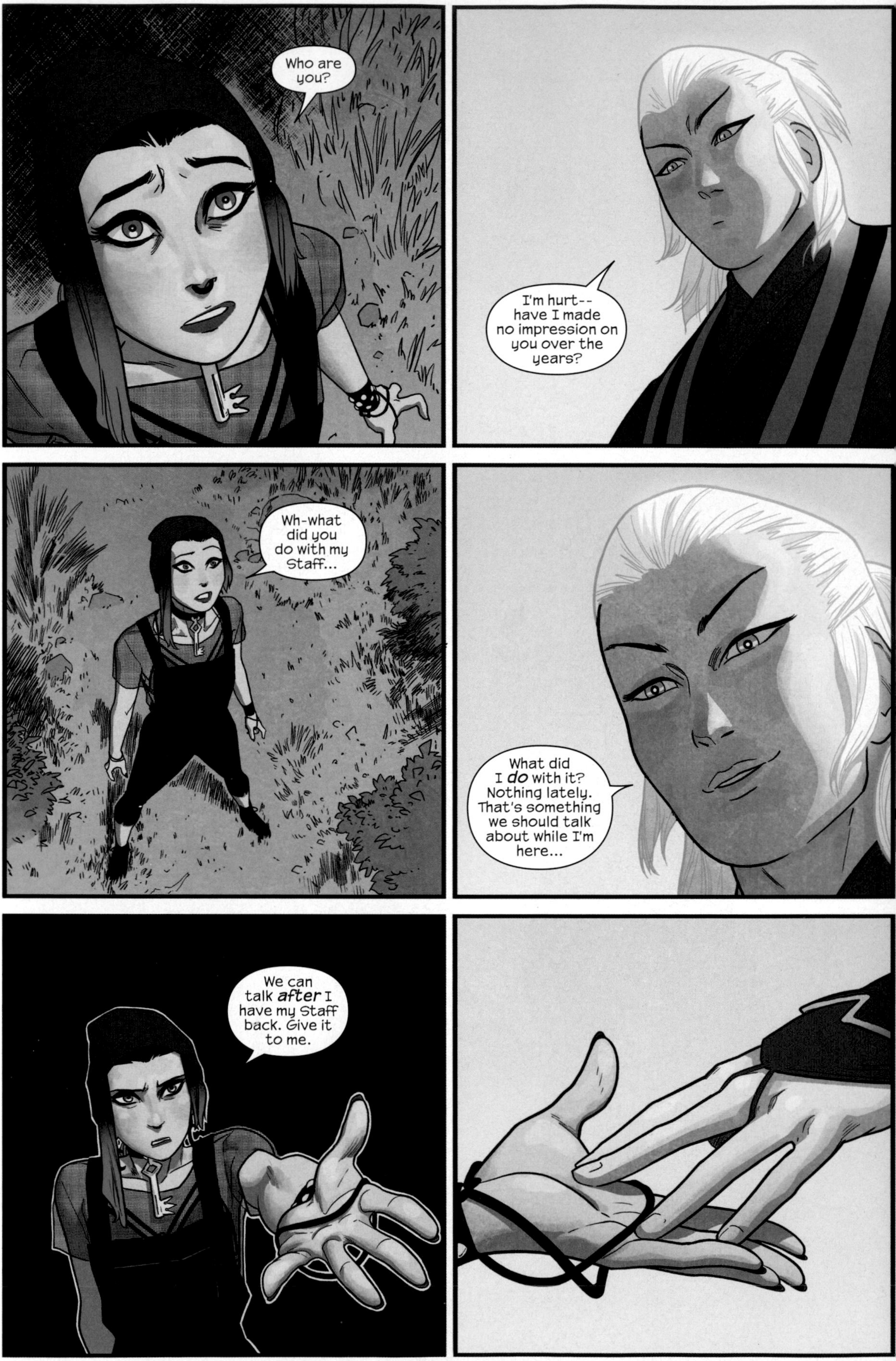
Who are you?
I'm hurt-- have I made no impression on you over the years?
Wh-what did you do with my Staff...
What did I *do* with it? Nothing lately. That's something we should talk about while I'm here...
We can talk *after* I have my Staff back. Give it to me.

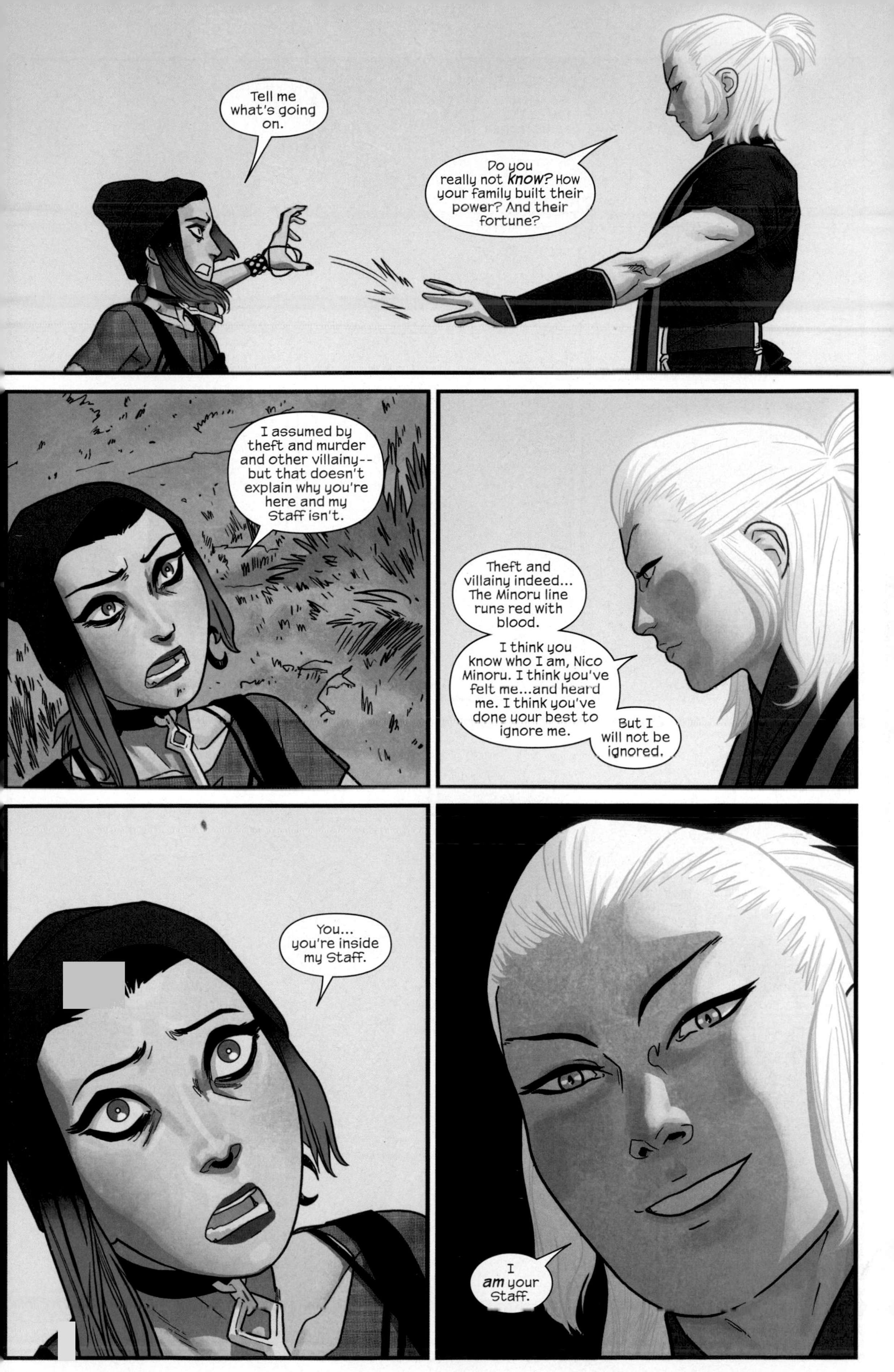
Tell me what's going on.
Do you really not *know?* How your family built their power? And their fortune?
I assumed by theft and murder and other villainy--but that doesn't explain why you're here and my Staff isn't.
Theft and villainy indeed... The Minoru line runs red with blood.
I think you know who I am, Nico Minoru. I think you've felt me...and heard me. I think you've done your best to ignore me.
But I will not be ignored.
You... you're inside my Staff.
I *am* your Staff.

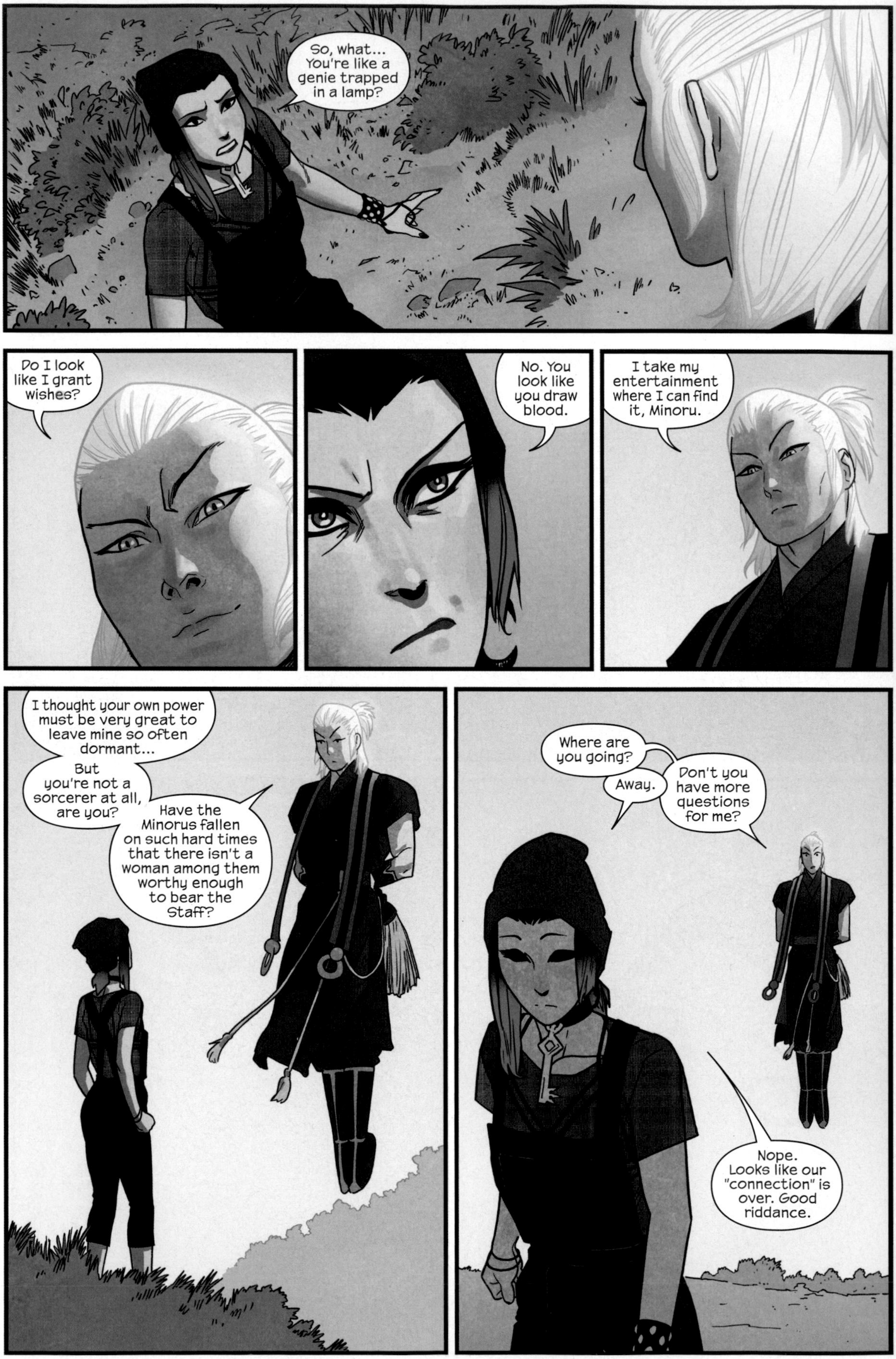
So, what... You're like a genie trapped in a lamp?
Do I look like I grant wishes?
No. You look like you draw blood.
I take my entertainment where I can find it, Minoru.
I thought your own power must be very great to leave mine so often dormant...
But you're not a sorcerer at all, are you?
Have the Minorus fallen on such hard times that there isn't a woman among them worthy enough to bear the Staff?
Where are you going?
Away.
Don't you have more questions for me?
Nope. Looks like our "connection" is over. Good riddance.

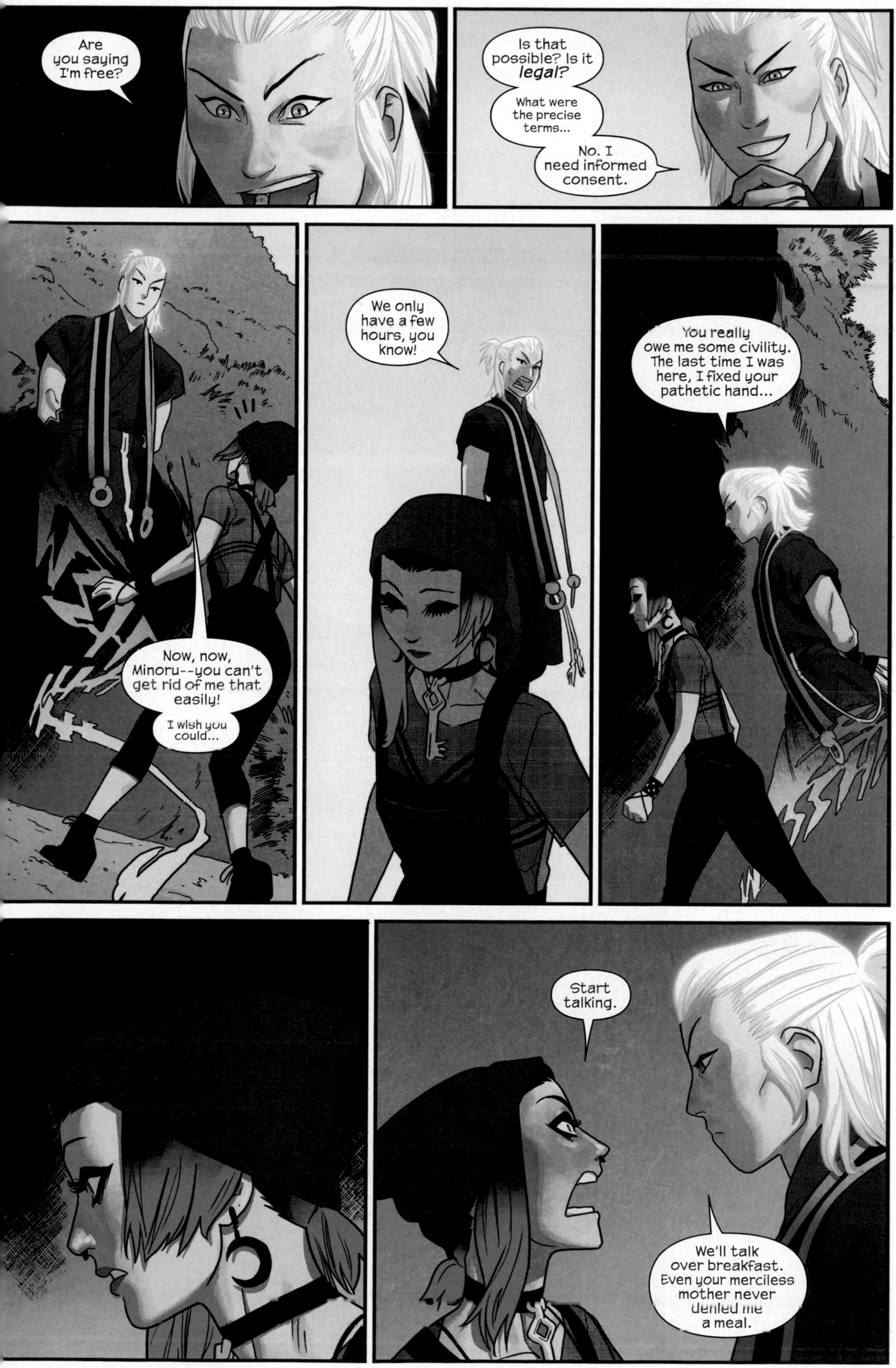
Are you saying I'm free?
Is that possible? Is it *legal?*
What were the precise terms...
No. I need informed consent.
Now, now, Minoru--you can't get rid of me that easily!
I wish you could...
We only have a few hours, you know!
You really owe me some civility. The last time I was here, I fixed your pathetic hand...
Start talking.
We'll talk over breakfast. Even your merciless mother never denied me a meal.

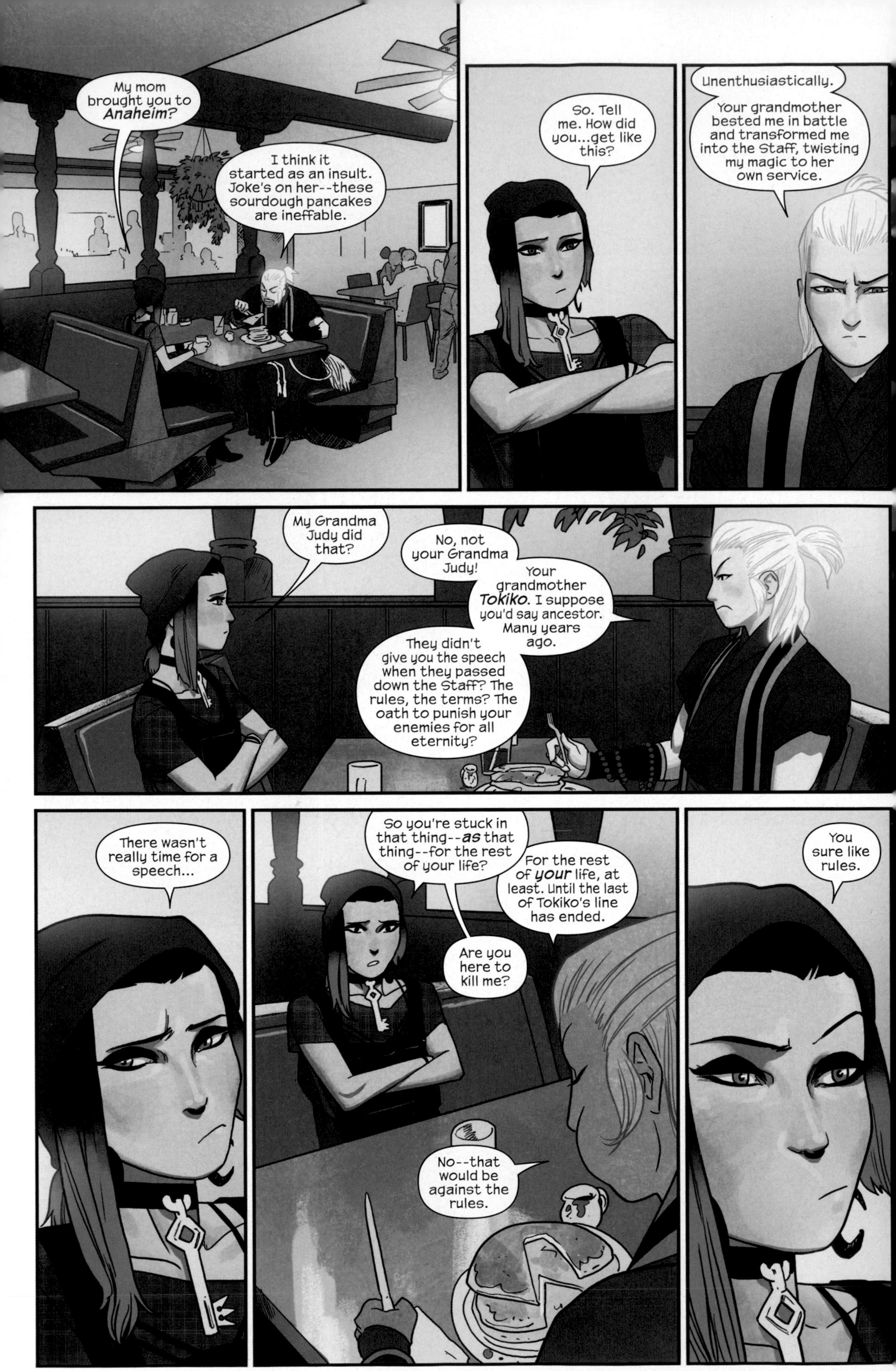

My mom brought you to Anaheim?
I think it started as an insult. Joke's on her--these sourdough pancakes are ineffable.
So. Tell me. How did you...get like this?
Unenthusiastically.
Your grandmother bested me in battle and transformed me into the Staff, twisting my magic to her own service.
My Grandma Judy did that?
No, not your Grandma Judy!
Your grandmother Tokiko. I suppose you'd say ancestor. Many years ago.
They didn't give you the speech when they passed down the Staff? The rules, the terms? The oath to punish your enemies for all eternity?
There wasn't really time for a speech...
So you're stuck in that thing--as that thing--for the rest of your life?
For the rest of your life, at least. Until the last of Tokiko's line has ended.
Are you here to kill me?
No--that would be against the rules.
You sure like rules.

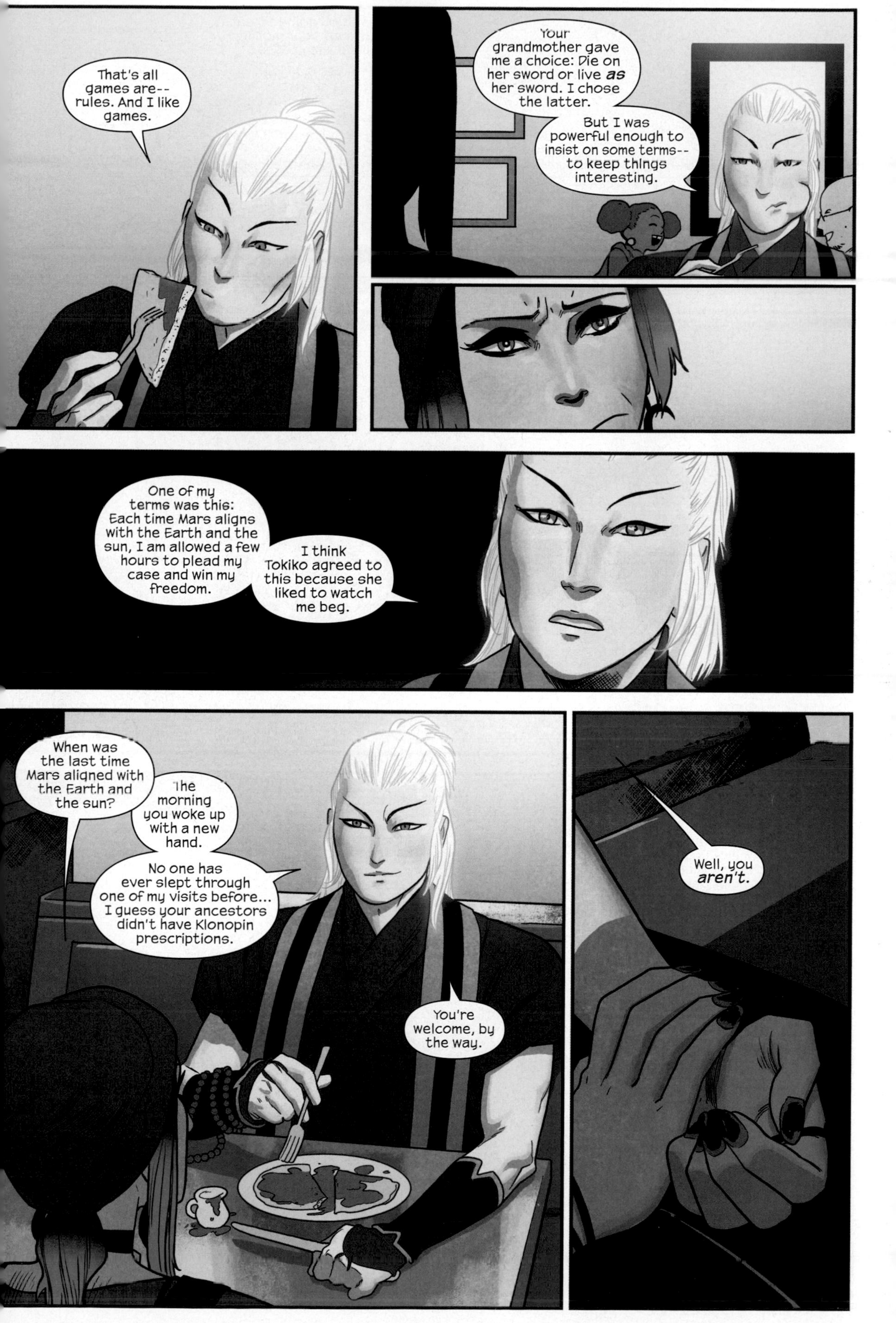
That's all games are-- rules. And I like games.
Your grandmother gave me a choice: Die on her sword or live *as* her sword. I chose the latter.
But I was powerful enough to insist on some terms-- to keep things interesting.
One of my terms was this: Each time Mars aligns with the Earth and the sun, I am allowed a few hours to plead my case and win my freedom.
I think Tokiko agreed to this because she liked to watch me beg.
When was the last time Mars aligned with the Earth and the sun?
The morning you woke up with a new hand.
No one has ever slept through one of my visits before... I guess your ancestors didn't have Klonopin prescriptions.
You're welcome, by the way.
Well, you *aren't*.

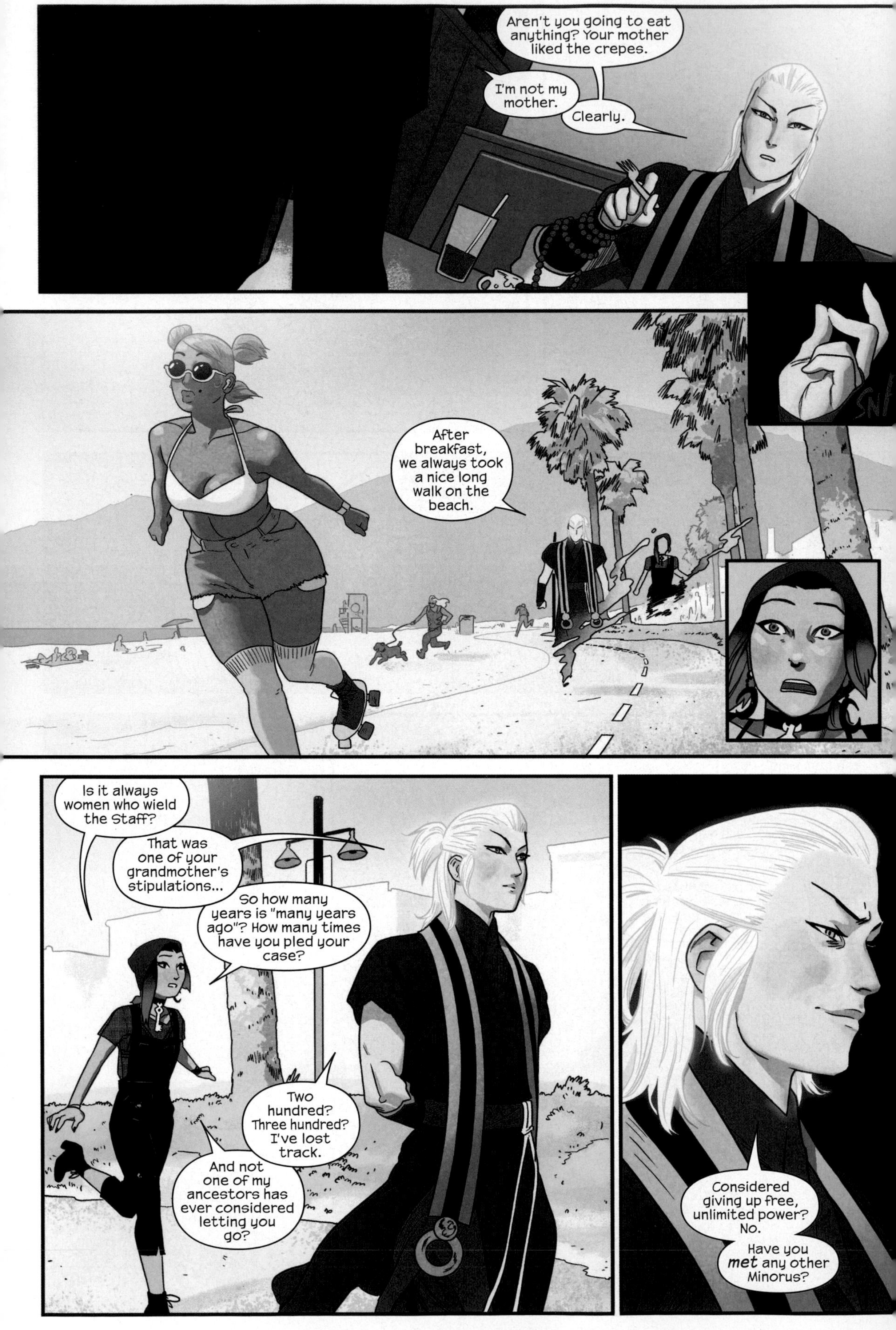
Aren't you going to eat anything? Your mother liked the crepes.
I'm not my mother.
Clearly.
SNF
After breakfast, we always took a nice long walk on the beach.
Is it always women who wield the Staff?
That was one of your grandmother's stipulations...
So how many years is "many years ago"? How many times have you pled your case?
Two hundred? Three hundred? I've lost track.
And not one of my ancestors has ever considered letting you go?
Considered giving up free, unlimited power? No.
Have you *met* any other Minorus?

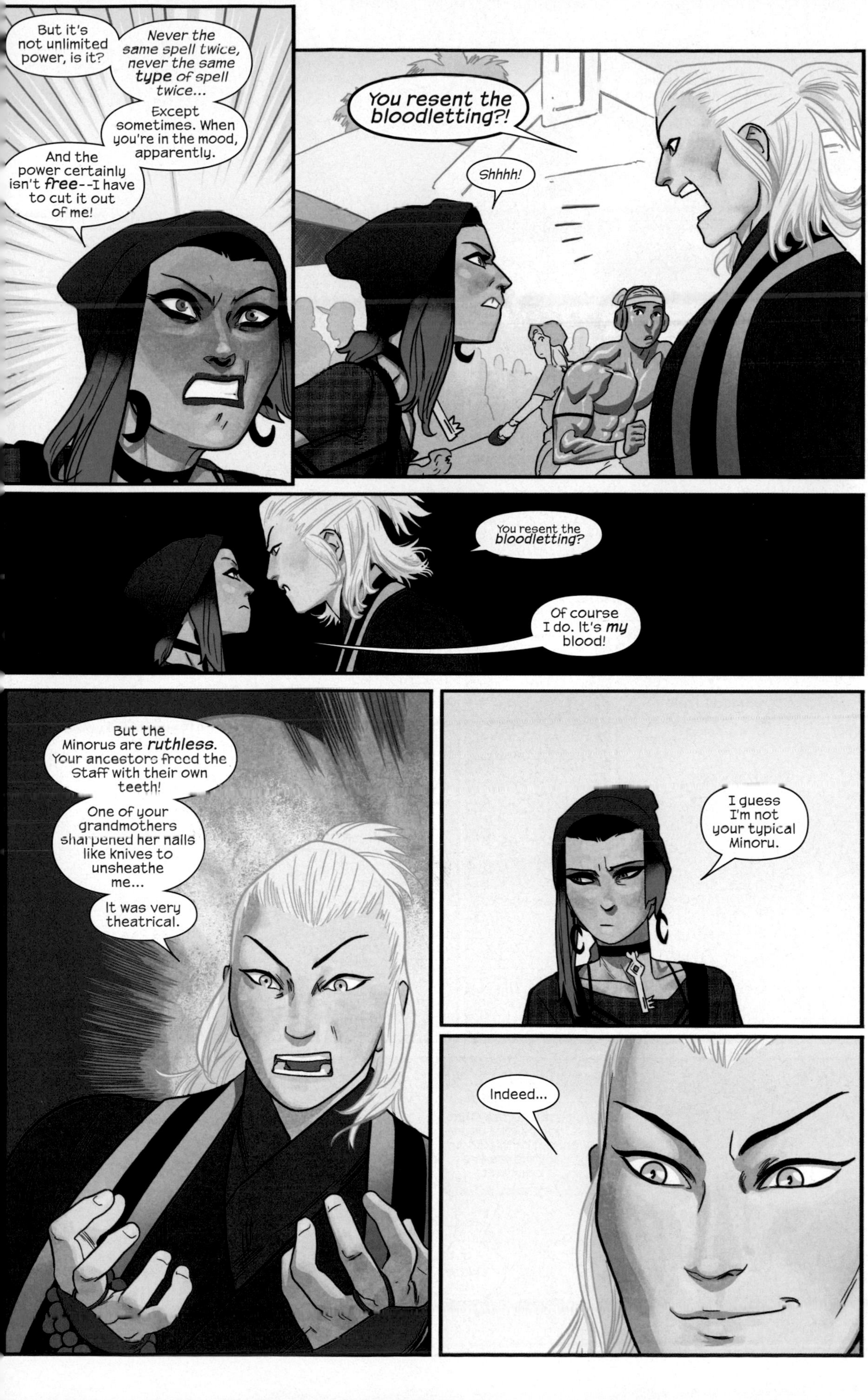

But it's not unlimited power, is it?
Never the same spell twice, never the same type of spell twice...
Except sometimes. When you're in the mood, apparently.
And the power certainly isn't free--I have to cut it out of me!
You resent the bloodletting?!
Shhhh!
You resent the bloodletting?
Of course I do. It's my blood!
But the Minorus are ruthless. Your ancestors freed the Staff with their own teeth!
One of your grandmothers sharpened her nails like knives to unsheathe me...
It was very theatrical.
I guess I'm not your typical Minoru.
Indeed...

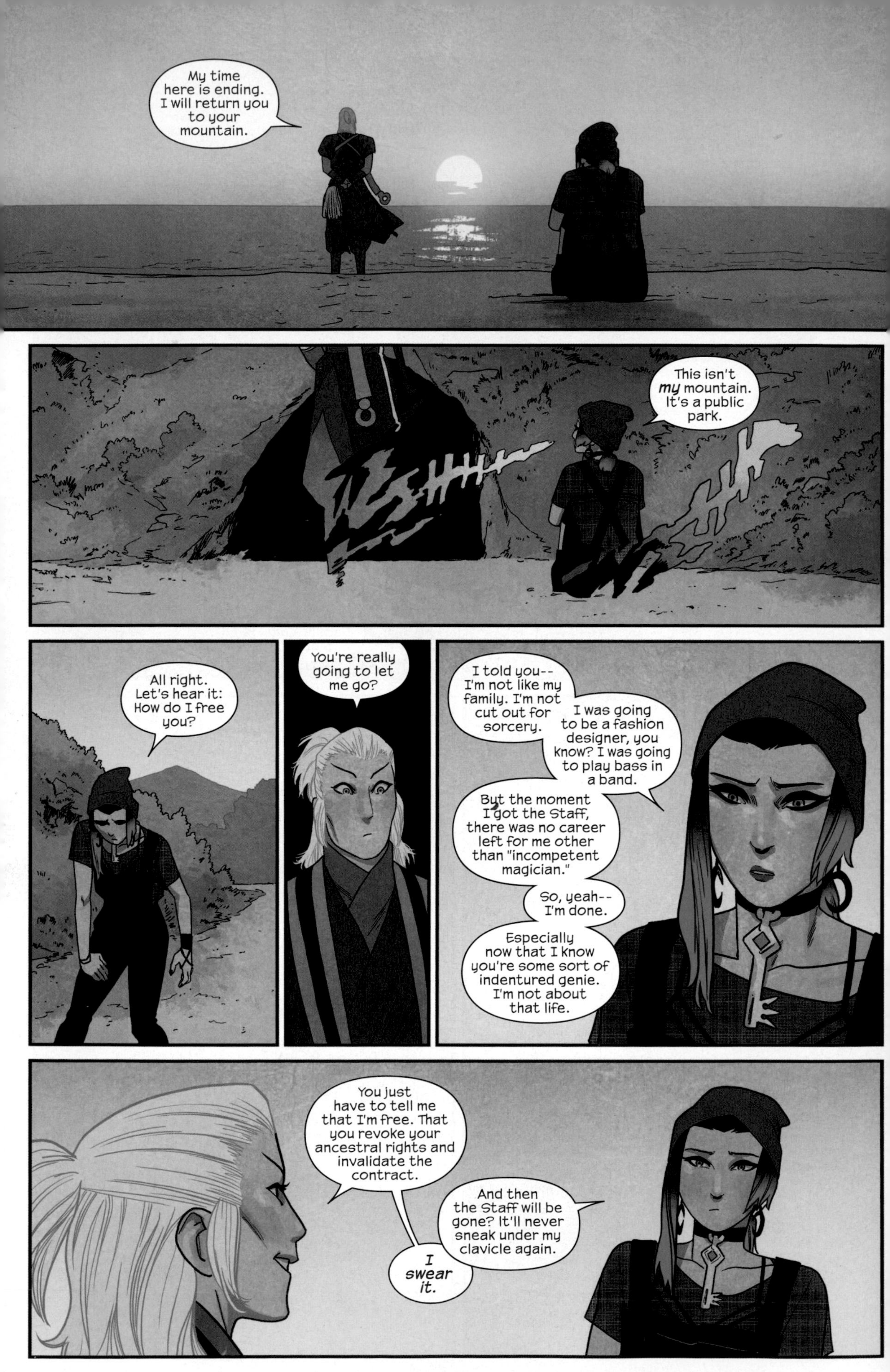
My time here is ending. I will return you to your mountain.
This isn't my mountain. It's a public park.
All right. Let's hear it: How do I free you?
You're really going to let me go?
I told you-- I'm not like my family. I'm not cut out for sorcery.
I was going to be a fashion designer, you know? I was going to play bass in a band.
But the moment I got the Staff, there was no career left for me other than "incompetent magician."
So, yeah-- I'm done.
Especially now that I know you're some sort of indentured genie. I'm not about that life.
You just have to tell me that I'm free. That you revoke your ancestral rights and invalidate the contract.
And then the Staff will be gone? It'll never sneak under my clavicle again.
I swear it.

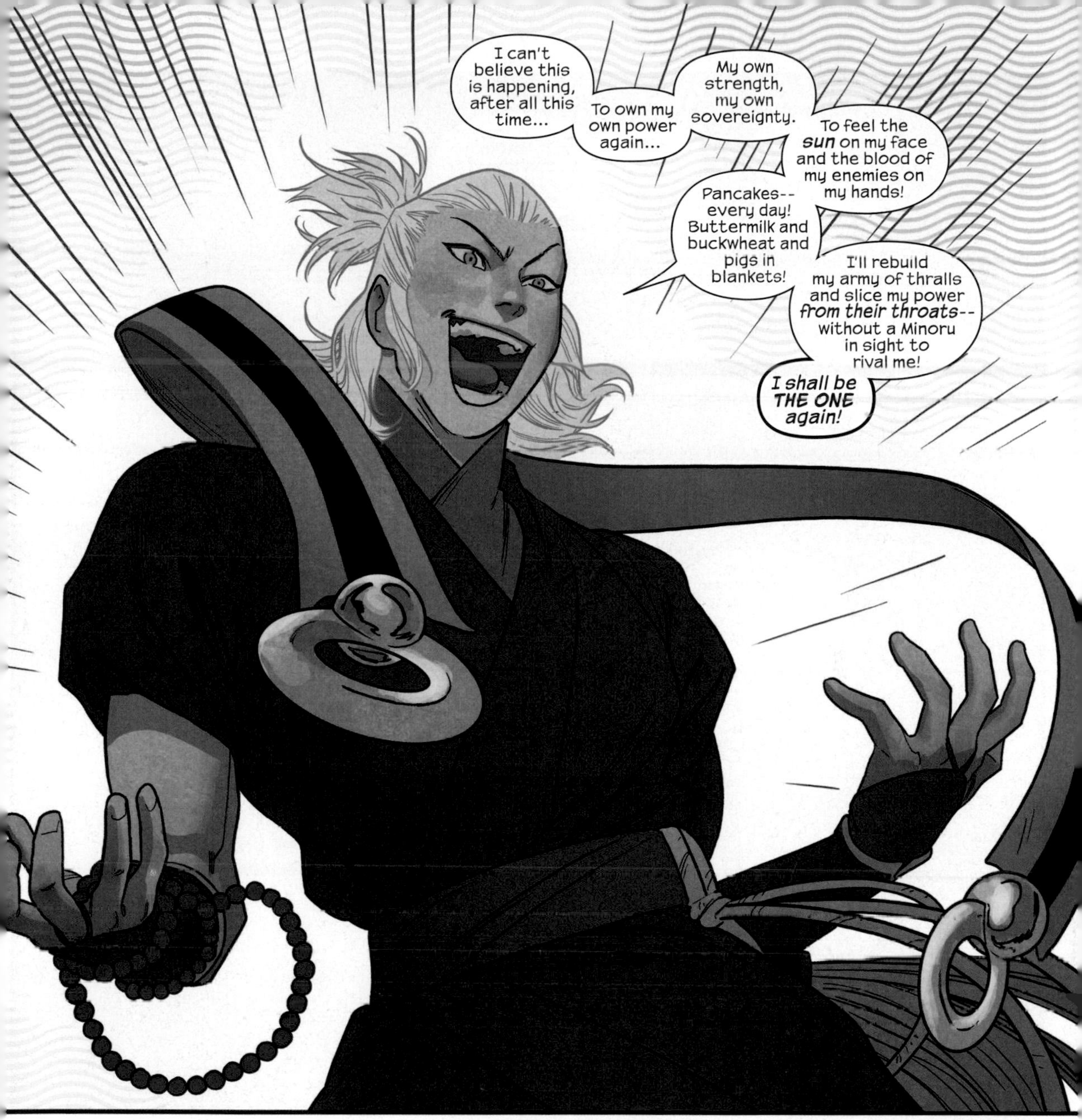

I can't believe this is happening, after all this time...
To own my own power again...
My own strength, my own sovereignty.
To feel the **sun** on my face and the blood of my enemies on my hands!
Pancakes--every day! Buttermilk and buckwheat and pigs in blankets!
I'll rebuild my army of thralls and slice my power *from their throats*--without a Minoru in sight to rival me!
I shall be ***THE ONE*** *again!*

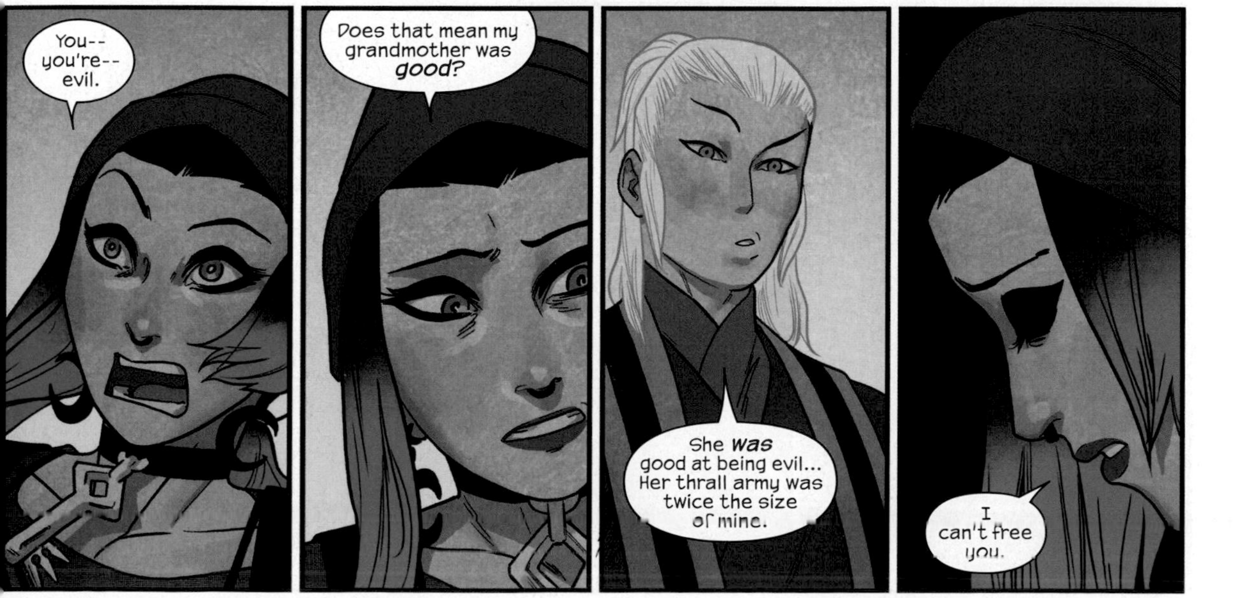

You--you're--evil.
Does that mean my grandmother was ***good?***
She ***was*** good at being evil... Her thrall army was twice the size of mine.
I can't free you.

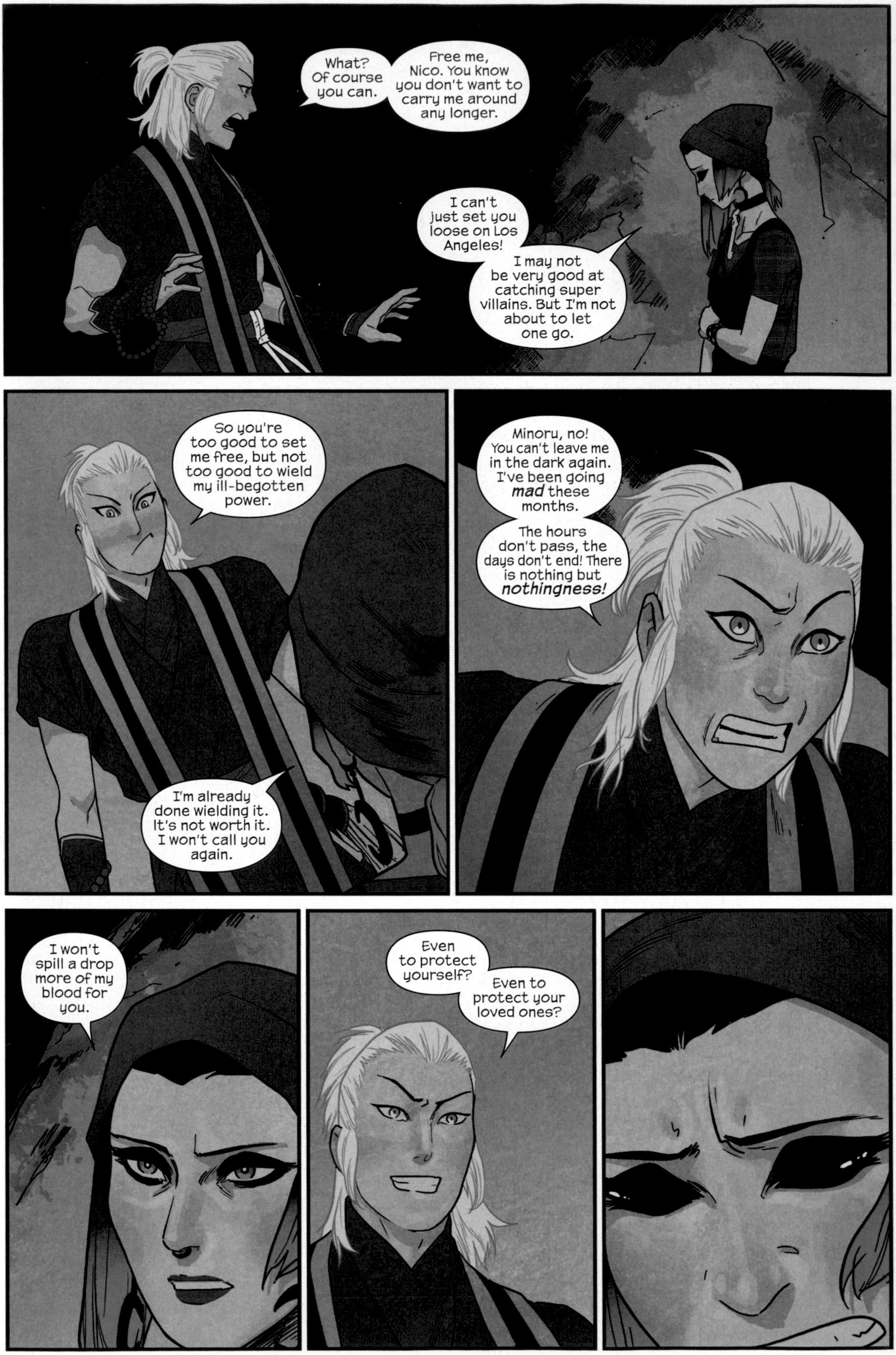
What? Of course you can.
Free me, Nico. You know you don't want to carry me around any longer.
I can't just set you loose on Los Angeles!
I may not be very good at catching super villains. But I'm not about to let one go.
So you're too good to set me free, but not too good to wield my ill-begotten power.
I'm already done wielding it. It's not worth it. I won't call you again.
Minoru, no! You can't leave me in the dark again. I've been going *mad* these months.
The hours don't pass, the days don't end! There is nothing but ***nothingness!***
I won't spill a drop more of my blood for you.
Even to protect yourself?
Even to protect your loved ones?

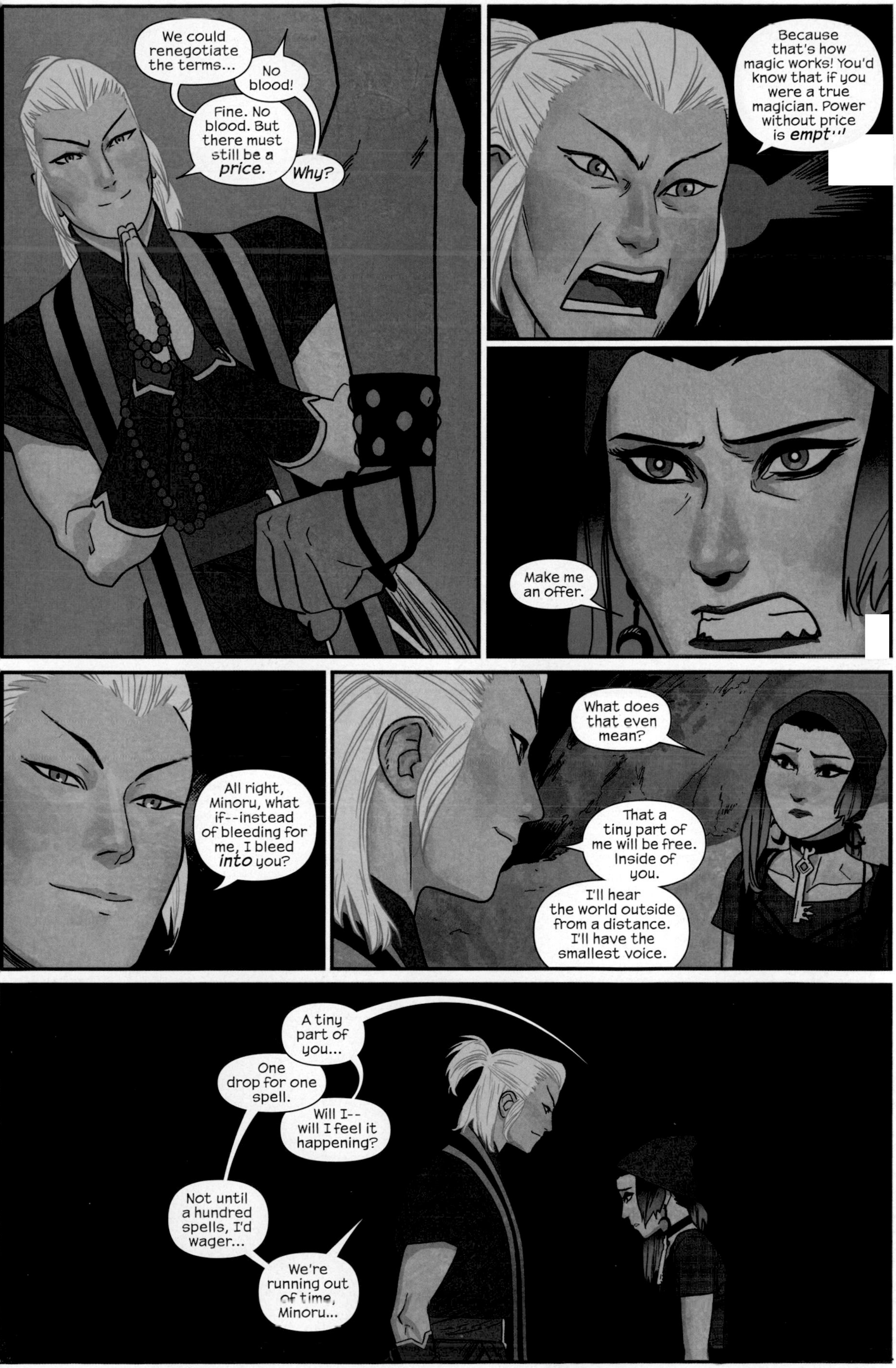
We could renegotiate the terms...
No blood!
Fine. No blood. But there must still be a *price.*
Why?
Because that's how magic works! You'd know that if you were a true magician. Power without price is *empt*
Make me an offer.
All right, Minoru, what if--instead of bleeding for me, I bleed *into* you?
What does that even mean?
That a tiny part of me will be free. Inside of you.
I'll hear the world outside from a distance. I'll have the smallest voice.
A tiny part of you...
One drop for one spell.
Will I--will I feel it happening?
Not until a hundred spells, I'd wager...
We're running out of time, Minoru...

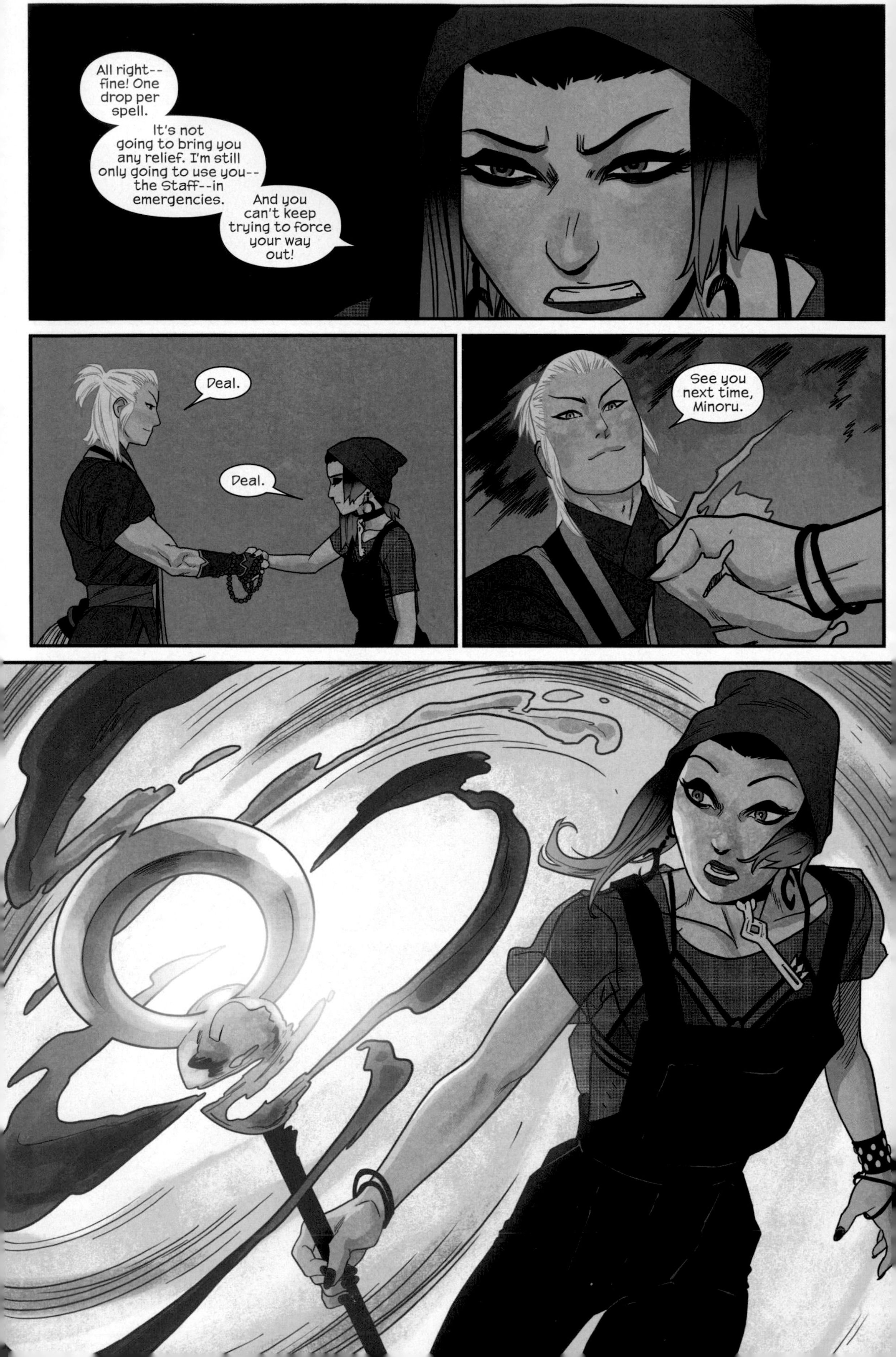
All right--fine! One drop per spell.
It's not going to bring you any relief. I'm still only going to use you--the Staff--in emergencies.
And you can't keep trying to force your way out!
Deal.
Deal.
See you next time, Minoru.

Nico! We looked everywhere! Where were you? Did you leave? Did Gib *let* you leave? Are you okay?

I'm fine. I promise.

You smell like...maple syrup. Did you break out of here to eat pancakes?

Sort of.

And you didn't even bring me some back? You are the worst girlfriend ever.

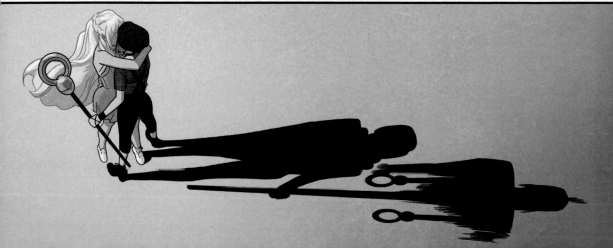

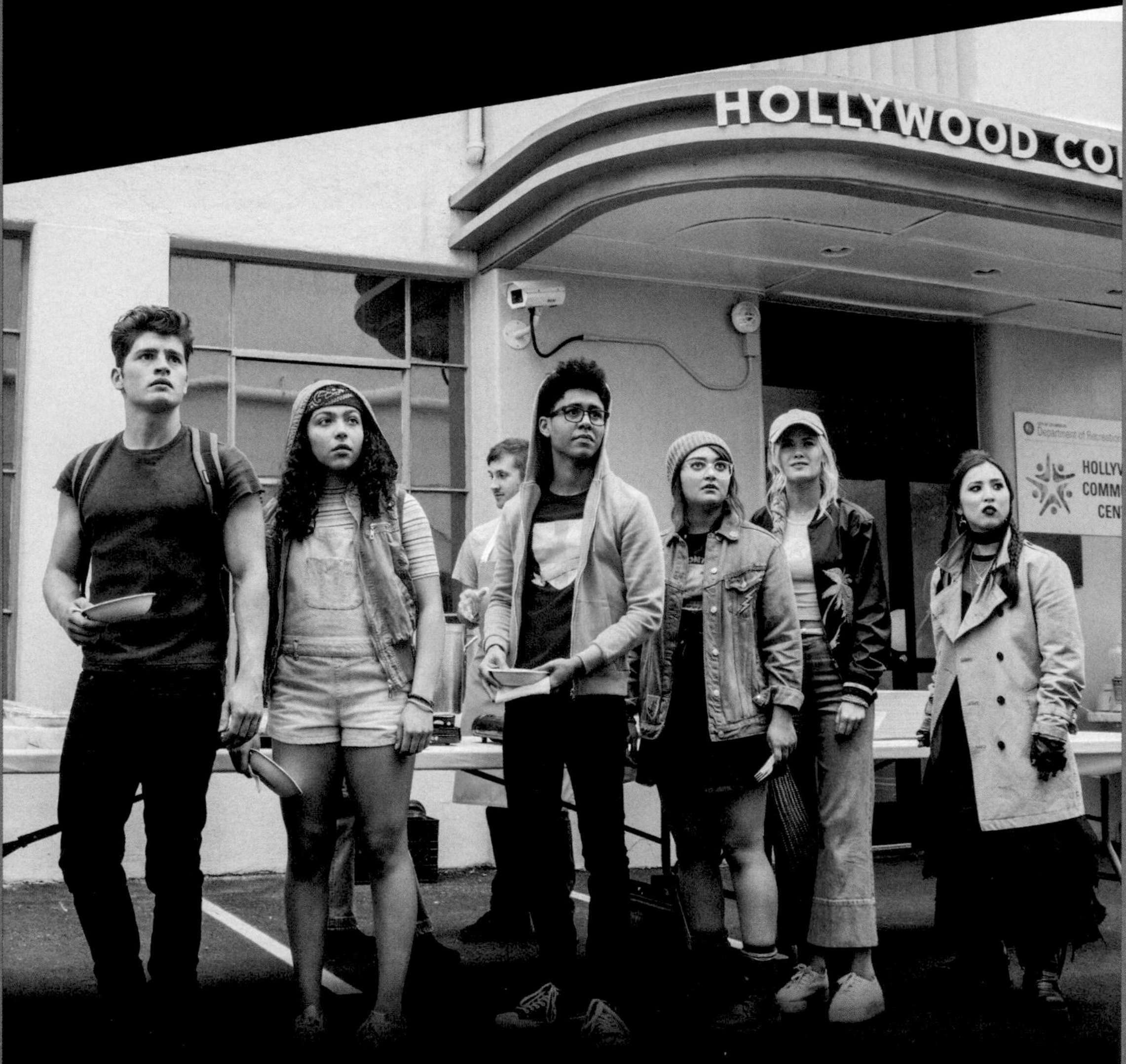
HOLLYWOOD

#15 TV VARIANT

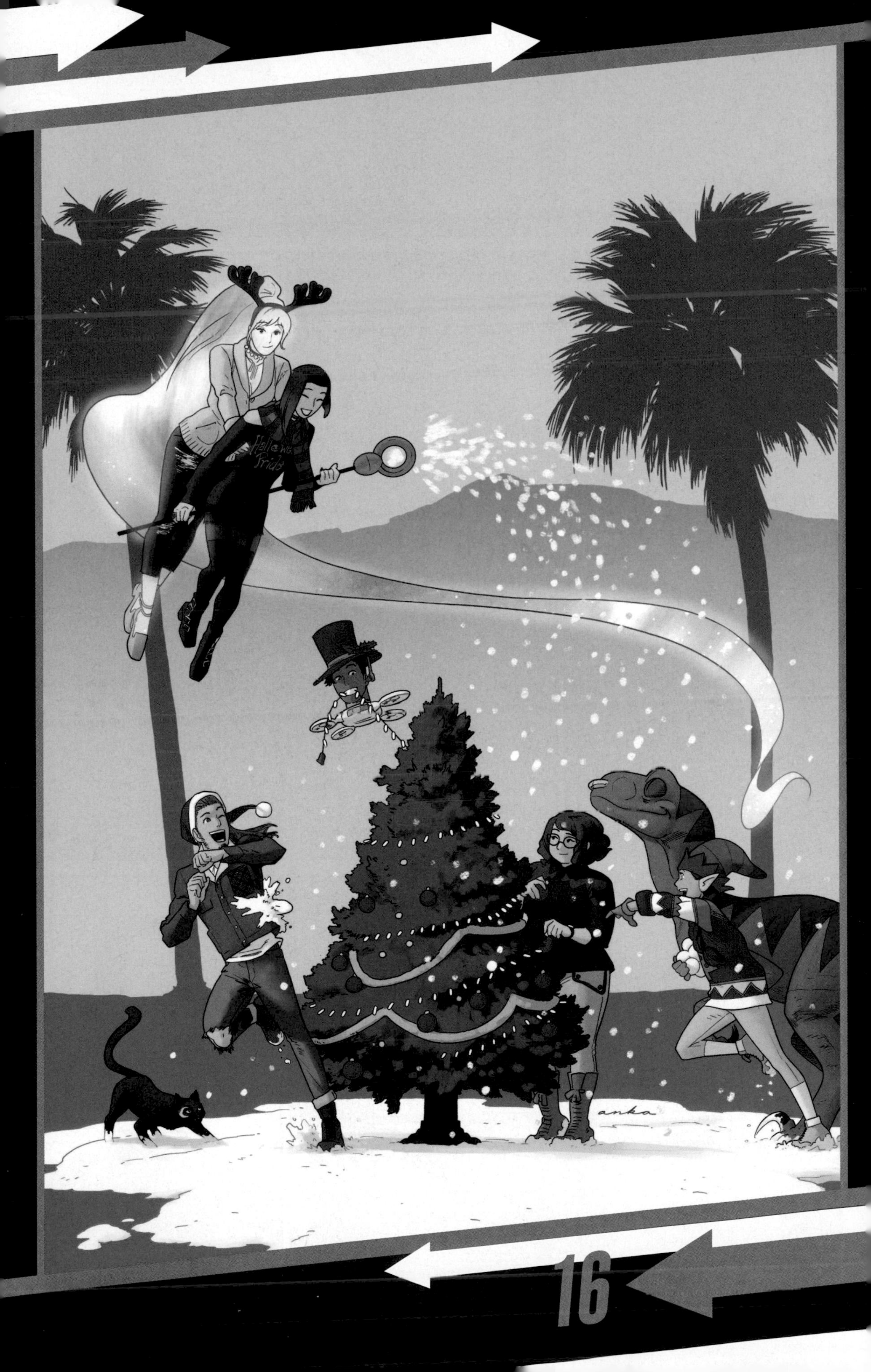
anka

16

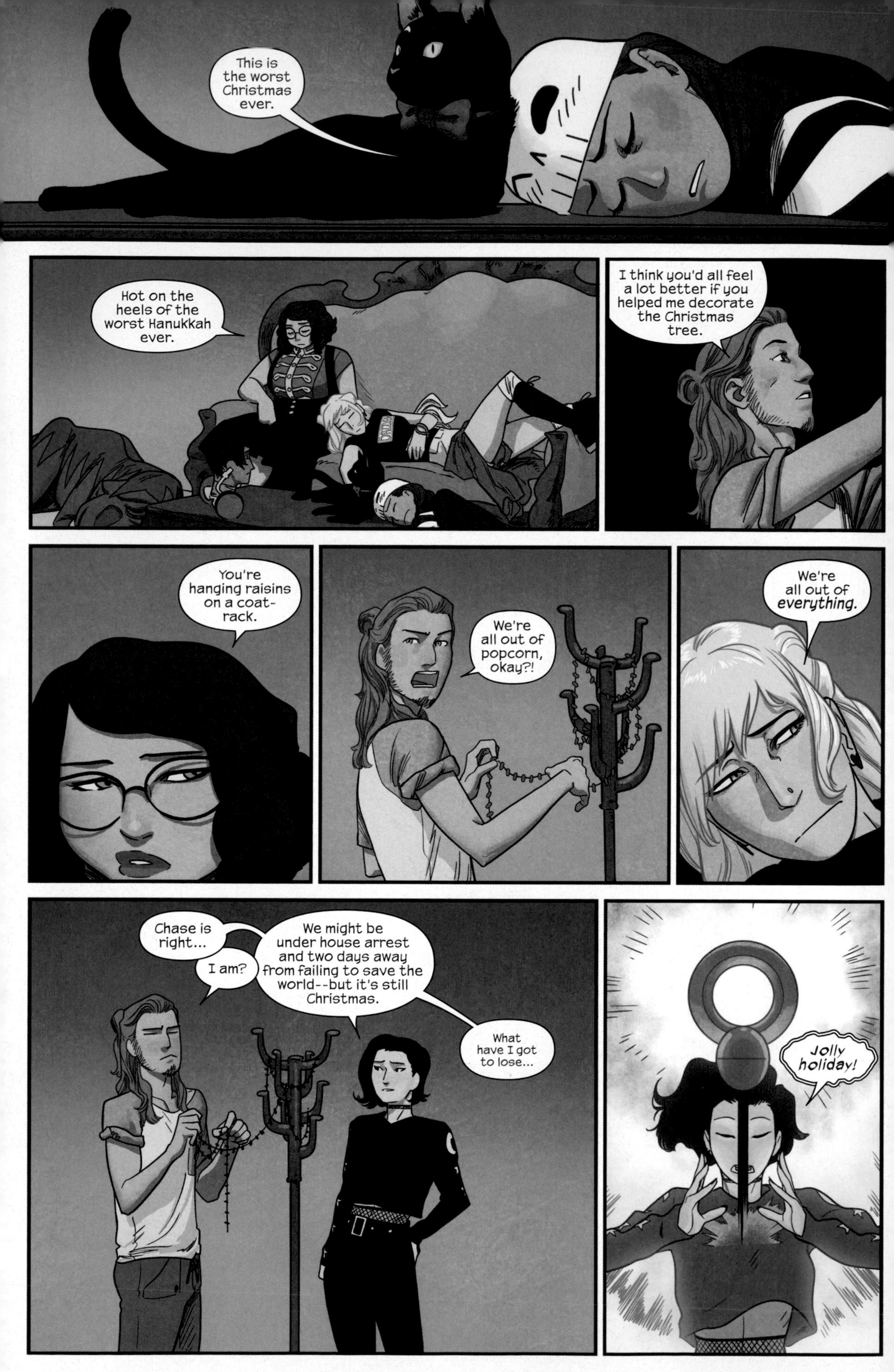
This is the worst Christmas ever.
Hot on the heels of the worst Hanukkah ever.
I think you'd all feel a lot better if you helped me decorate the Christmas tree.
You're hanging raisins on a coat-rack.
We're all out of popcorn, okay?!
We're all out of *everything.*
Chase is right...
I am?
We might be under house arrest and two days away from failing to save the world--but it's still Christmas.
What have I got to lose...
Jolly holiday!

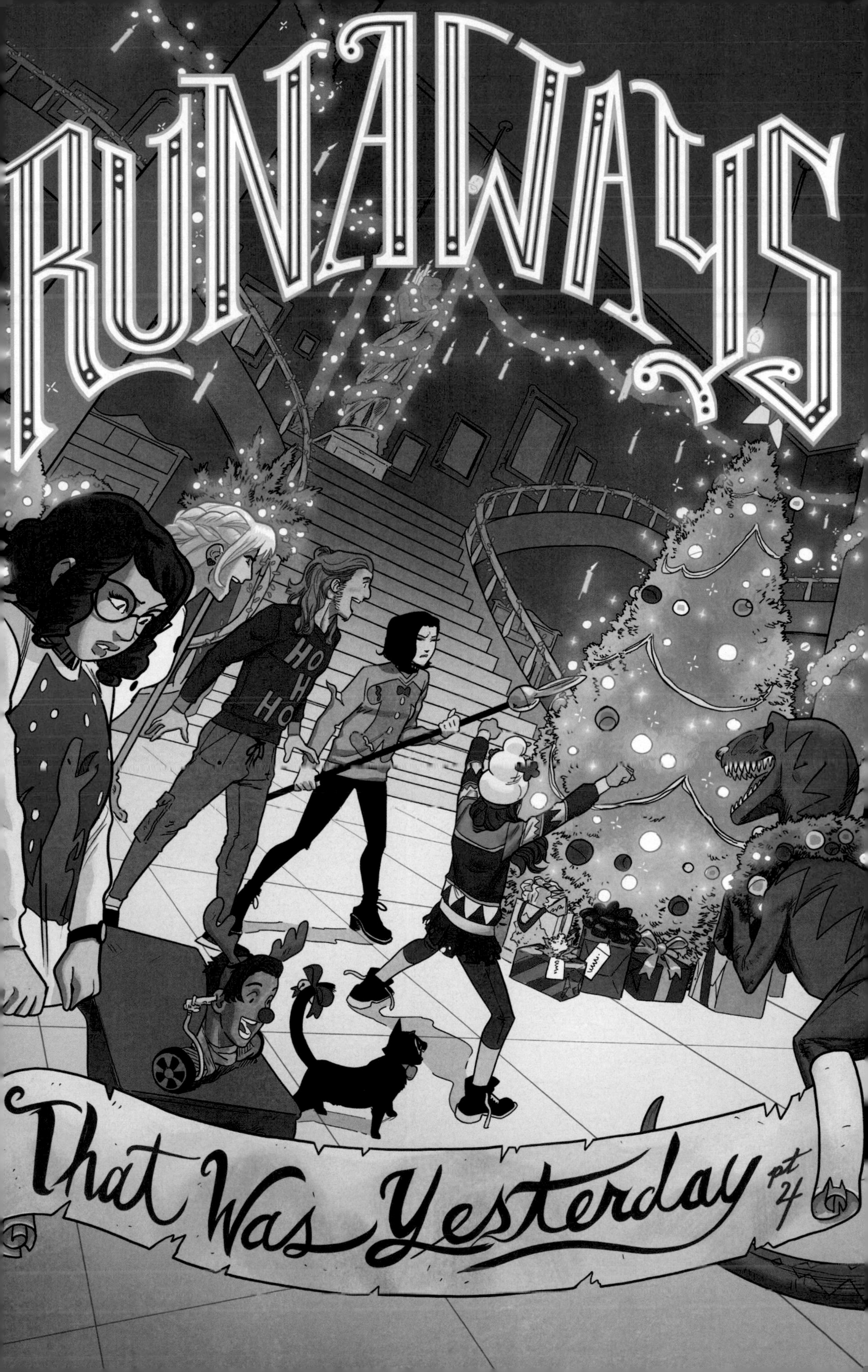
RUNAWAYS
HO HO HO
That Was Yesterday pt 4

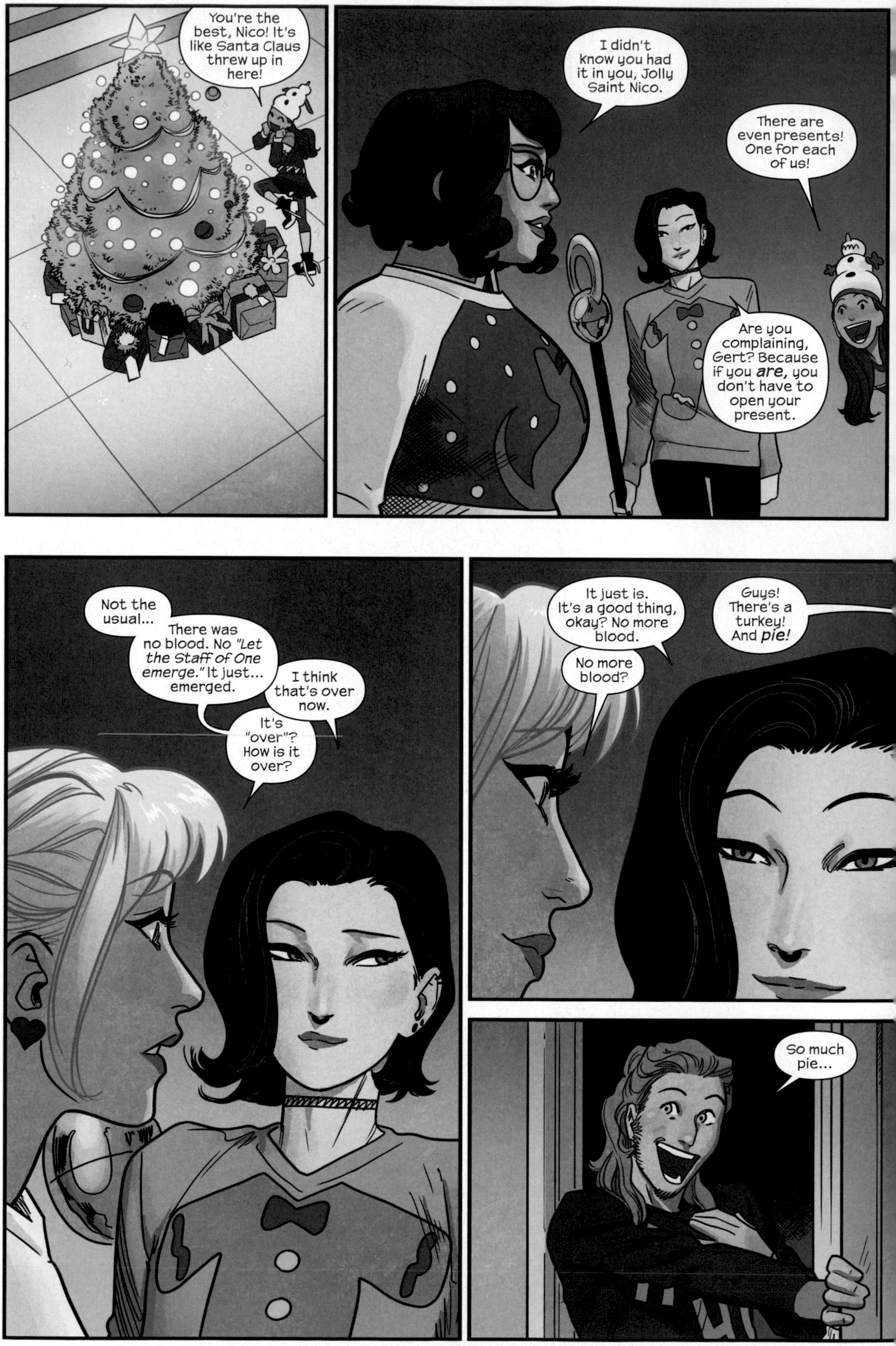
You're the best, Nico! It's like Santa Claus threw up in here!
I didn't know you had it in you, Jolly Saint Nico.
There are even presents! One for each of us!
Are you complaining, Gert? Because if you *are,* you don't have to open your present.
Not the usual...
There was no blood. No *"Let the Staff of One emerge."* It just... emerged.
I think that's over now.
It's "over"? How is it over?
It just is. It's a good thing, okay? No more blood.
No more blood?
Guys! There's a turkey! And *pie!*
So much pie...

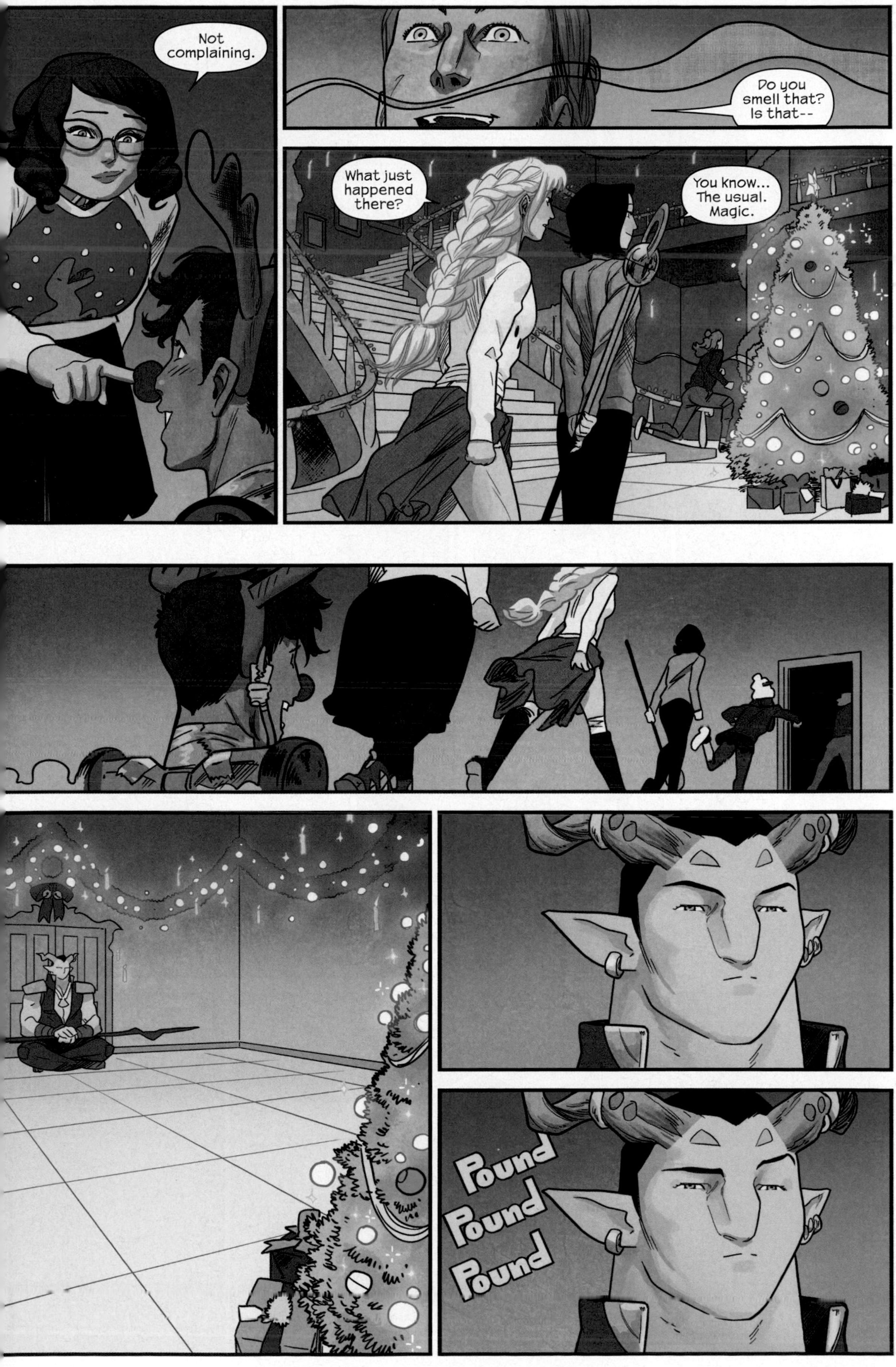
Not complaining.
Do you smell that? Is that--
What just happened there?
You know... The usual. Magic.
Pound
Pound
Pound

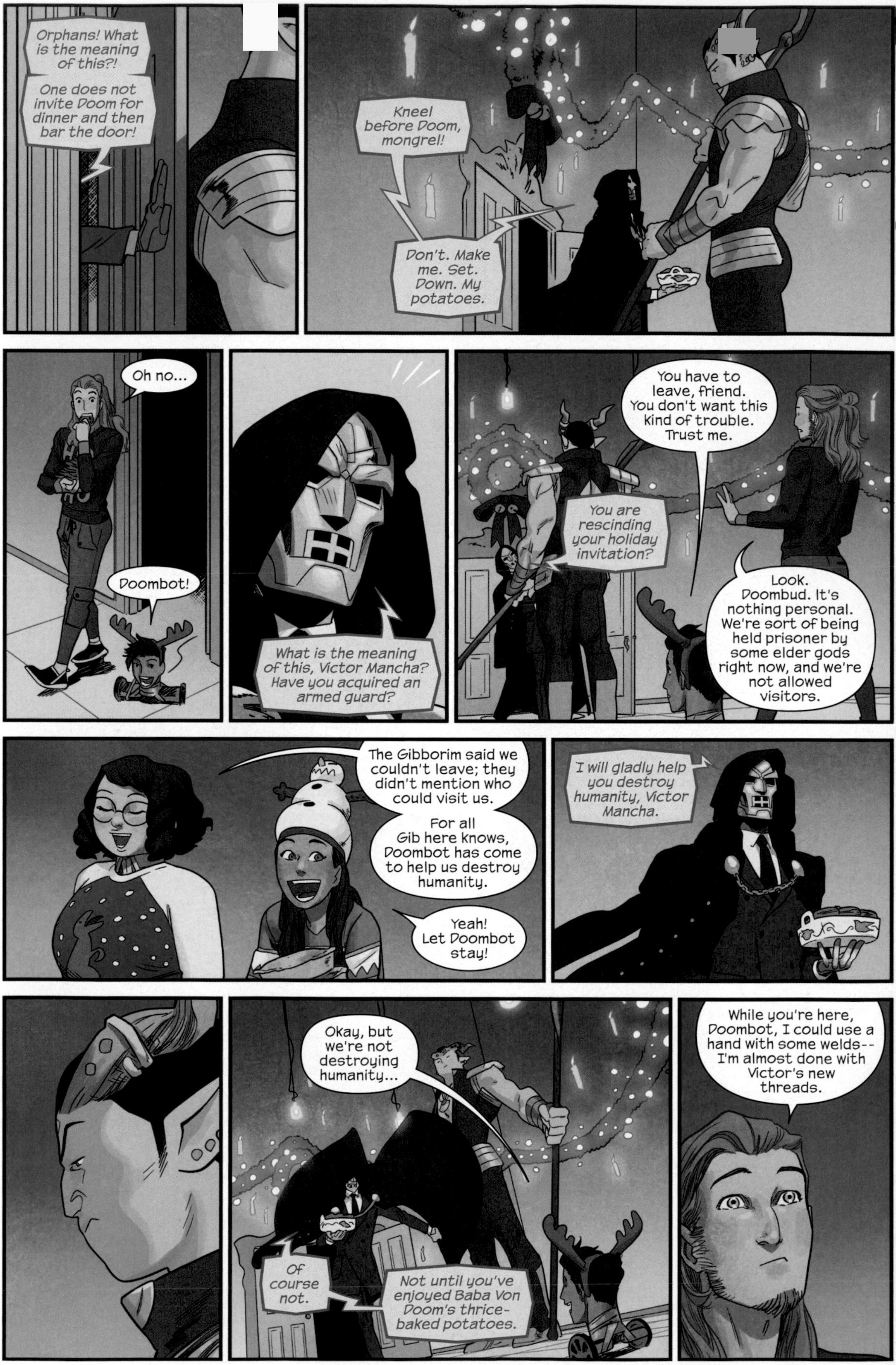

Orphans! What is the meaning of this?!
One does not invite Doom for dinner and then bar the door!
Kneel before Doom, mongrel!
Don't. Make me. Set. Down. My potatoes.
Oh no...
Doombot!
What is the meaning of this, Victor Mancha? Have you acquired an armed guard?
You have to leave, friend. You don't want this kind of trouble. Trust me.
You are rescinding your holiday invitation?
Look. Doombud. It's nothing personal. We're sort of being held prisoner by some elder gods right now, and we're not allowed visitors.
The Gibborim said we couldn't leave; they didn't mention who could visit us.
For all Gib here knows, Doombot has come to help us destroy humanity.
Yeah! Let Doombot stay!
I will gladly help you destroy humanity, Victor Mancha.
Okay, but we're not destroying humanity...
Of course not.
Not until you've enjoyed Baba Von Doom's thrice-baked potatoes.
While you're here, Doombot, I could use a hand with some welds-- I'm almost done with Victor's new threads.

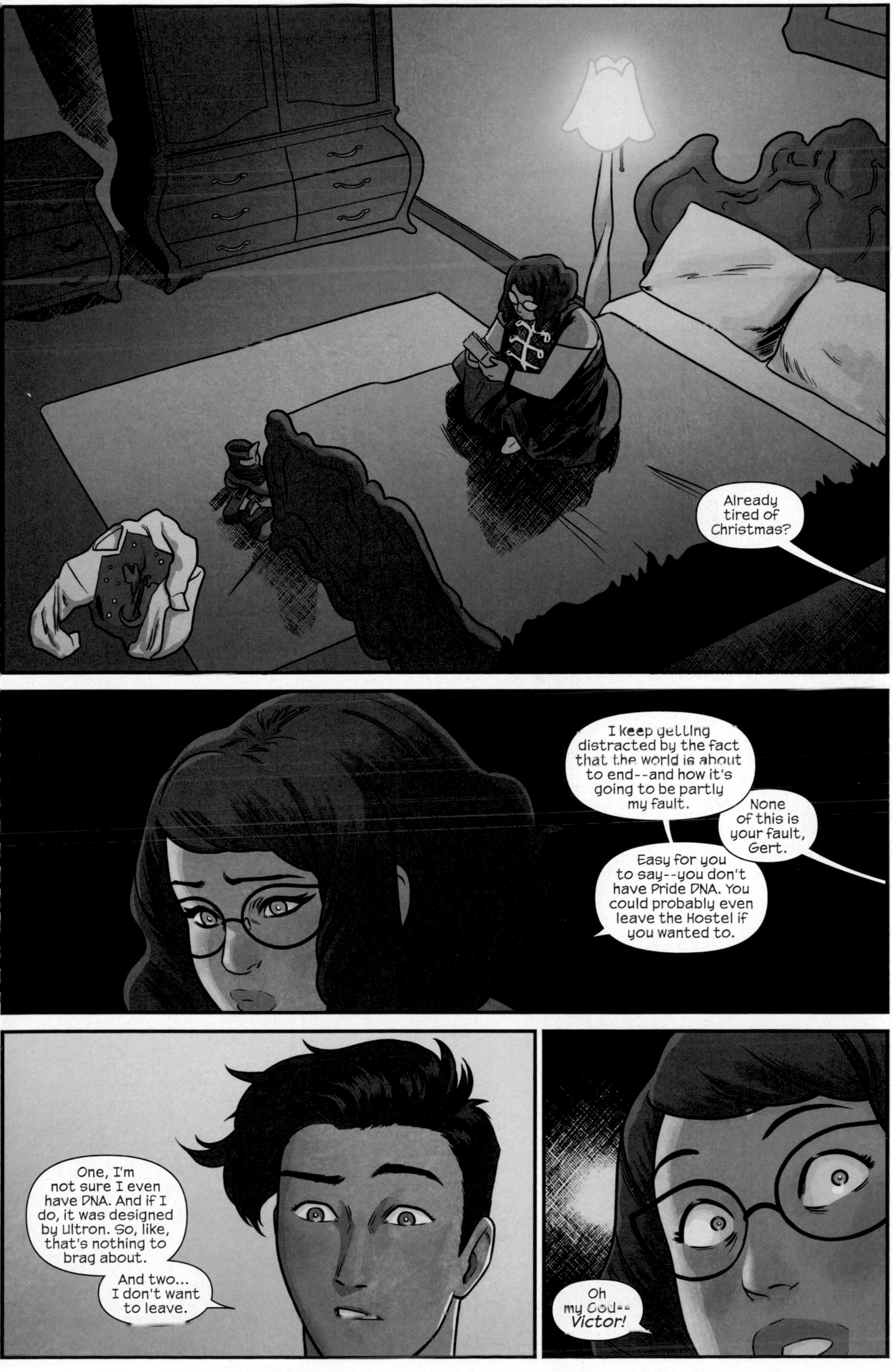
Already tired of Christmas?
I keep getting distracted by the fact that the world is about to end--and how it's going to be partly my fault.
None of this is your fault, Gert.
Easy for you to say--you don't have Pride DNA. You could probably even leave the Hostel if you wanted to.
One, I'm not sure I even have DNA. And if I do, it was designed by Ultron. So, like, that's nothing to brag about.
And two... I don't want to leave.
Oh my God--
Victor!

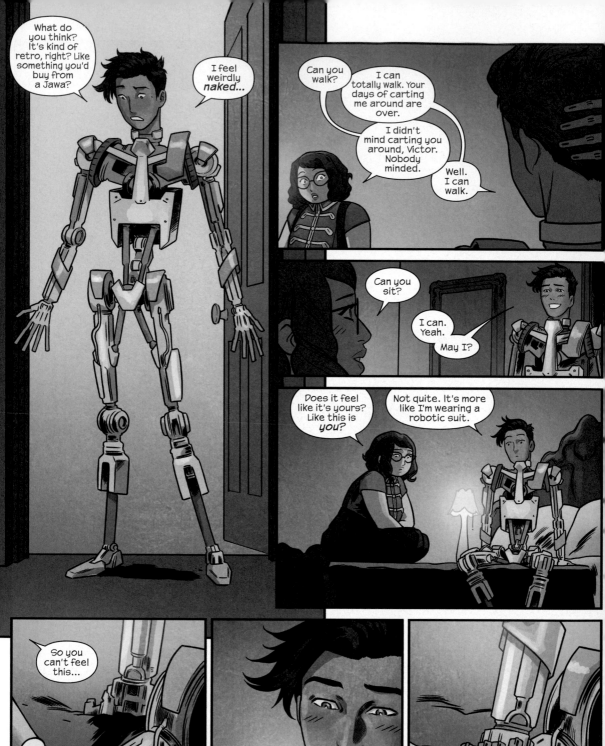

What do you think? It's kind of retro, right? Like something you'd buy from a Jawa?

I feel weirdly *naked*...

Can you walk?

I can totally walk. Your days of carting me around are over.

I didn't mind carting you around, Victor. Nobody minded.

Well. I can walk.

Can you sit?

I can. Yeah.

May I?

Does it feel like it's yours? Like this is *you*?

Not quite. It's more like I'm wearing a robotic suit.

So you can't feel this...

Not really. Not there.

But seeing is feeling-- *knowing* is feeling.

I know I'm sitting next to you.

I know...

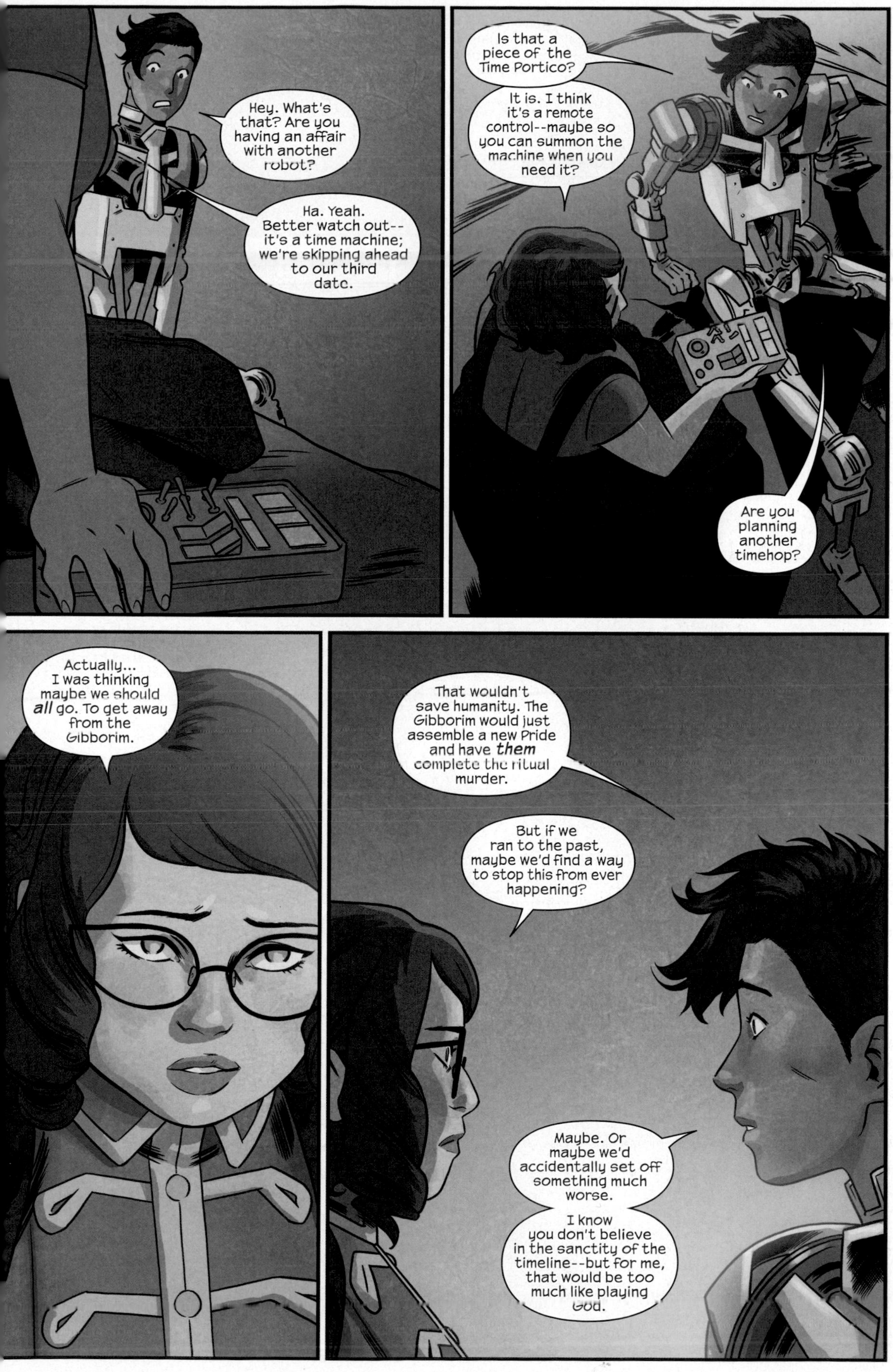
Hey. What's that? Are you having an affair with another robot?
Ha. Yeah. Better watch out-- it's a time machine; we're skipping ahead to our third date.
Is that a piece of the Time Portico?
It is. I think it's a remote control--maybe so you can summon the machine when you need it?
Are you planning another timehop?
Actually... I was thinking maybe we should *all* go. To get away from the Gibborim.
That wouldn't save humanity. The Gibborim would just assemble a new Pride and have *them* complete the ritual murder.
But if we ran to the past, maybe we'd find a way to stop this from ever happening?
Maybe. Or maybe we'd accidentally set off something much worse.
I know you don't believe in the sanctity of the timeline--but for me, that would be too much like playing God.

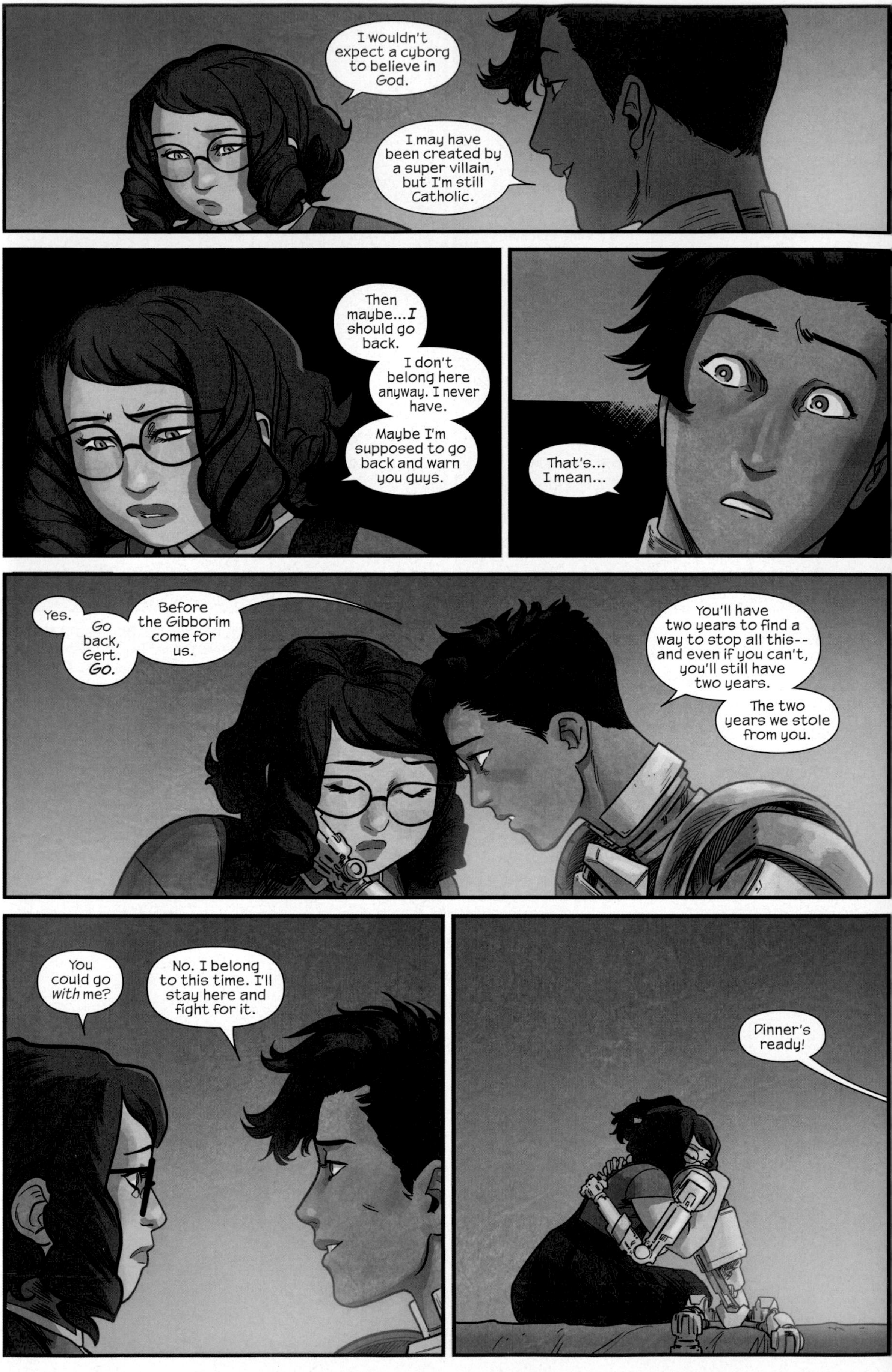
I wouldn't expect a cyborg to believe in God.
I may have been created by a super villain, but I'm still Catholic.
Then maybe...*I* should go back.
I don't belong here anyway. I never have.
Maybe I'm supposed to go back and warn you guys.
That's... I mean...
Yes.
Go back, Gert. *Go.*
Before the Gibborim come for us.
You'll have two years to find a way to stop all this-- and even if you can't, you'll still have two years.
The two years we stole from you.
You could go *with* me?
No. I belong to this time. I'll stay here and fight for it.
Dinner's ready!

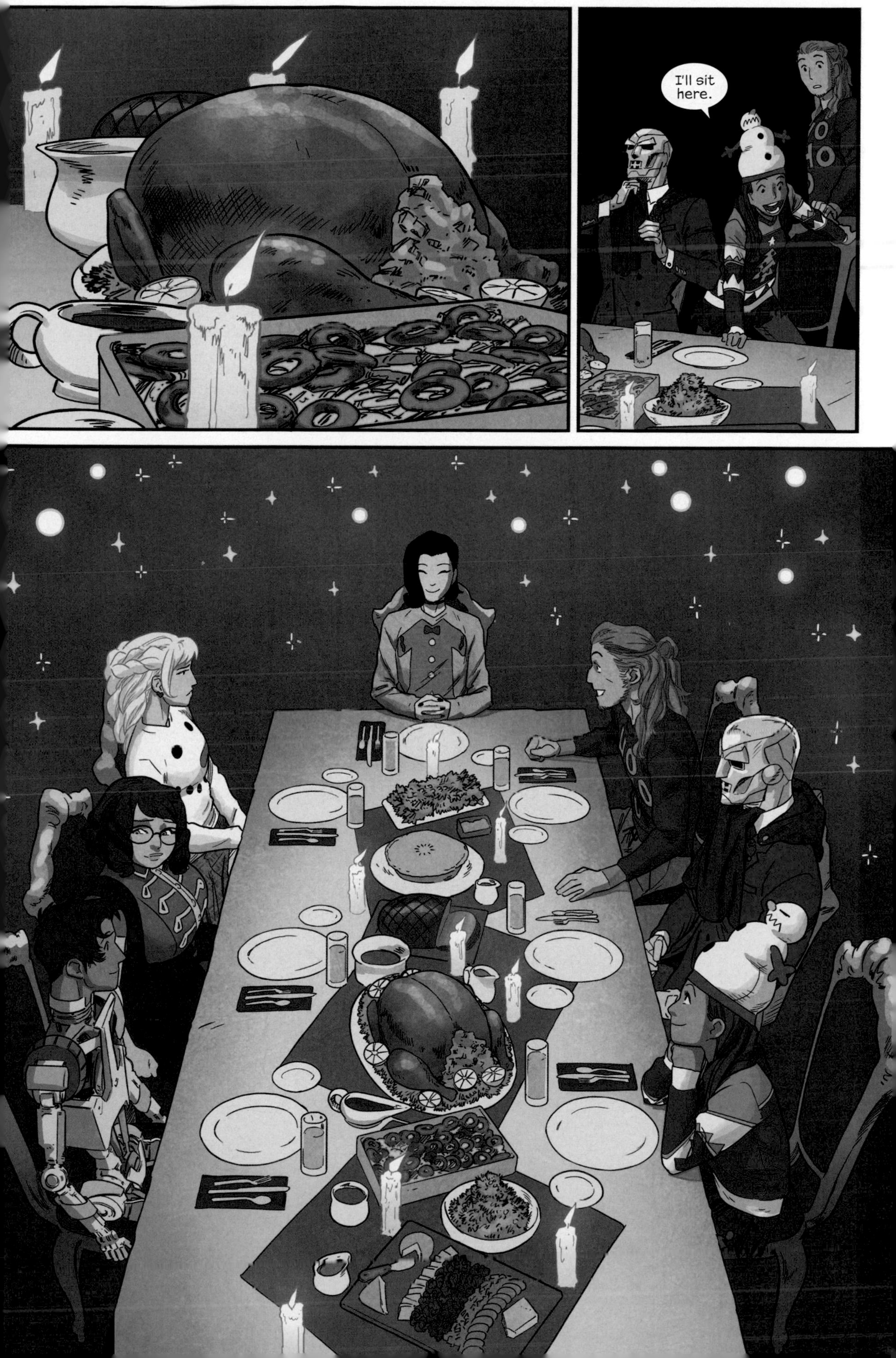
I'll sit here.

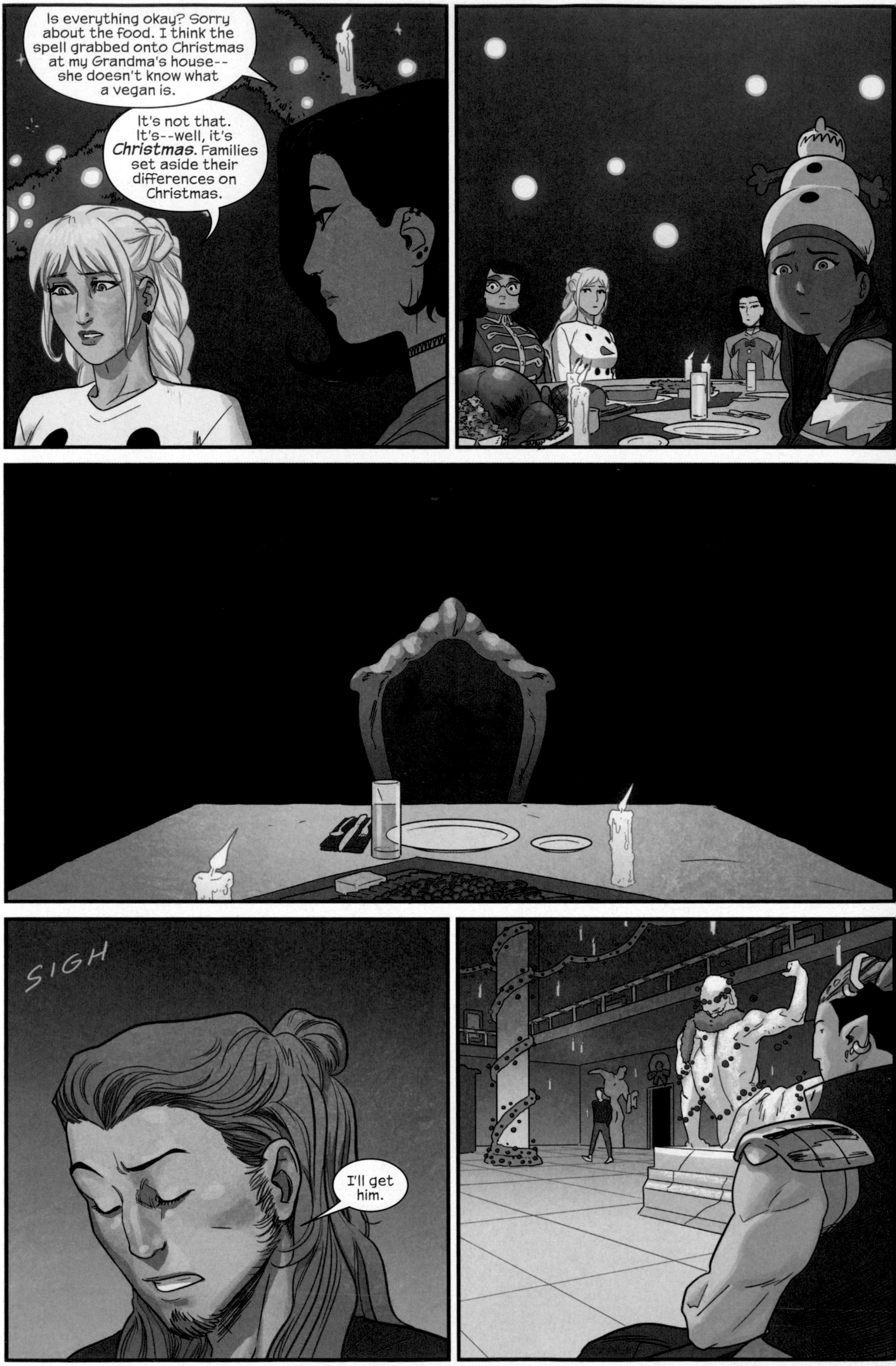
Is everything okay? Sorry about the food. I think the spell grabbed onto Christmas at my Grandma's house--she doesn't know what a vegan is.
It's not that. It's--well, it's *Christmas*. Families set aside their differences on Christmas.
SIGH
I'll get him.

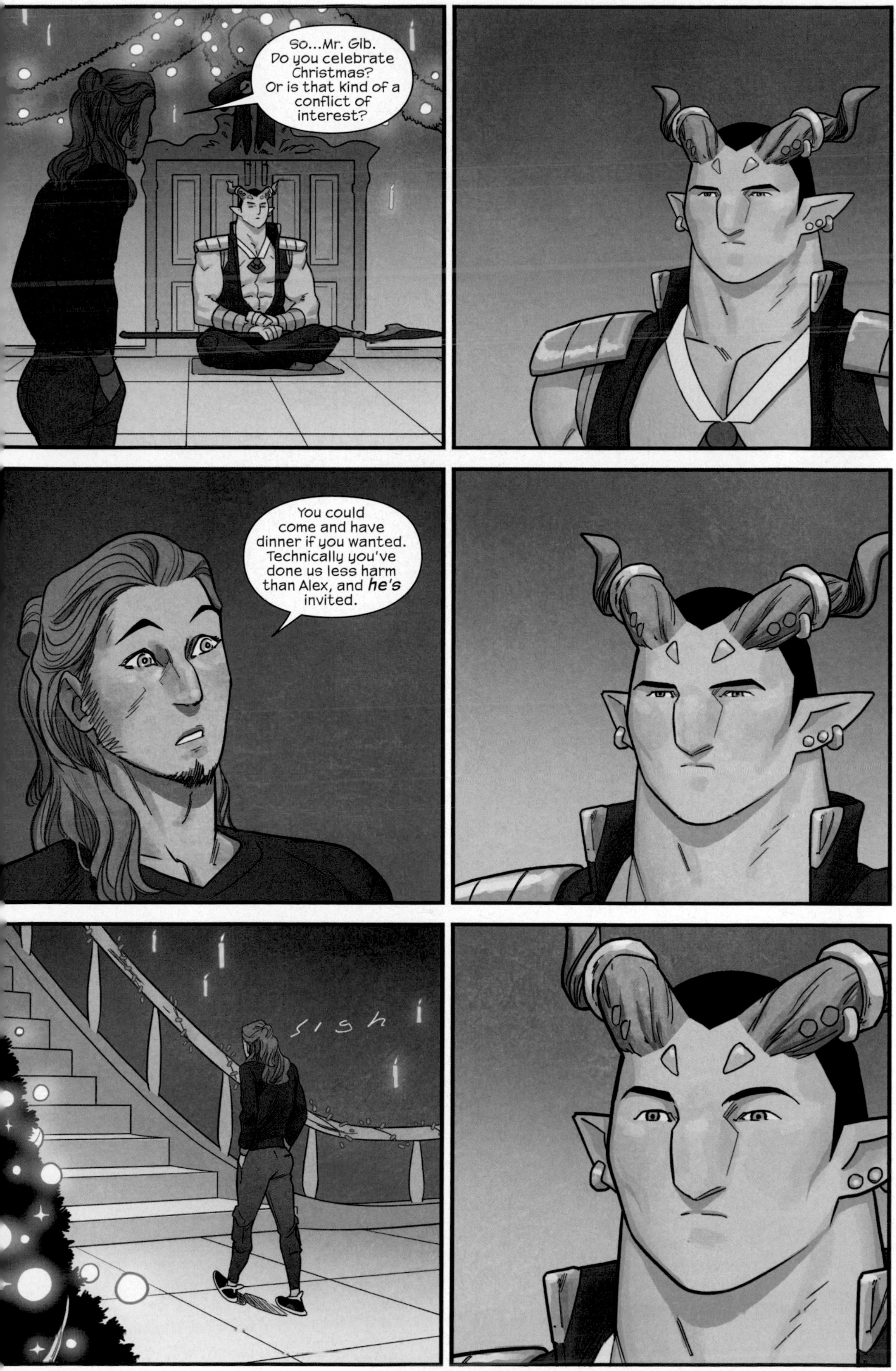
So...Mr. Glb. Do you celebrate Christmas? Or is that kind of a conflict of interest?
You could come and have dinner if you wanted. Technically you've done us less harm than Alex, and *he's* invited.
sish

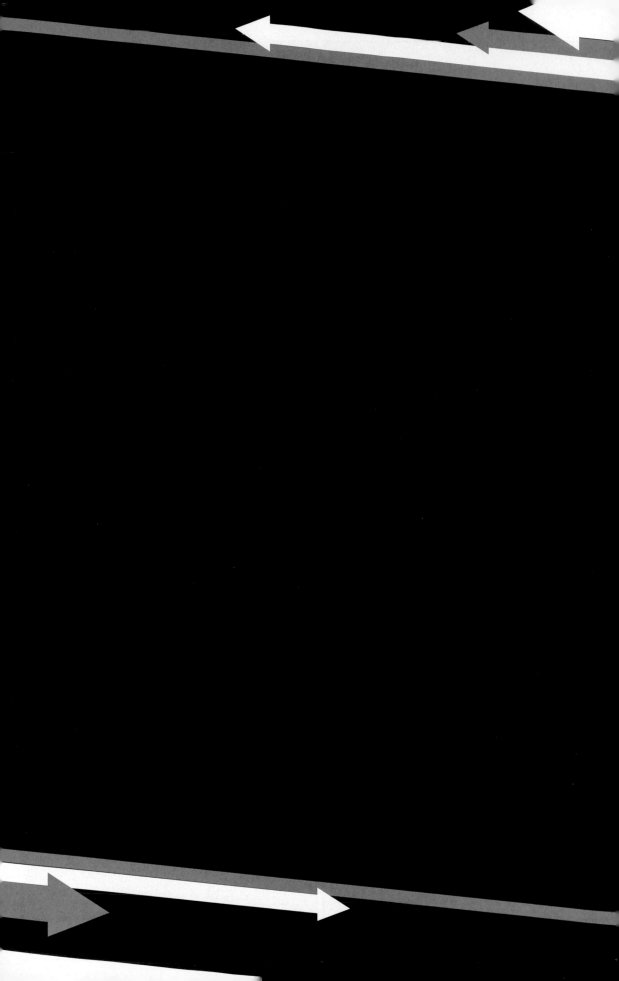

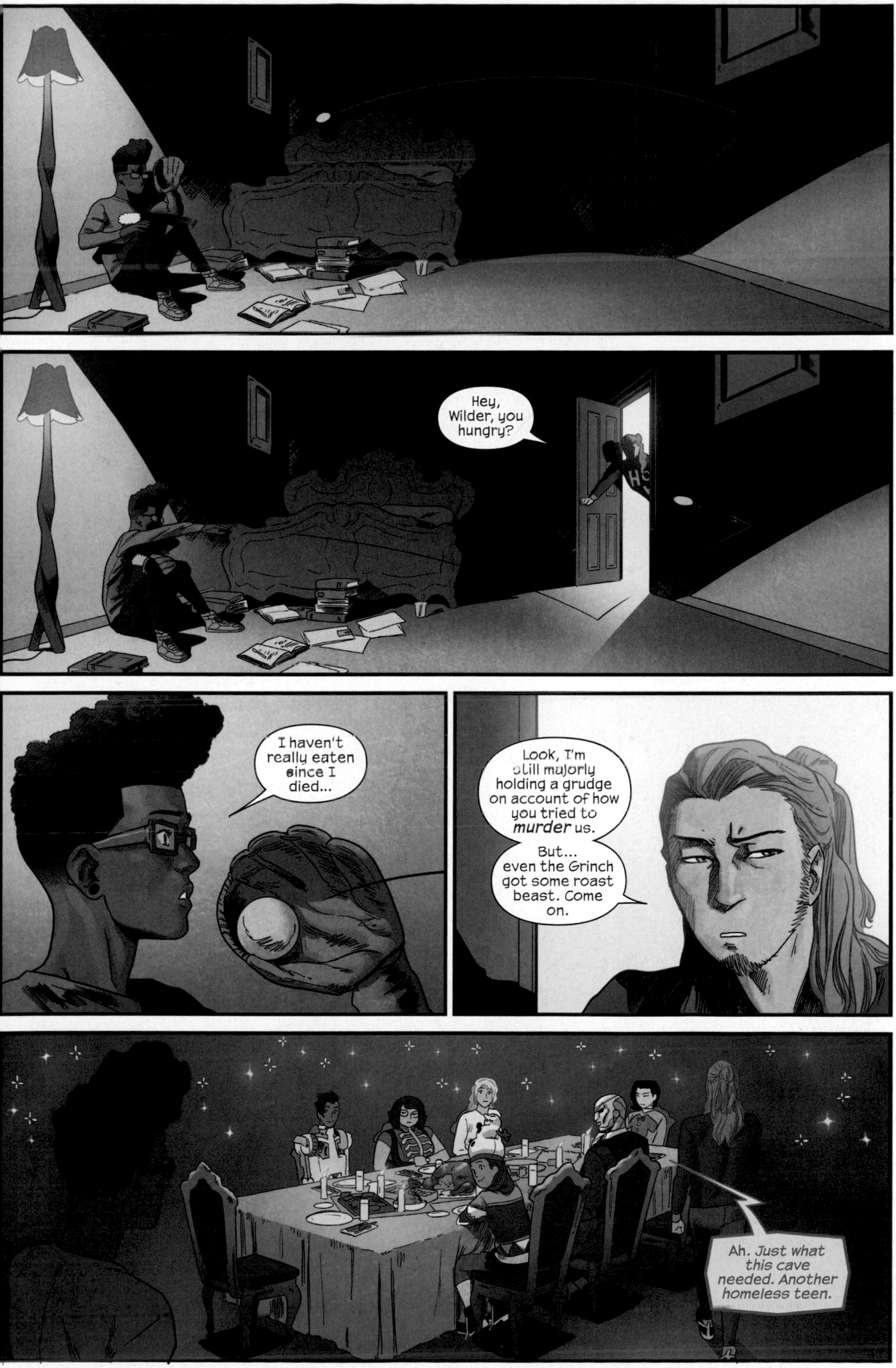
Hey, Wilder, you hungry?
I haven't really eaten since I died...
Look, I'm still majorly holding a grudge on account of how you tried to *murder* us.
But... even the Grinch got some roast beast. Come on.
Ah. Just what this cave needed. Another homeless teen.

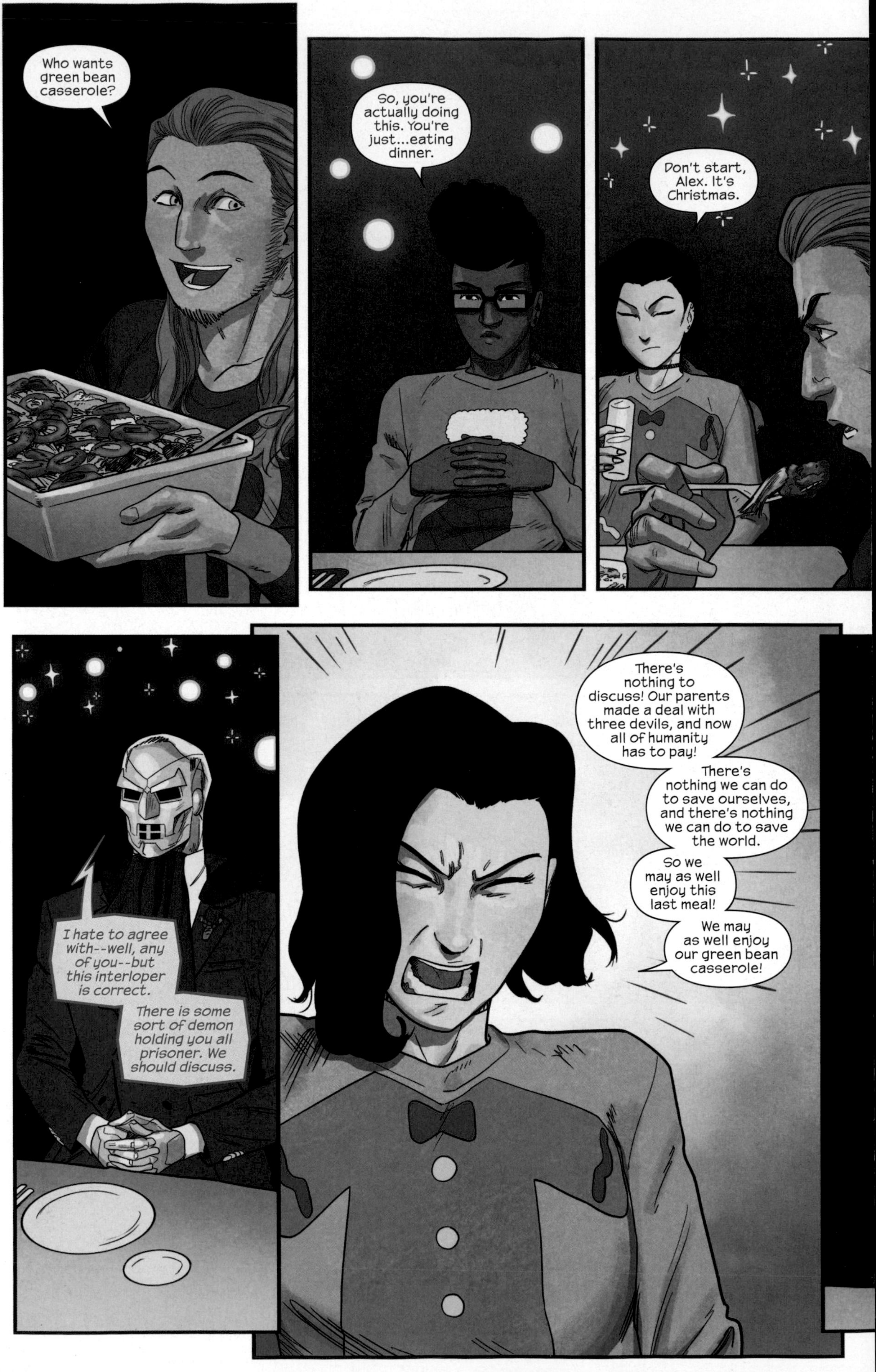
Who wants green bean casserole?
So, you're actually doing this. You're just...eating dinner.
Don't start, Alex. It's Christmas.
I hate to agree with--well, any of you--but this interloper is correct.
There is some sort of demon holding you all prisoner. We should discuss.
There's nothing to discuss! Our parents made a deal with three devils, and now all of humanity has to pay!
There's nothing we can do to save ourselves, and there's nothing we can do to save the world.
So we may as well enjoy this last meal!
We may as well enjoy our green bean casserole!

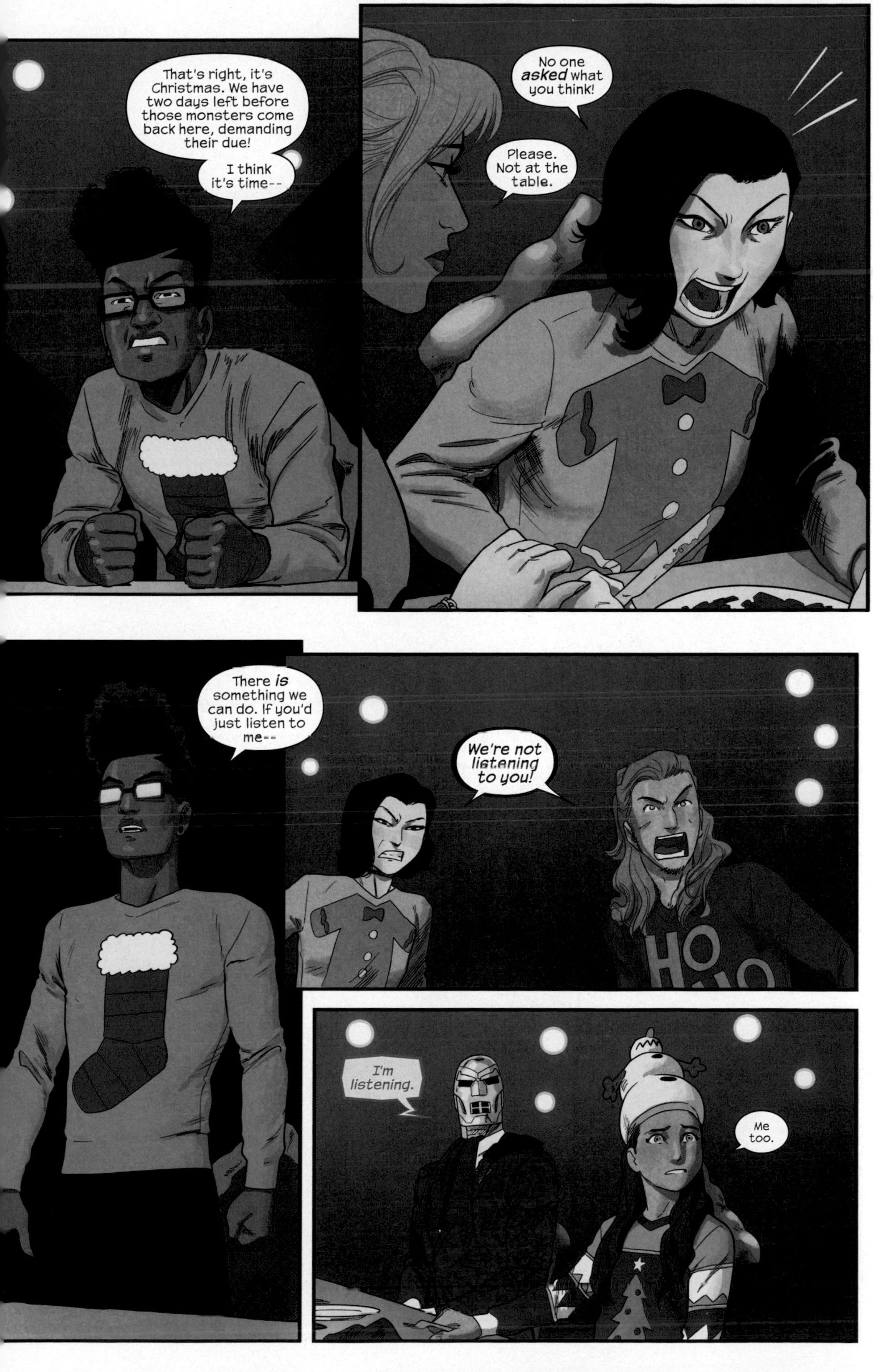
That's right, it's Christmas. We have two days left before those monsters come back here, demanding their due!
I think it's time--
No one *asked* what you think!
Please. Not at the table.
There *is* something we can do. If you'd just listen to me--
We're not listening to you!
I'm listening.
Me too.

After I died, I was stuck in limbo with the Gibborim.

They were incensed. All their plans were undone. They ranted and raged for a year.

And I just listened.

Were-- were our *parents* in limbo with you?

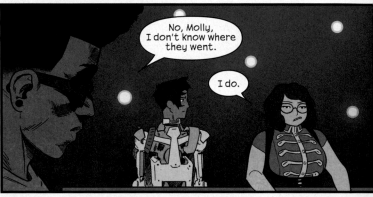

No, Molly, I don't know where they went.

I do.

The Gibborim talked about the father they'd disappointed, and the children they'd abandoned on Earth.

That's who our captors are. That's *what* they are-- *children*.

They're weaker than their parents. They need *us* to make them strong. With sacrifice.

If they're weak--does that mean we can clobber them?

Yes. We clobber them. Doom will lead the charge.

We can't exactly clobber them--they're still gods.

But there *is* a way to *flip* the ritual...

The Gibborim were afraid our parents would figure it out.

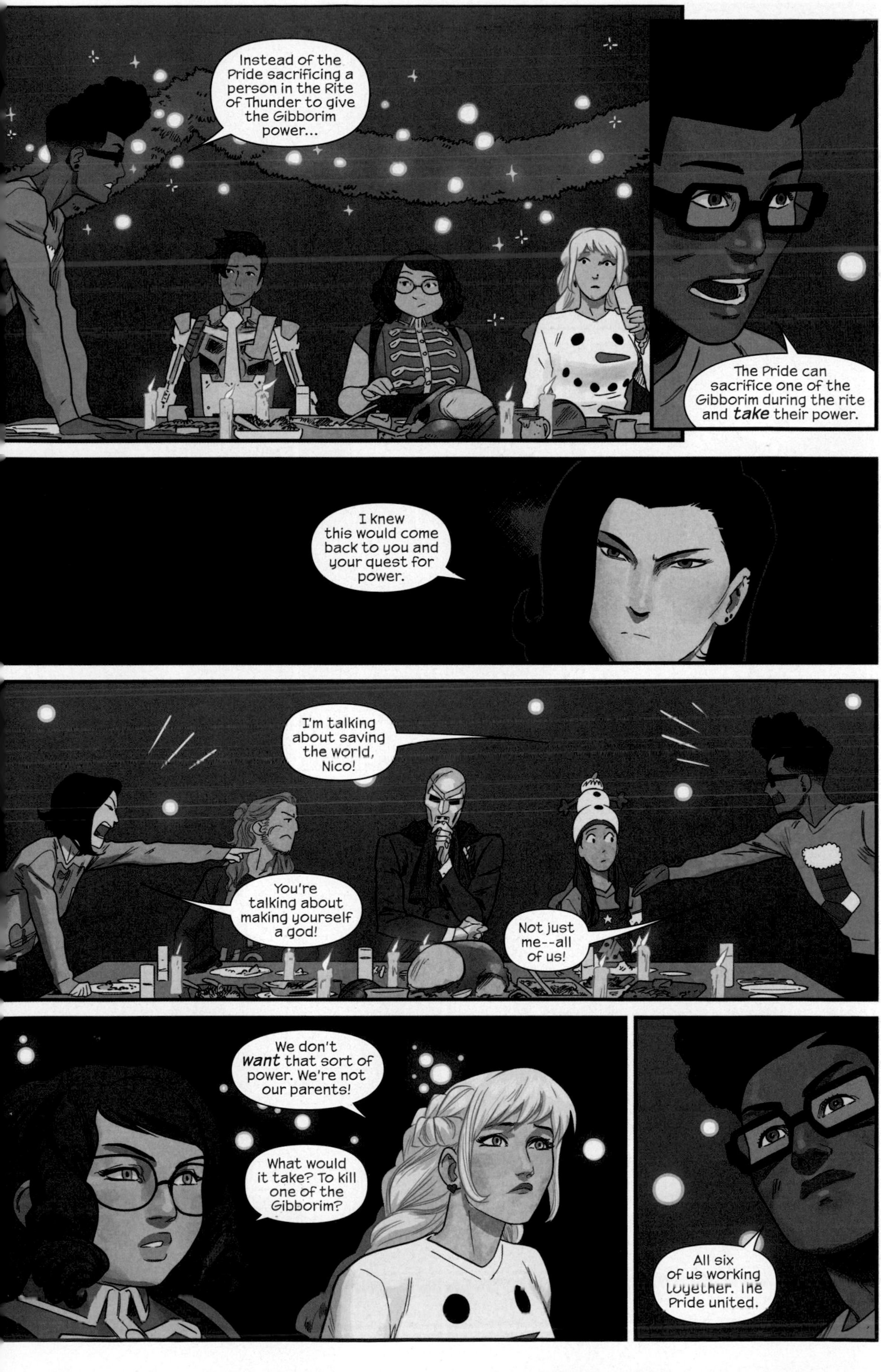
Instead of the Pride sacrificing a person in the Rite of Thunder to give the Gibborim power...
The Pride can sacrifice one of the Gibborim during the rite and take their power.
I knew this would come back to you and your quest for power.
I'm talking about saving the world, Nico!
You're talking about making yourself a god!
Not just me--all of us!
We don't want that sort of power. We're not our parents!
What would it take? To kill one of the Gibborim?
All six of us working together. The Pride united.

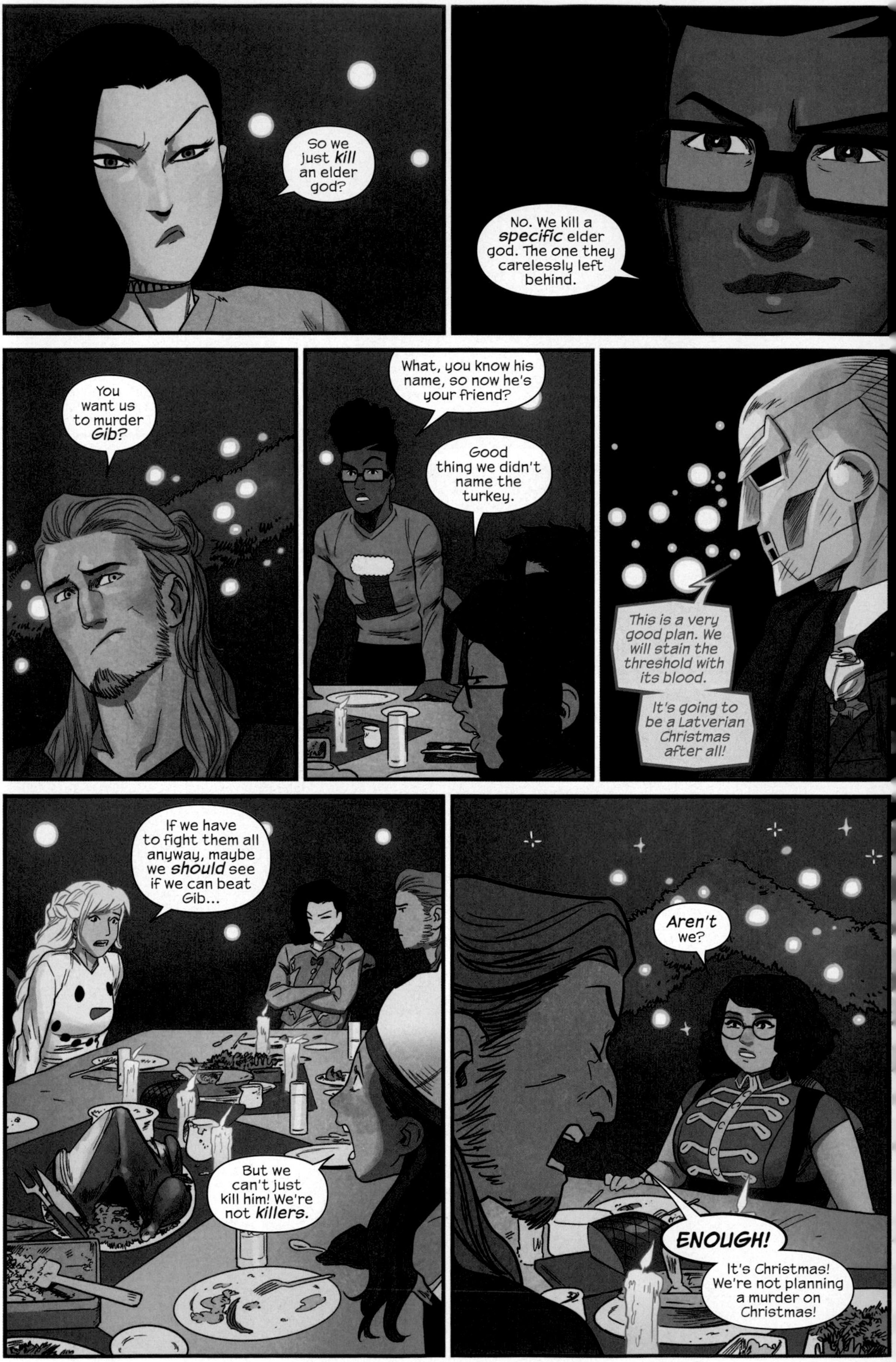
So we just kill an elder god?
No. We kill a specific elder god. The one they carelessly left behind.
You want us to murder Gib?
What, you know his name, so now he's your friend?
Good thing we didn't name the turkey.
This is a very good plan. We will stain the threshold with its blood.
It's going to be a Latverian Christmas after all!
If we have to fight them all anyway, maybe we should see if we can beat Gib...
But we can't just kill him! We're not killers.
Aren't we?
ENOUGH!
It's Christmas! We're not planning a murder on Christmas!

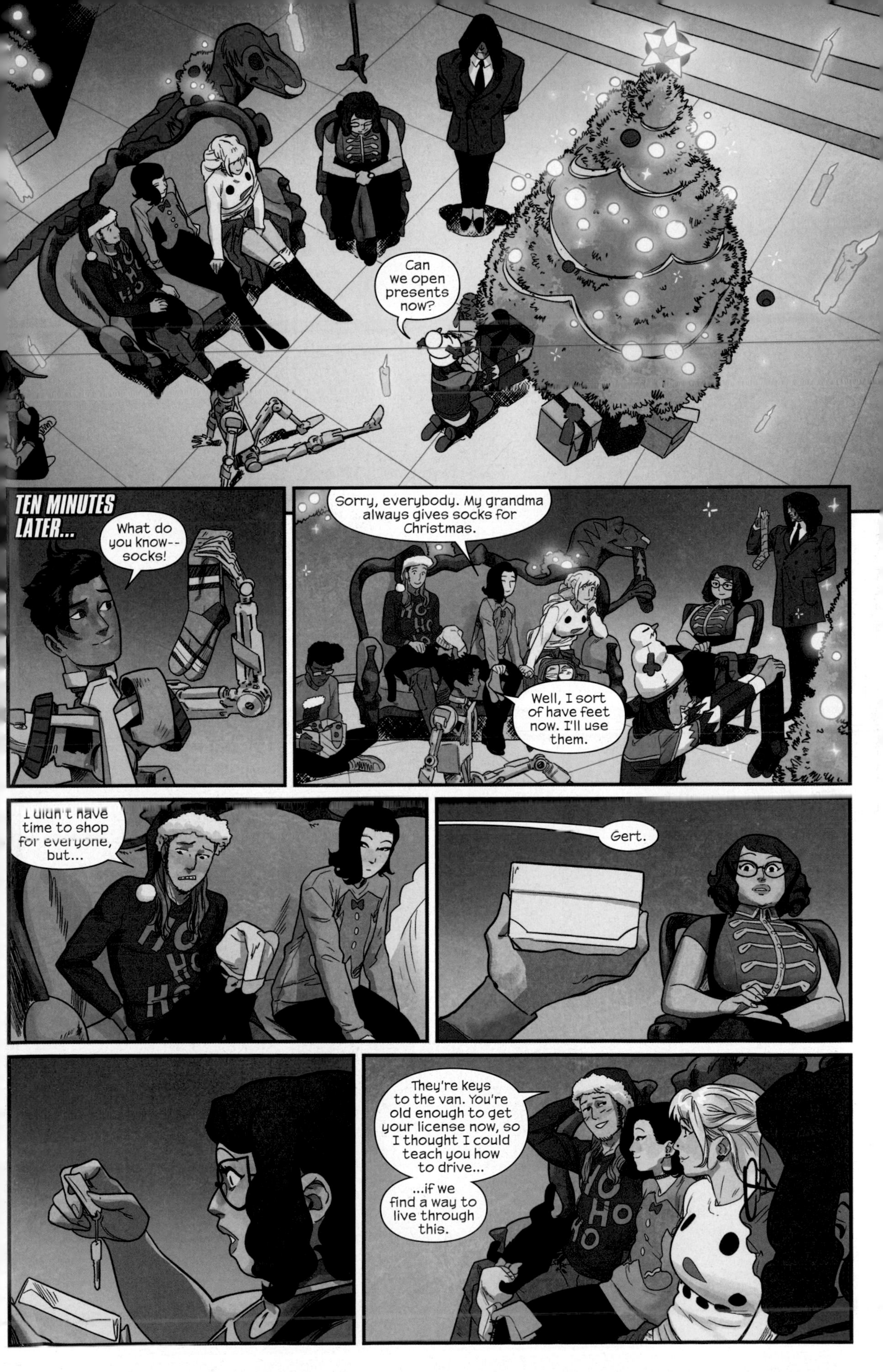
Can we open presents now?
TEN MINUTES LATER...
What do you know--socks!
Sorry, everybody. My grandma always gives socks for Christmas.
Well, I sort of have feet now. I'll use them.
I didn't have time to shop for everyone, but...
Gert.
They're keys to the van. You're old enough to get your license now, so I thought I could teach you how to drive...
...if we find a way to live through this.

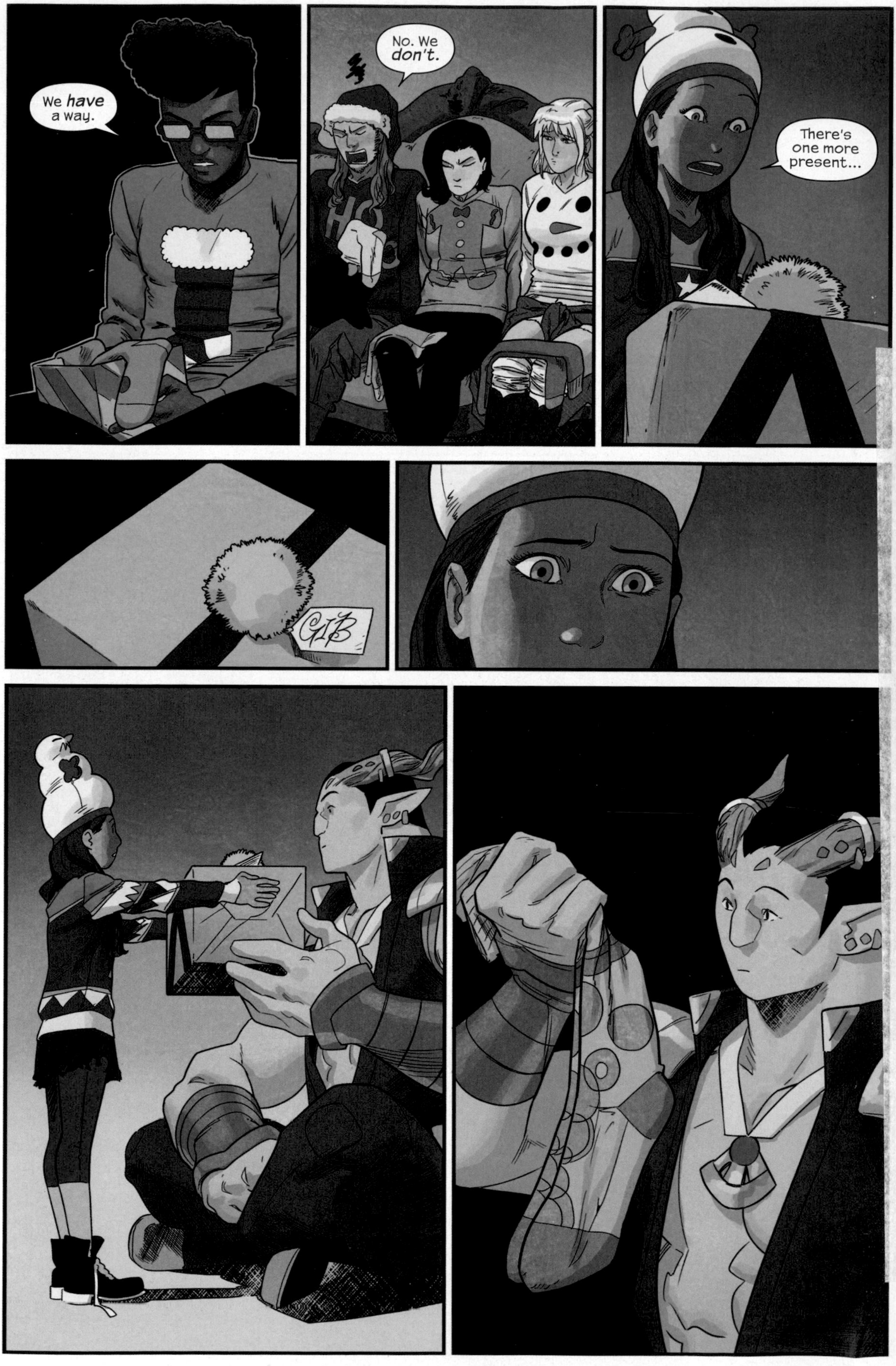
We have a way.
No. We don't.
There's one more present...
GIB

HERE
LIES
ALEX
WILDER

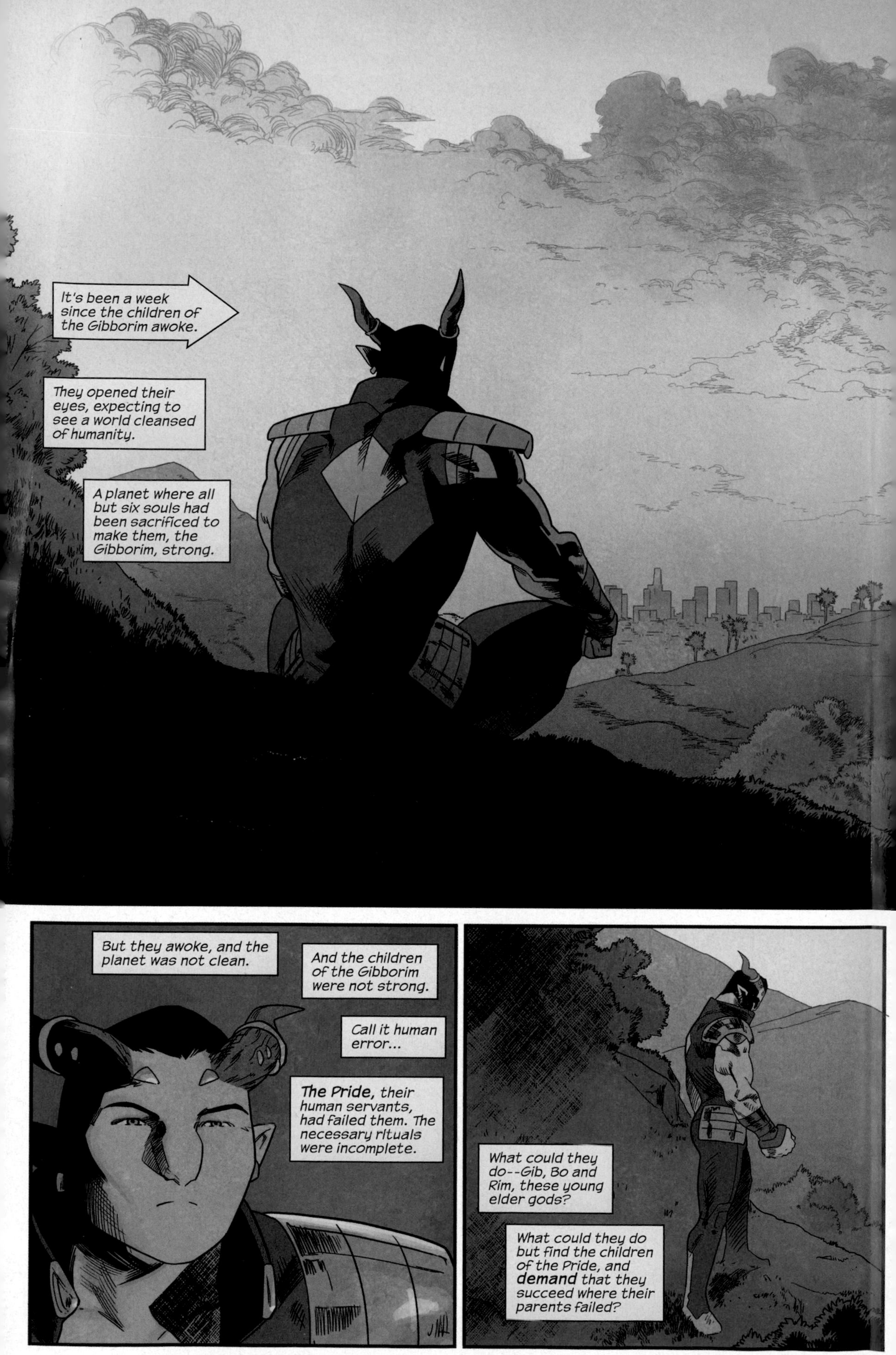
It's been a week since the children of the Gibborim awoke.
They opened their eyes, expecting to see a world cleansed of humanity.
A planet where all but six souls had been sacrificed to make them, the Gibborim, strong.
But they awoke, and the planet was not clean.
And the children of the Gibborim were not strong.
Call it human error...
The Pride, their human servants, had failed them. The necessary rituals were incomplete.
What could they do--Gib, Bo and Rim, these young elder gods?
What could they do but find the children of the Pride, and **demand** that they succeed where their parents failed?

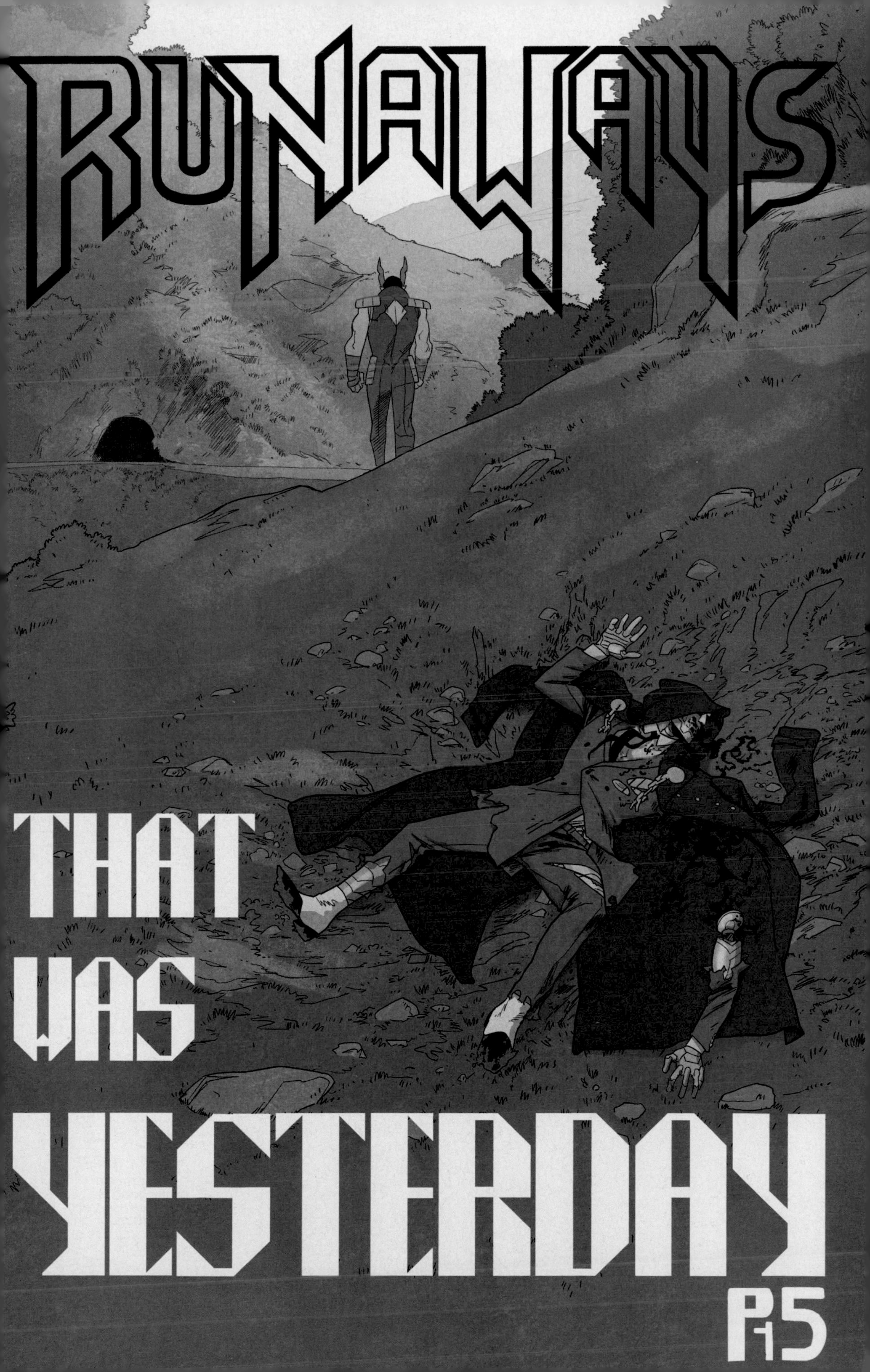
RUNAWAYS
THAT WAS YESTERDAY
P.15

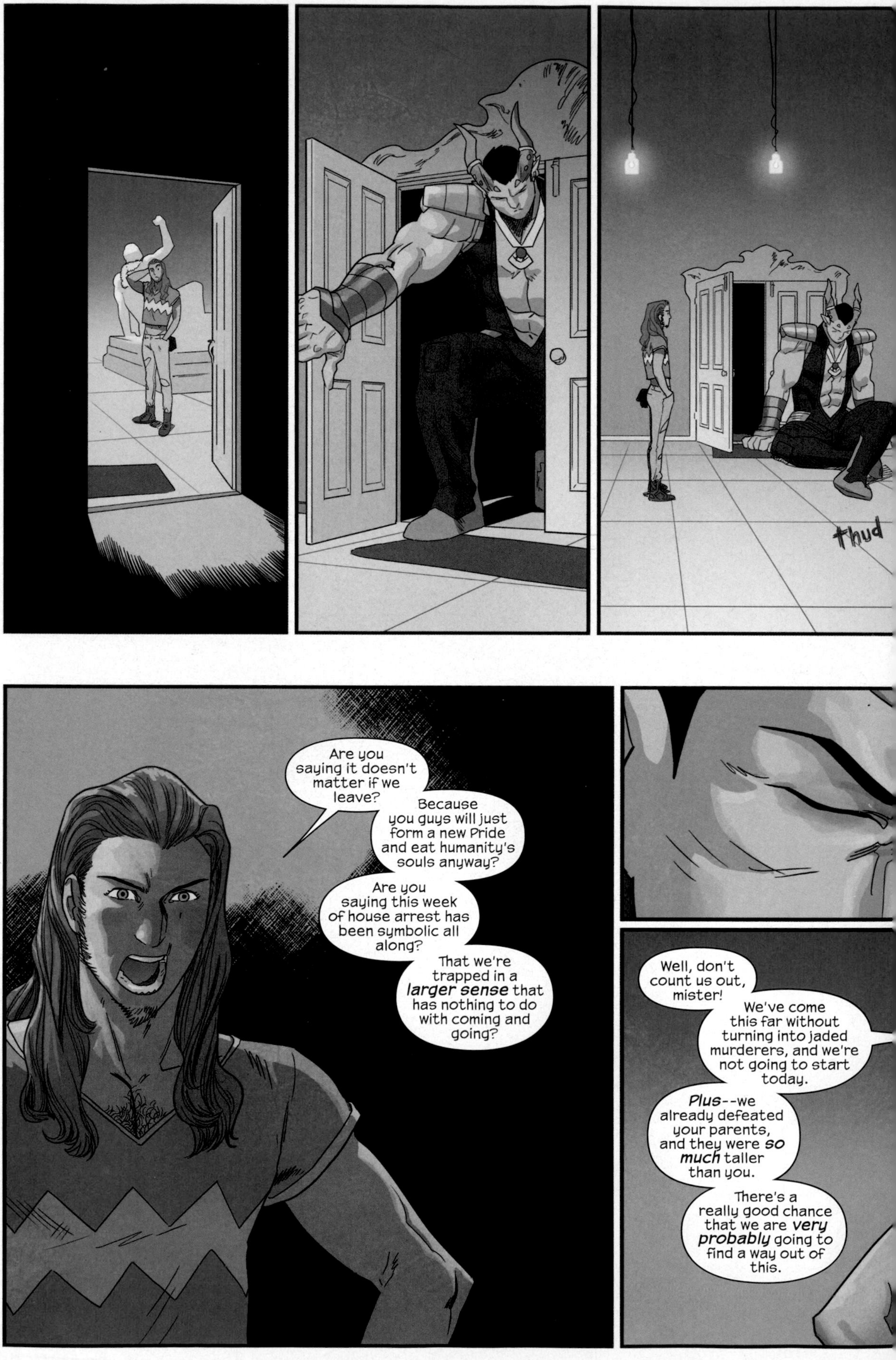
thud
Are you saying it doesn't matter if we leave?
Because you guys will just form a new Pride and eat humanity's souls anyway?
Are you saying this week of house arrest has been symbolic all along?
That we're trapped in a *larger sense* that has nothing to do with coming and going?
Well, don't count us out, mister!
We've come this far without turning into jaded murderers, and we're not going to start today.
Plus--we already defeated your parents, and they were *so much* taller than you.
There's a really good chance that we are *very probably* going to find a way out of this.

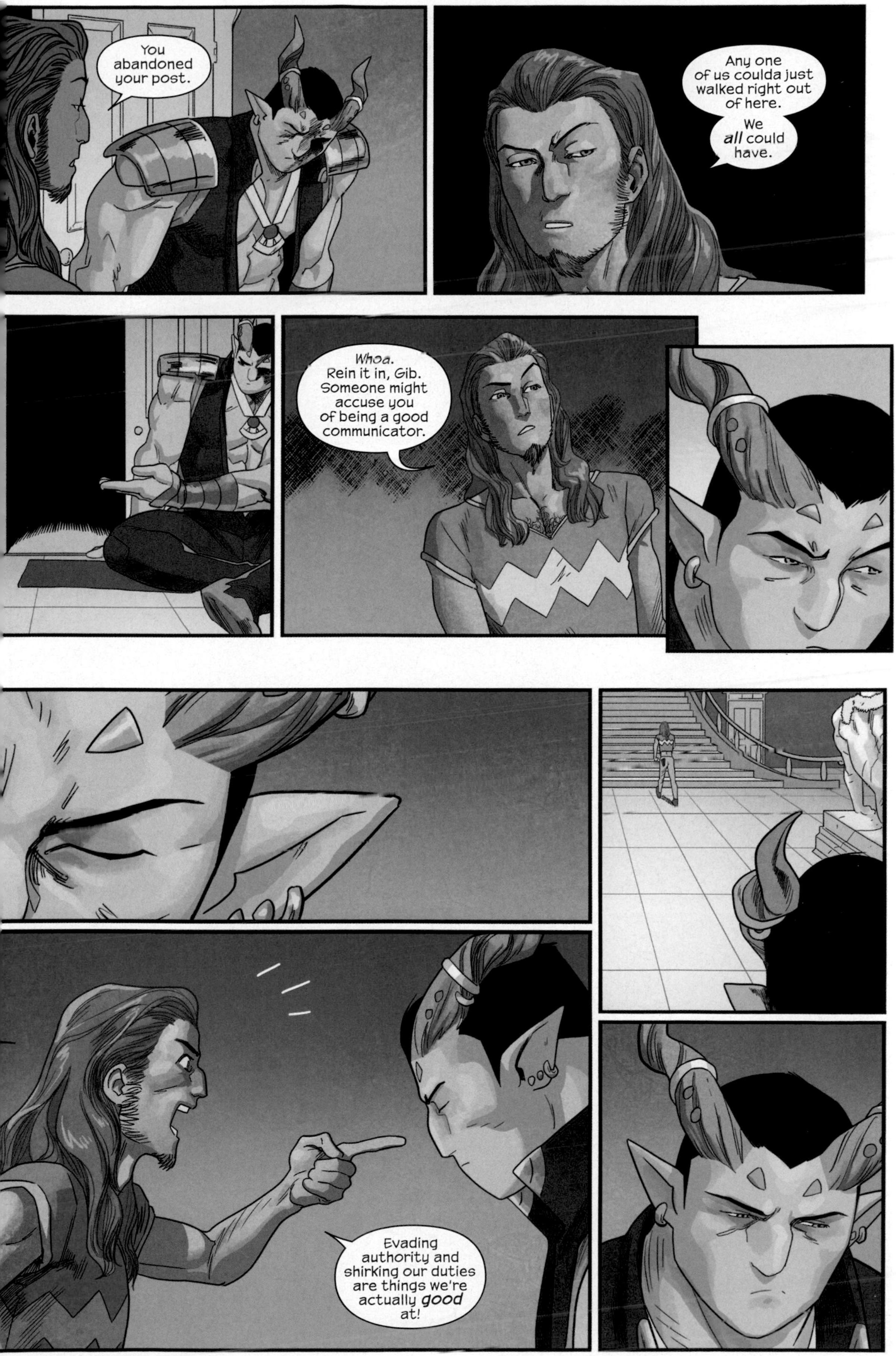

You abandoned your post.
Any one of us coulda just walked right out of here.
We *all* could have.
Whoa. Rein it in, Gib. Someone might accuse you of being a good communicator.
Evading authority and shirking our duties are things we're actually *good* at!

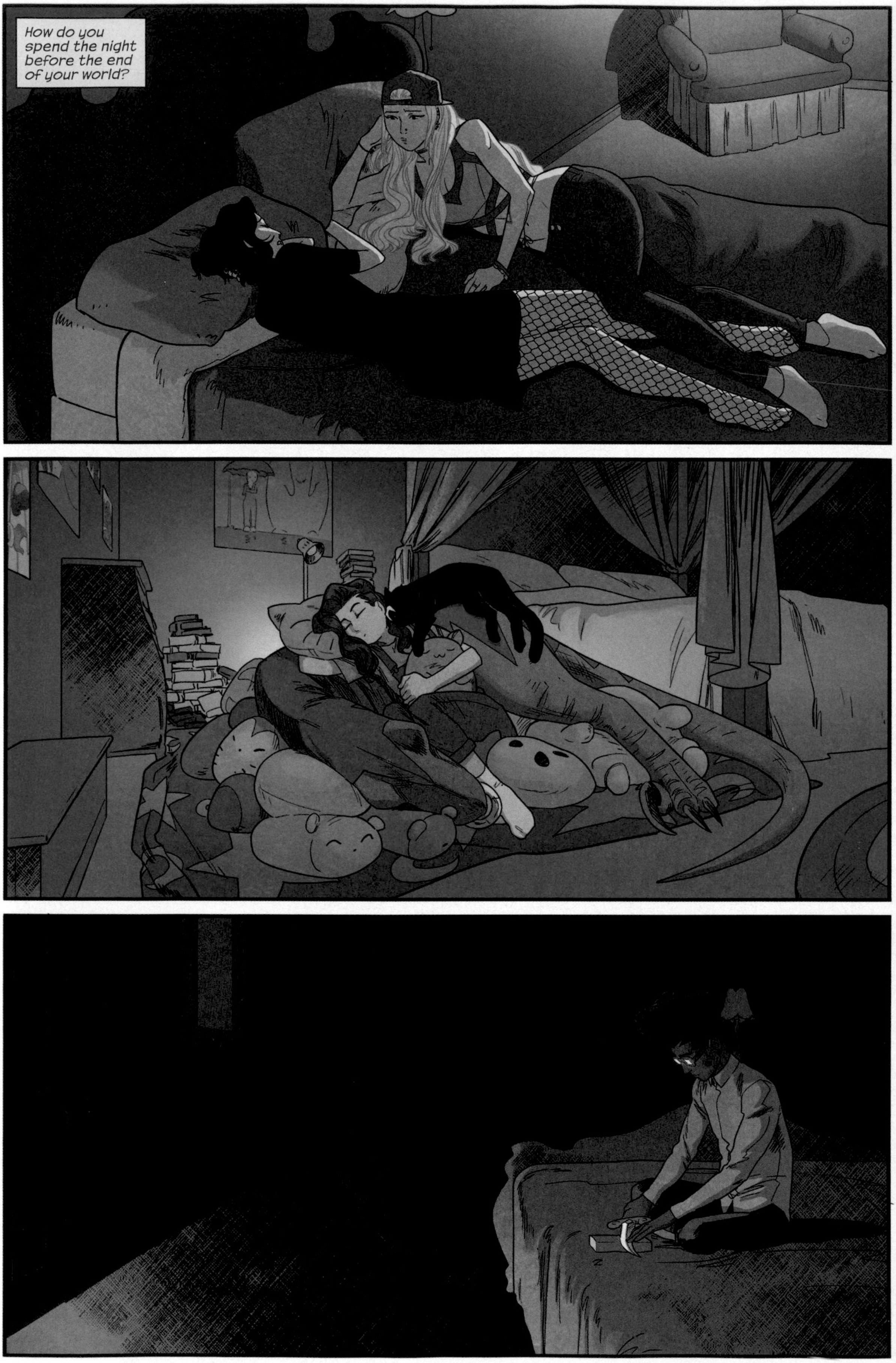
How do you spend the night before the end of your world?

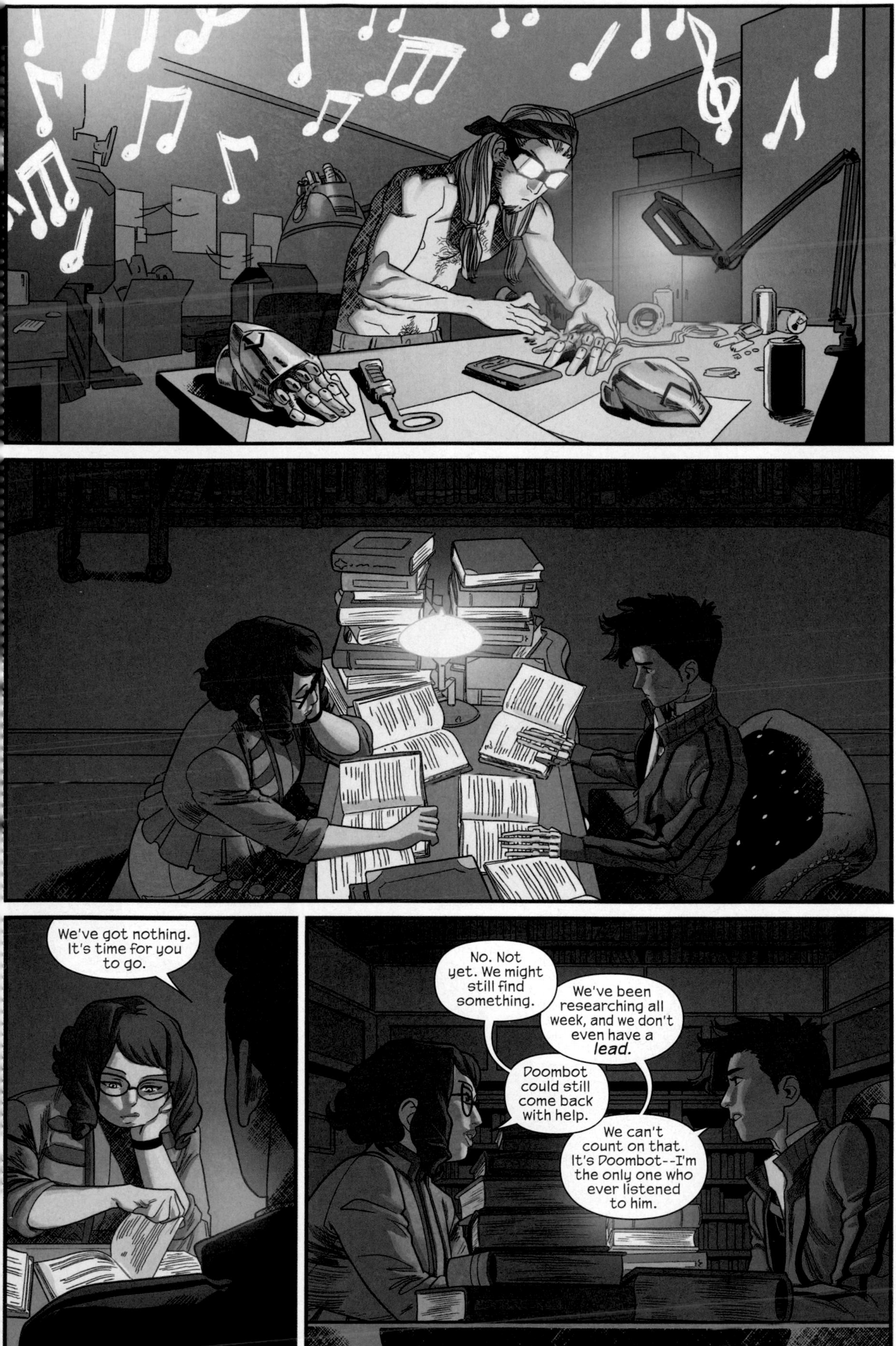
We've got nothing. It's time for you to go.
No. Not yet. We might still find something.
We've been researching all week, and we don't even have a *lead.*
Doombot could still come back with help.
We can't count on that. It's Doombot--I'm the only one who ever listened to him.

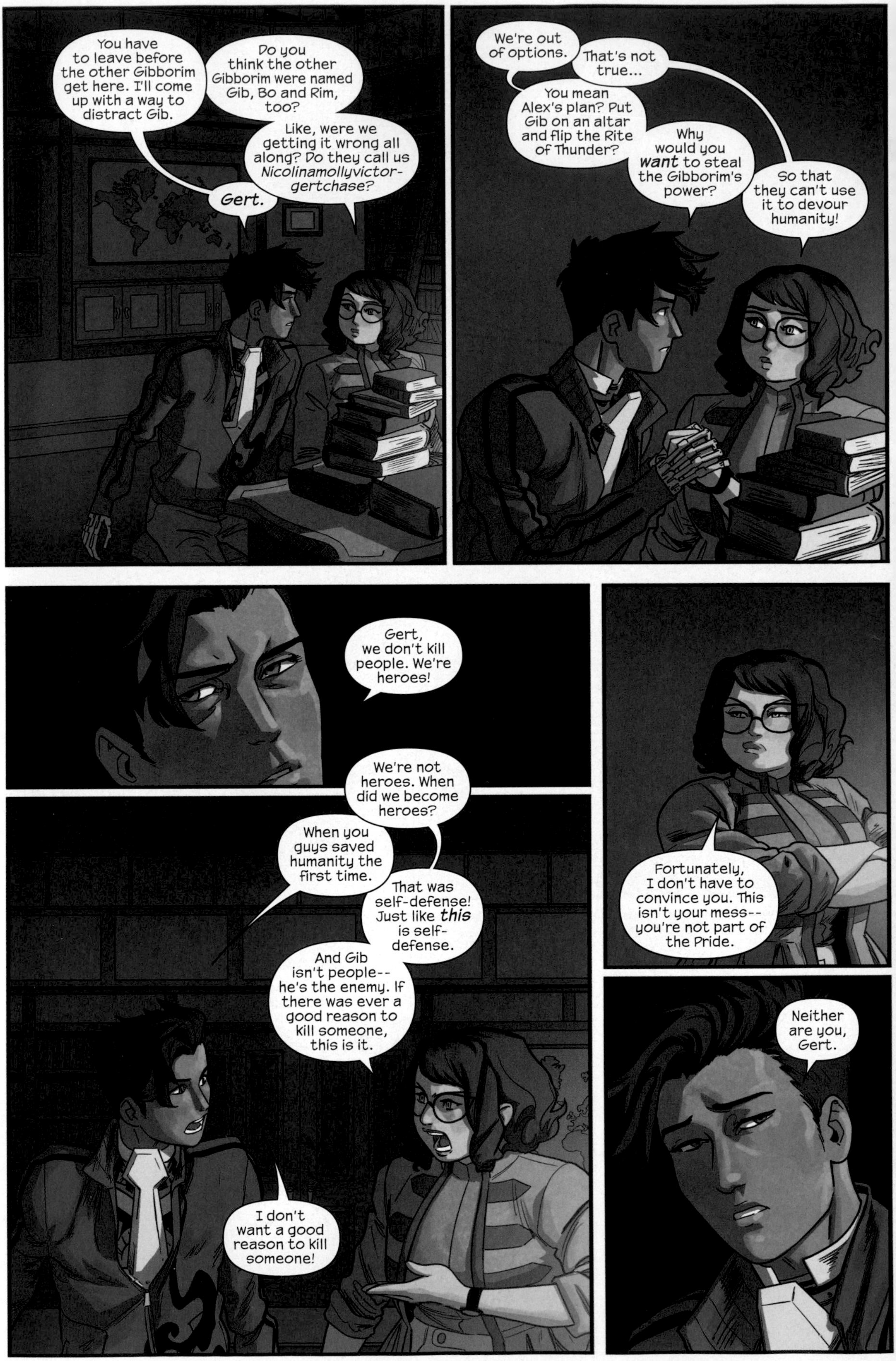
You have to leave before the other Gibborim get here. I'll come up with a way to distract Gib.
Do you think the other Gibborim were named Gib, Bo and Rim, too?
Like, were we getting it wrong all along? Do they call us *Nicolinamollyvictor-gertchase*?
Gert.
We're out of options.
That's not true...
You mean Alex's plan? Put Gib on an altar and flip the Rite of Thunder?
Why would you ***want*** to steal the Gibborim's power?
So that they can't use it to devour humanity!
Gert, we don't kill people. We're heroes!
We're not heroes. When did we become heroes?
When you guys saved humanity the first time.
That was self-defense! Just like ***this*** is self-defense.
And Gib isn't people--he's the enemy. If there was ever a good reason to kill someone, this is it.
I don't want a good reason to kill someone!
Fortunately, I don't have to convince you. This isn't your mess--you're not part of the Pride.
Neither are you, Gert.

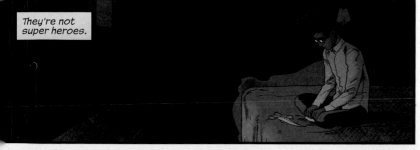

They're not super heroes.

They're not a team.

Maybe the *right spell* would work against them. Like, what if the spell was, "Exception to all the Gibborim's rules!"

Maybe. I'll try it.

And I'll fight, too. I've been hoarding my sun energy.

Okay.

And if that doesn't work...

Alex's plan.

Right.

Or maybe we *lead* with Alex's plan...

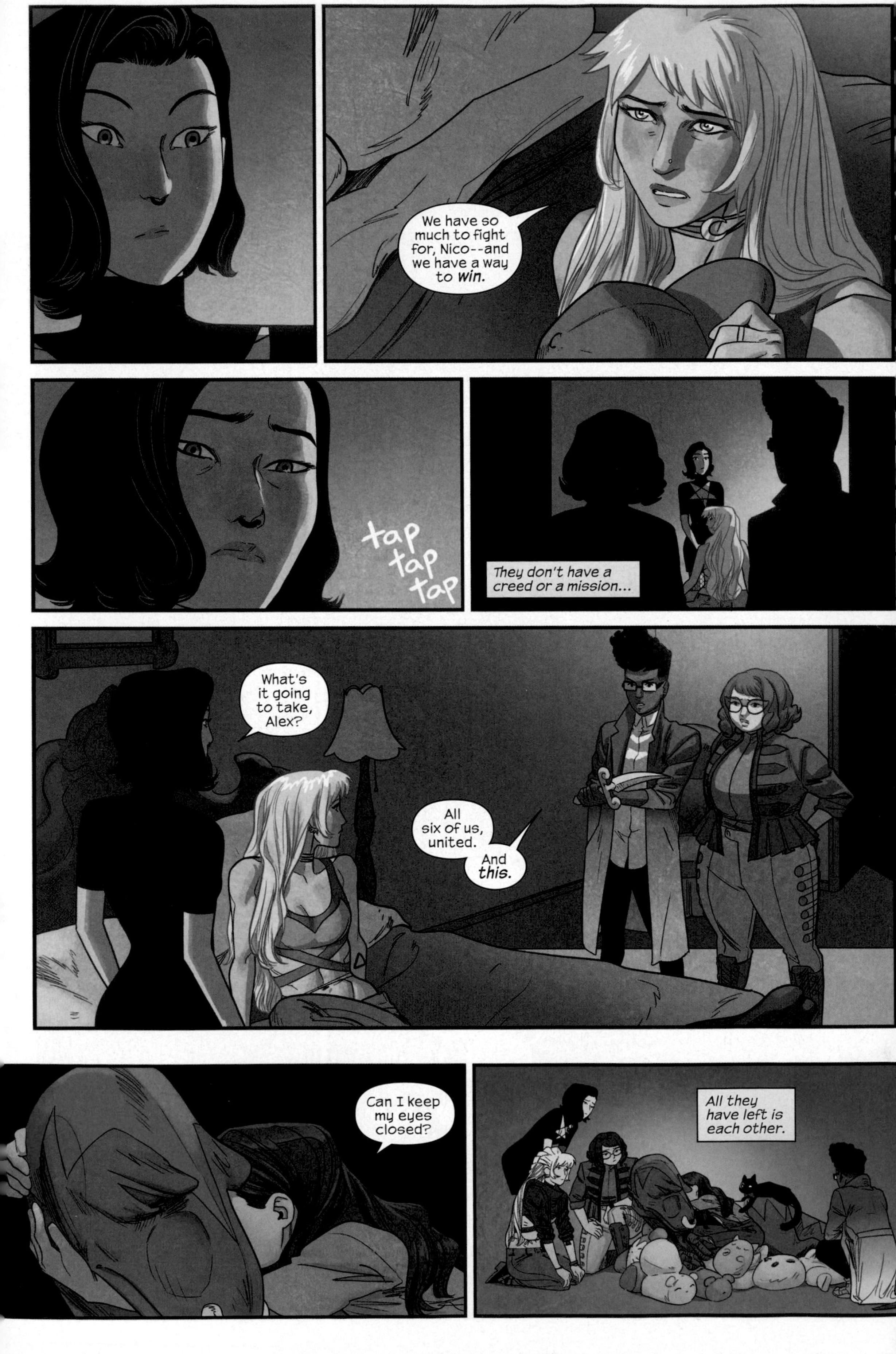
We have so much to fight for, Nico--and we have a way to win.
tap tap tap
They don't have a creed or a mission...
What's it going to take, Alex?
All six of us, united.
And this.
Can I keep my eyes closed?
All they have left is each other.

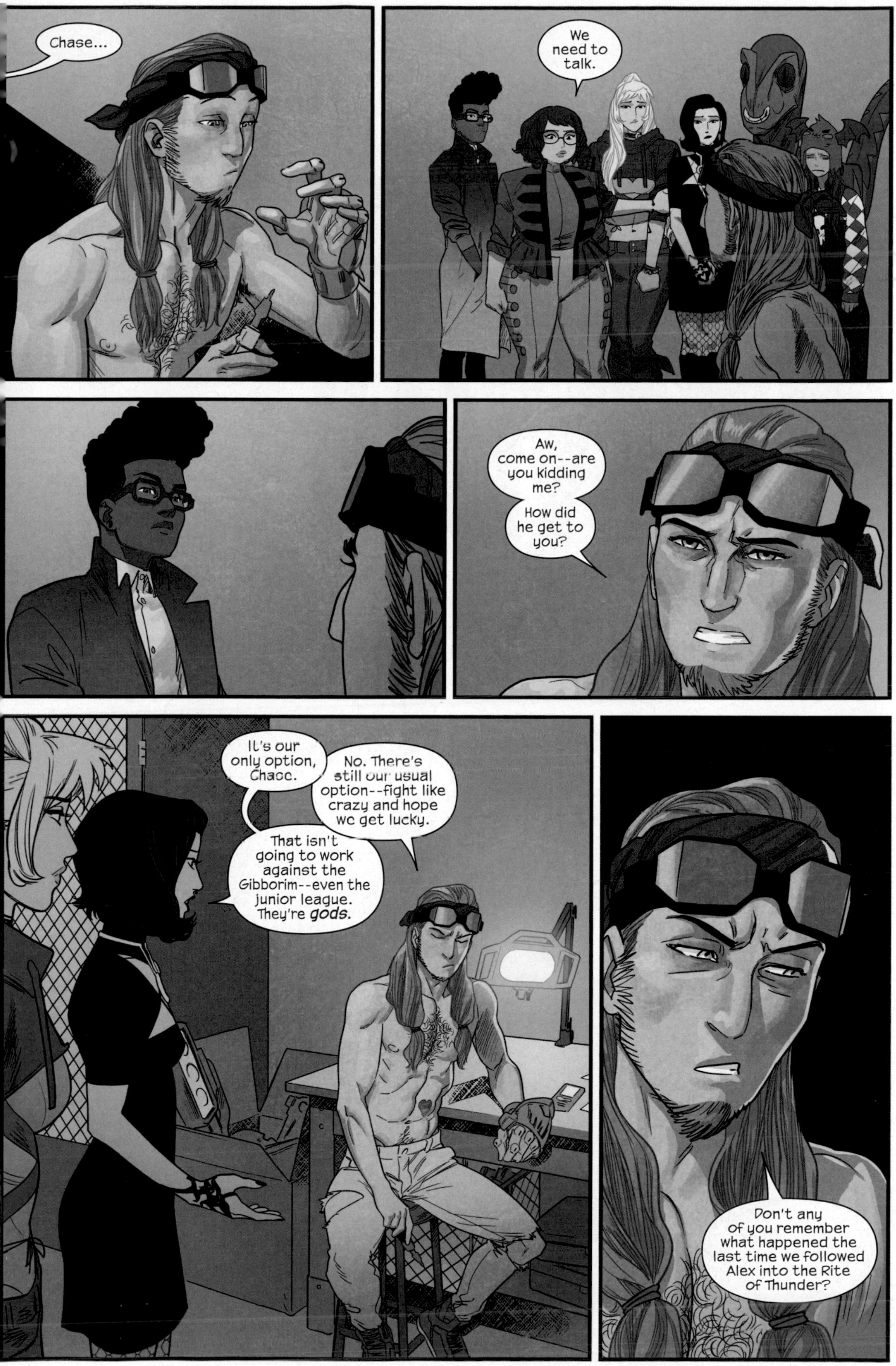
Chase...
We need to talk.
Aw, come on--are you kidding me?
How did he get to you?
It's our only option, Chase.
No. There's still our usual option--fight like crazy and hope we get lucky.
That isn't going to work against the Gibborim--even the junior league. They're *gods.*
Don't any of you remember what happened the last time we followed Alex into the Rite of Thunder?

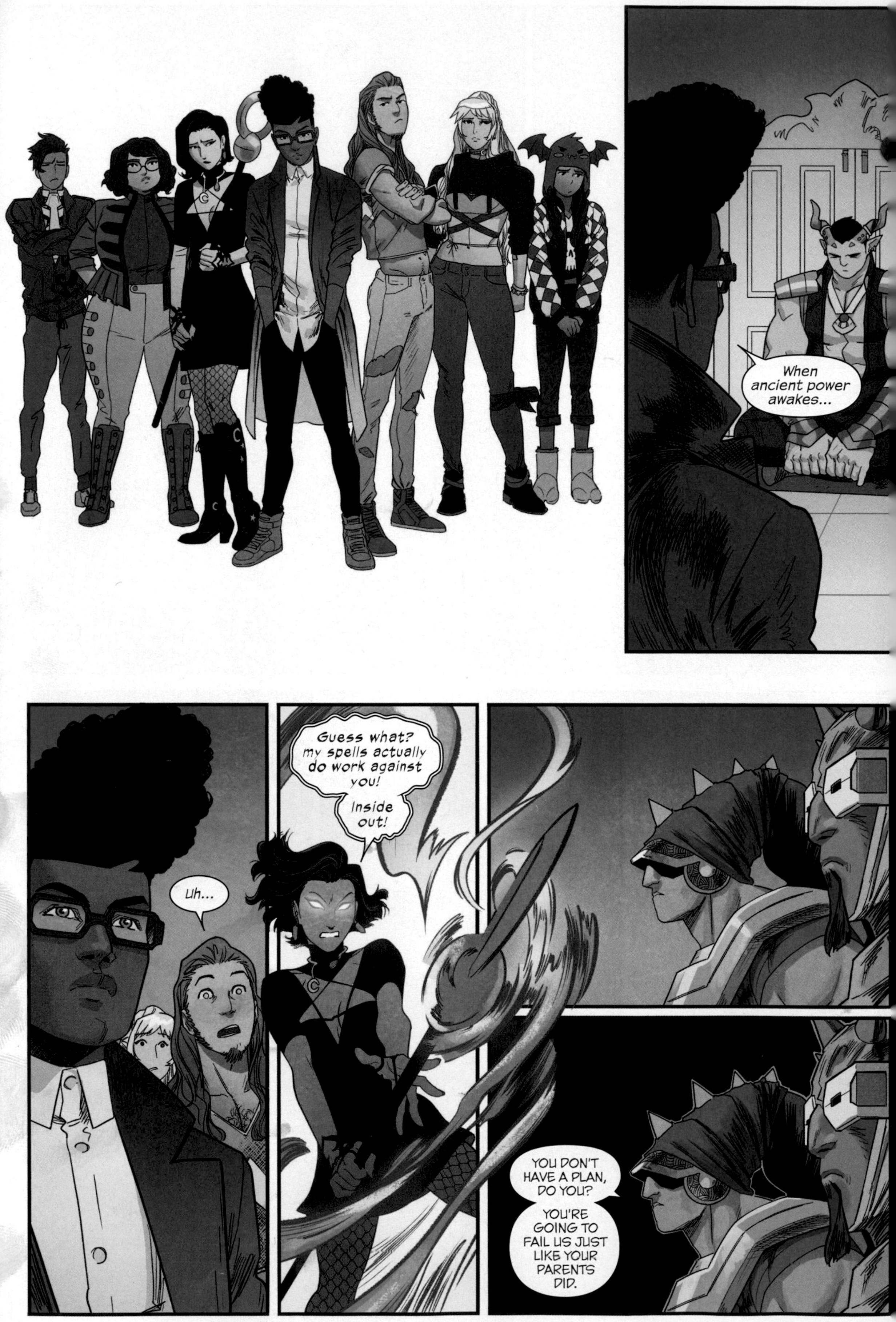
When ancient power awakes...
Uh...
Guess what? my spells actually do work against you!
Inside out!
YOU DON'T HAVE A PLAN, DO YOU?
YOU'RE GOING TO FAIL US JUST LIKE YOUR PARENTS DID.

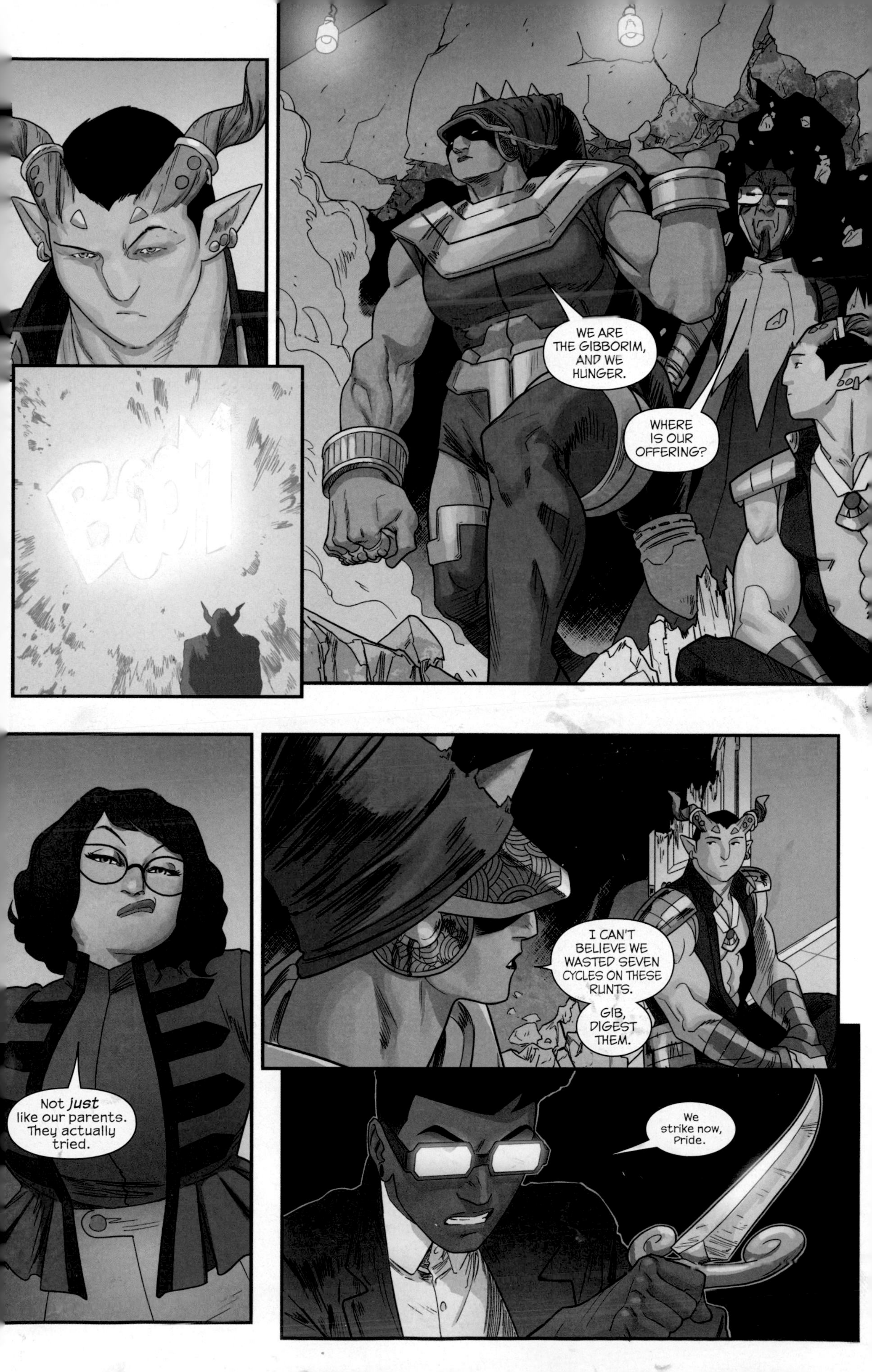

BOOM
WE ARE THE GIBBORIM, AND WE HUNGER.
WHERE IS OUR OFFERING?
Not *just* like our parents. They actually tried.
I CAN'T BELIEVE WE WASTED SEVEN CYCLES ON THESE RUNTS.
GIB, DIGEST THEM.
We strike now, Pride.

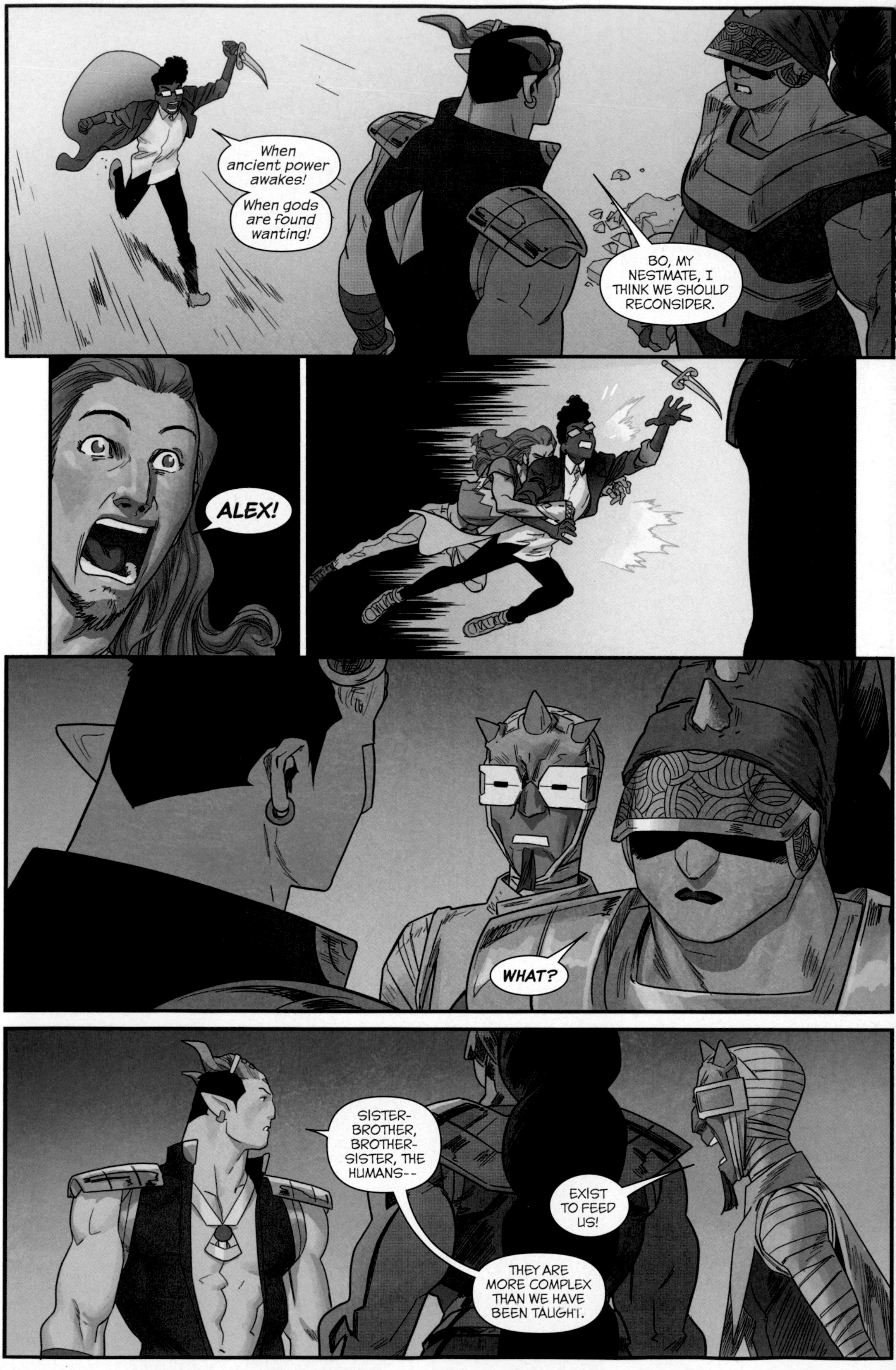
When ancient power awakes!
When gods are found wanting!
BO, MY NESTMATE, I THINK WE SHOULD RECONSIDER.
ALEX!
WHAT?
SISTER-BROTHER, BROTHER-SISTER, THE HUMANS--
EXIST TO FEED US!
THEY ARE MORE COMPLEX THAN WE HAVE BEEN TAUGHT.

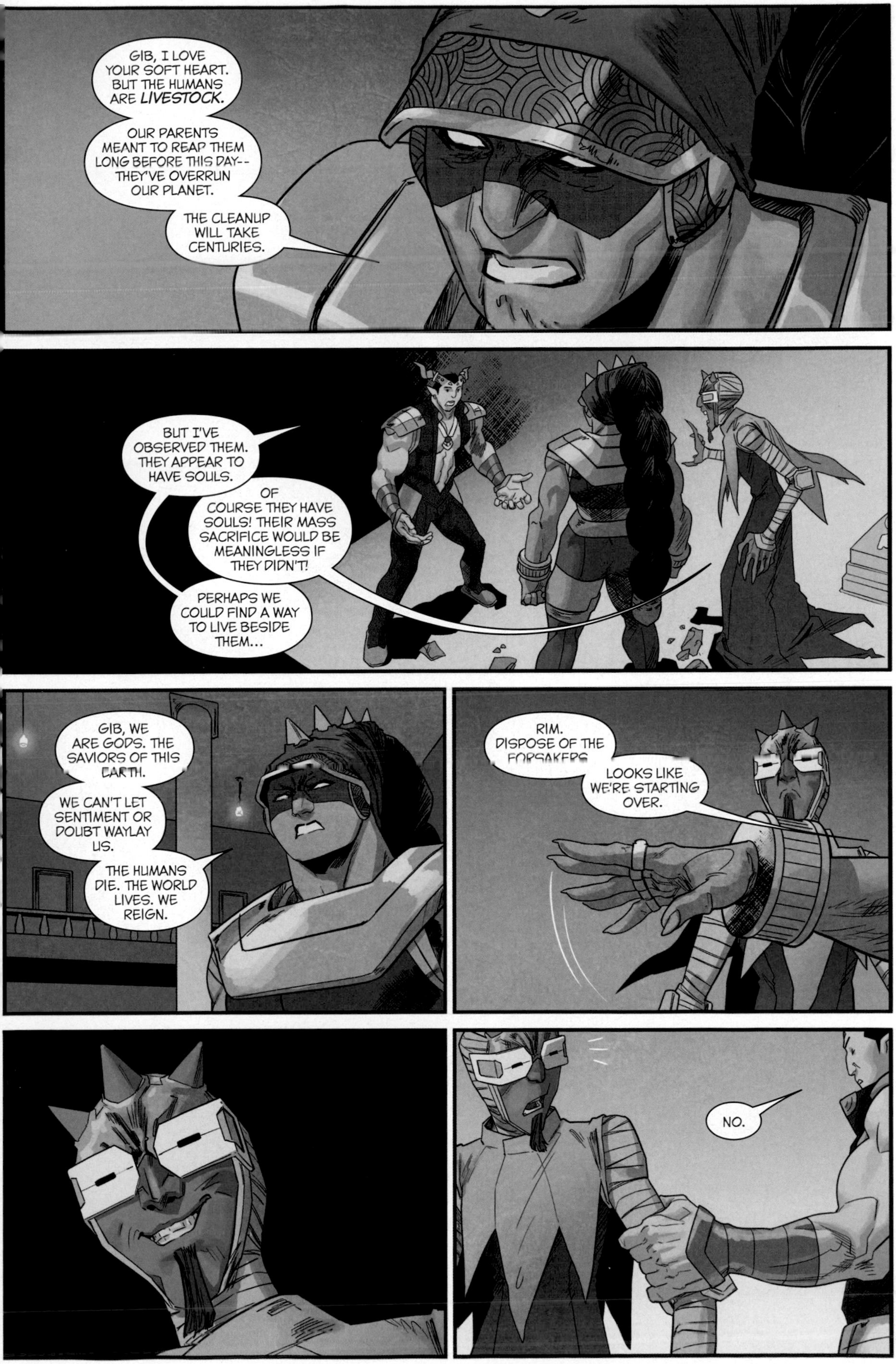
GIB, I LOVE YOUR SOFT HEART. BUT THE HUMANS ARE *LIVESTOCK.*
OUR PARENTS MEANT TO REAP THEM LONG BEFORE THIS DAY-- THEY'VE OVERRUN OUR PLANET.
THE CLEANUP WILL TAKE CENTURIES.
BUT I'VE OBSERVED THEM. THEY APPEAR TO HAVE SOULS.
OF COURSE THEY HAVE SOULS! THEIR MASS SACRIFICE WOULD BE MEANINGLESS IF THEY DIDN'T!
PERHAPS WE COULD FIND A WAY TO LIVE BESIDE THEM...
GIB, WE ARE GODS. THE SAVIORS OF THIS EARTH.
WE CAN'T LET SENTIMENT OR DOUBT WAYLAY US.
THE HUMANS DIE. THE WORLD LIVES. WE REIGN.
RIM. DISPOSE OF THE FORSAKERS.
LOOKS LIKE WE'RE STARTING OVER.
NO.

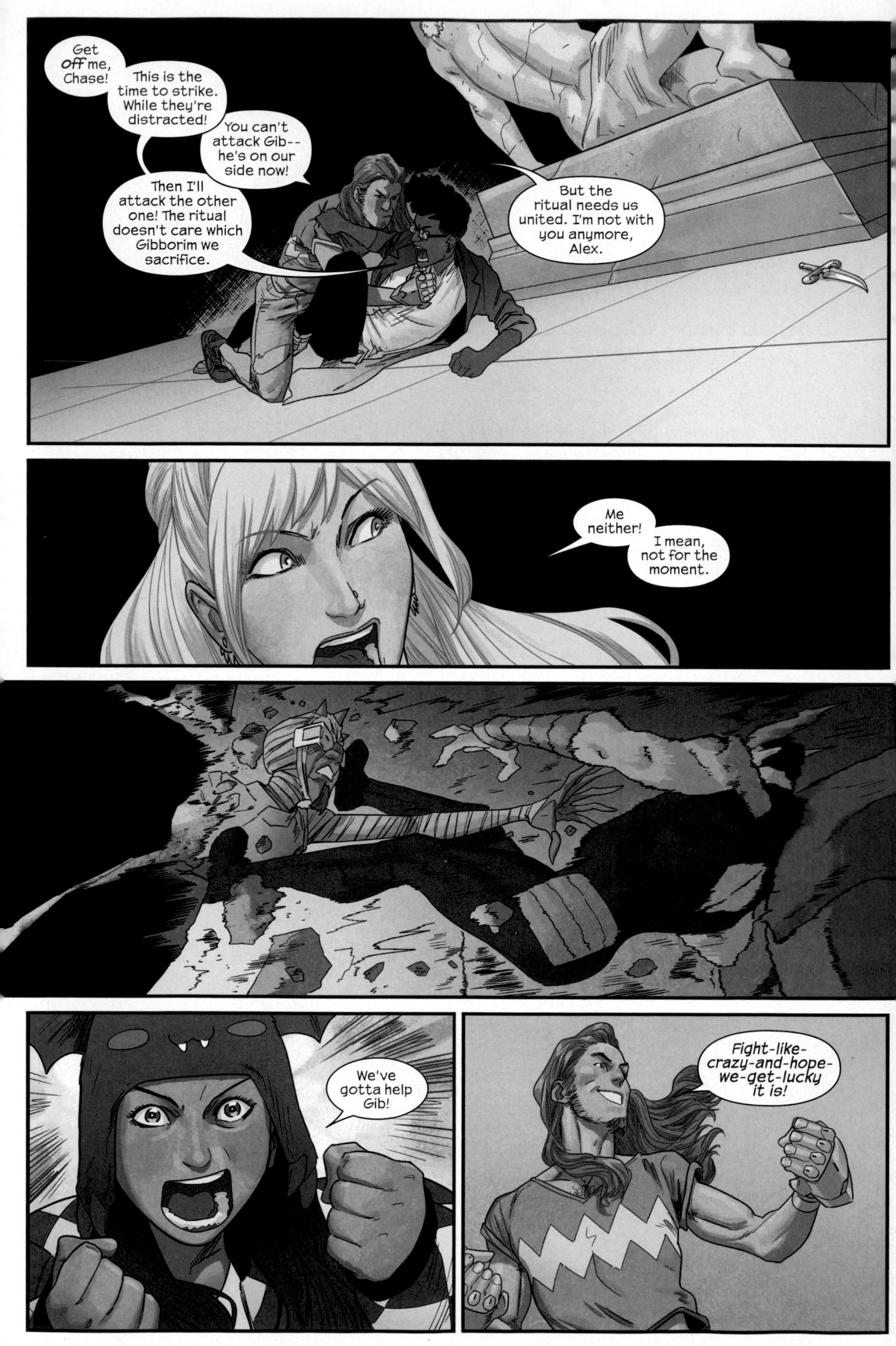
Get OFF me, Chase!
This is the time to strike. While they're distracted!
You can't attack Gib-- he's on our side now!
Then I'll attack the other one! The ritual doesn't care which Gibborim we sacrifice.
But the ritual needs us united. I'm not with you anymore, Alex.
Me neither!
I mean, not for the moment.
We've gotta help Gib!
Fight-like-crazy-and-hope-we-get-lucky it is!

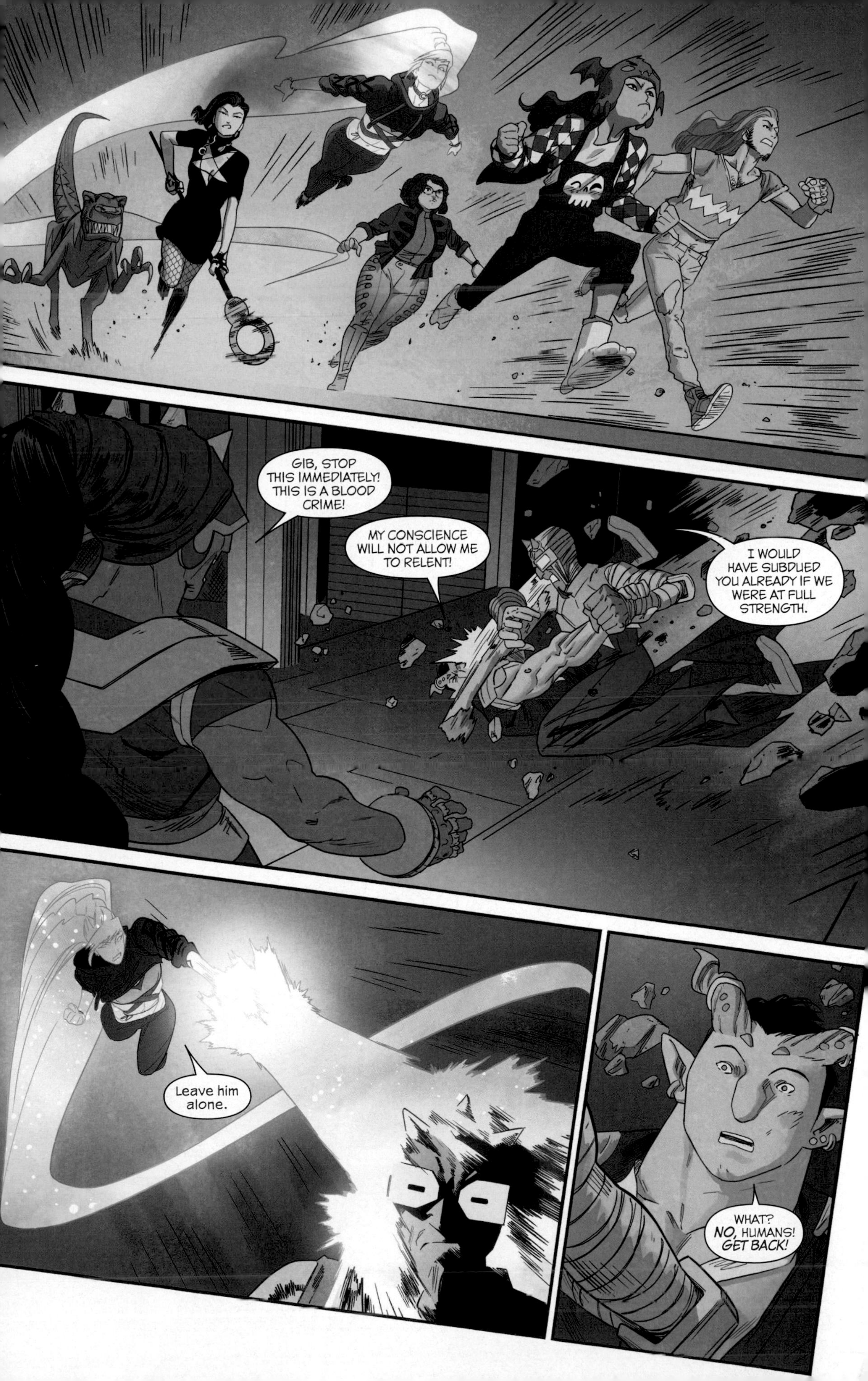
GIB, STOP THIS IMMEDIATELY! THIS IS A BLOOD CRIME!
MY CONSCIENCE WILL NOT ALLOW ME TO RELENT!
I WOULD HAVE SUBDUED YOU ALREADY IF WE WERE AT FULL STRENGTH.
Leave him alone.
WHAT? NO, HUMANS! GET BACK!

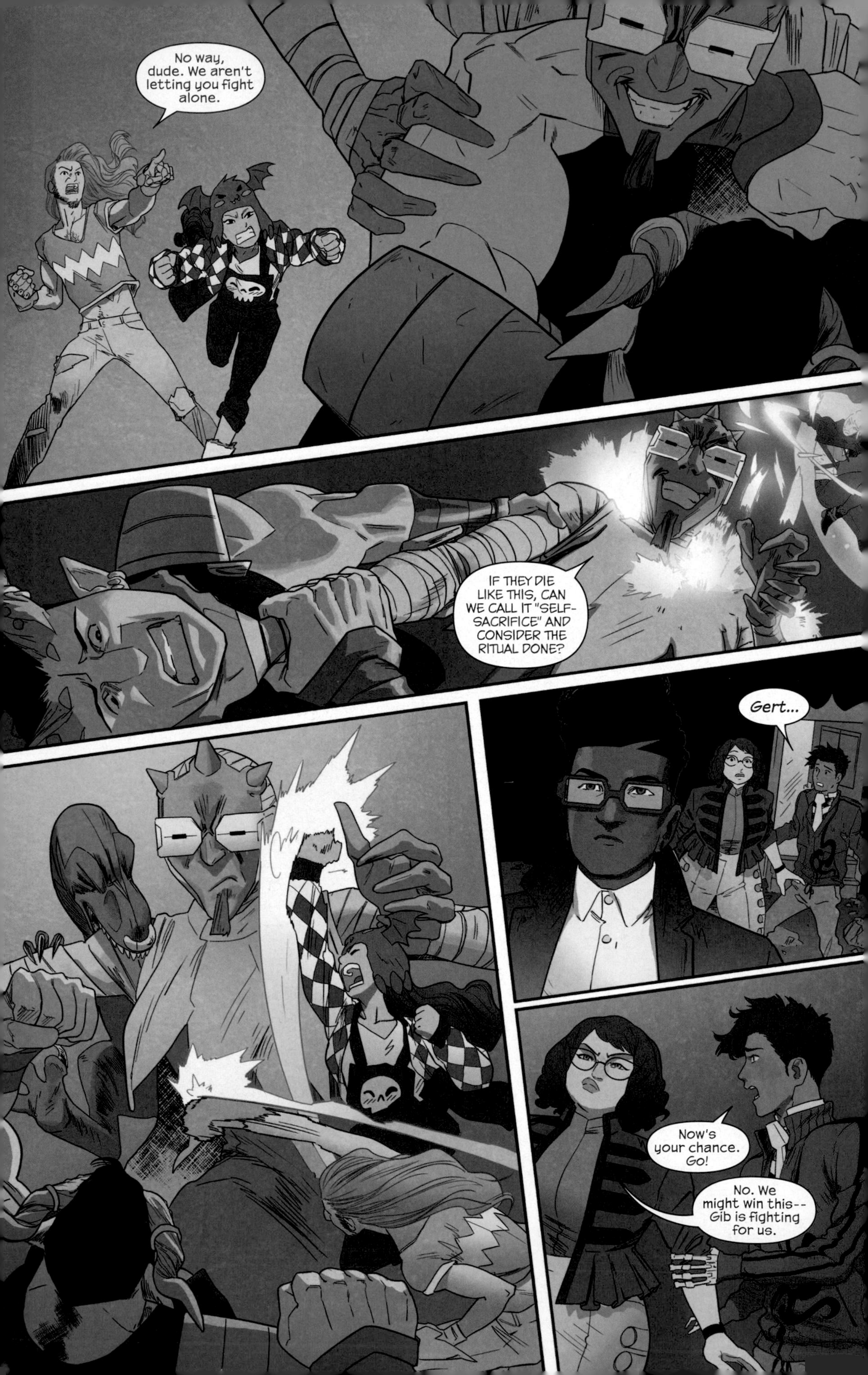
No way, dude. We aren't letting you fight alone.
IF THEY DIE LIKE THIS, CAN WE CALL IT "SELF-SACRIFICE" AND CONSIDER THE RITUAL DONE?
Gert...
Now's your chance. Go!
No. We might win this-- Gib is fighting for us.

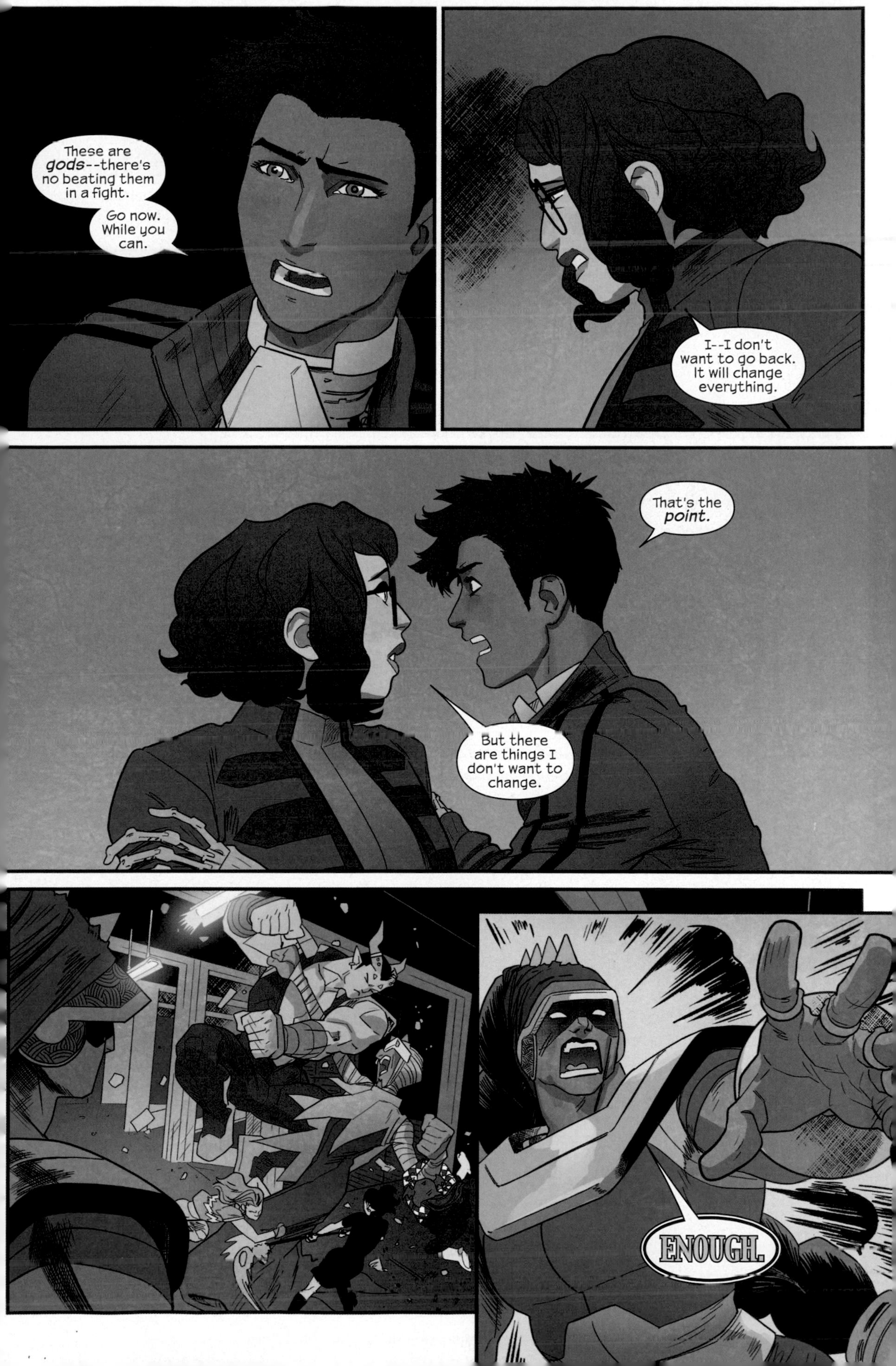
These are gods--there's no beating them in a fight.
Go now. While you can.
I--I don't want to go back. It will change everything.
That's the point.
But there are things I don't want to change.
ENOUGH.

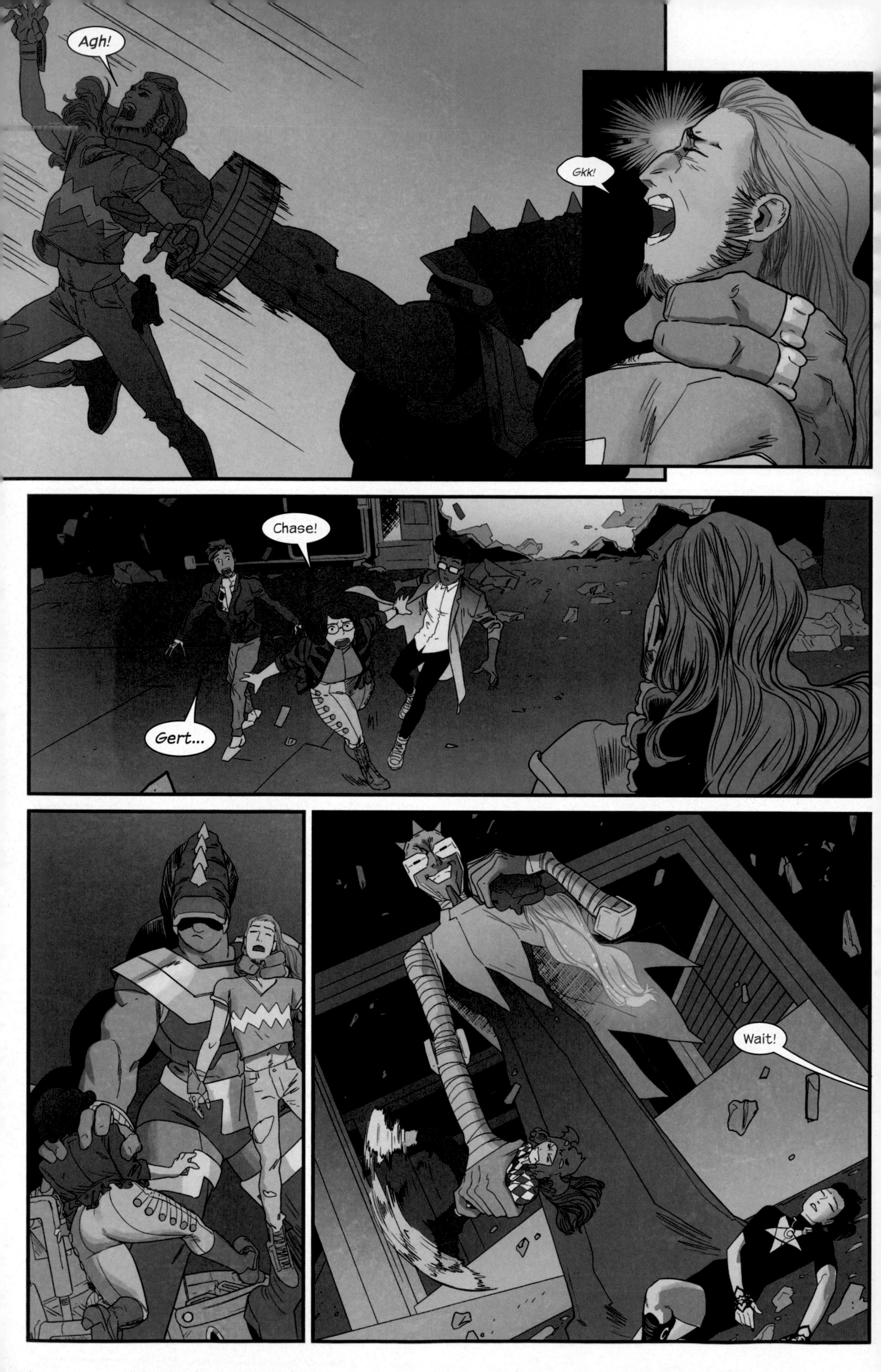
Agh!
Gkk!
Chase!
Gert...
Wait!

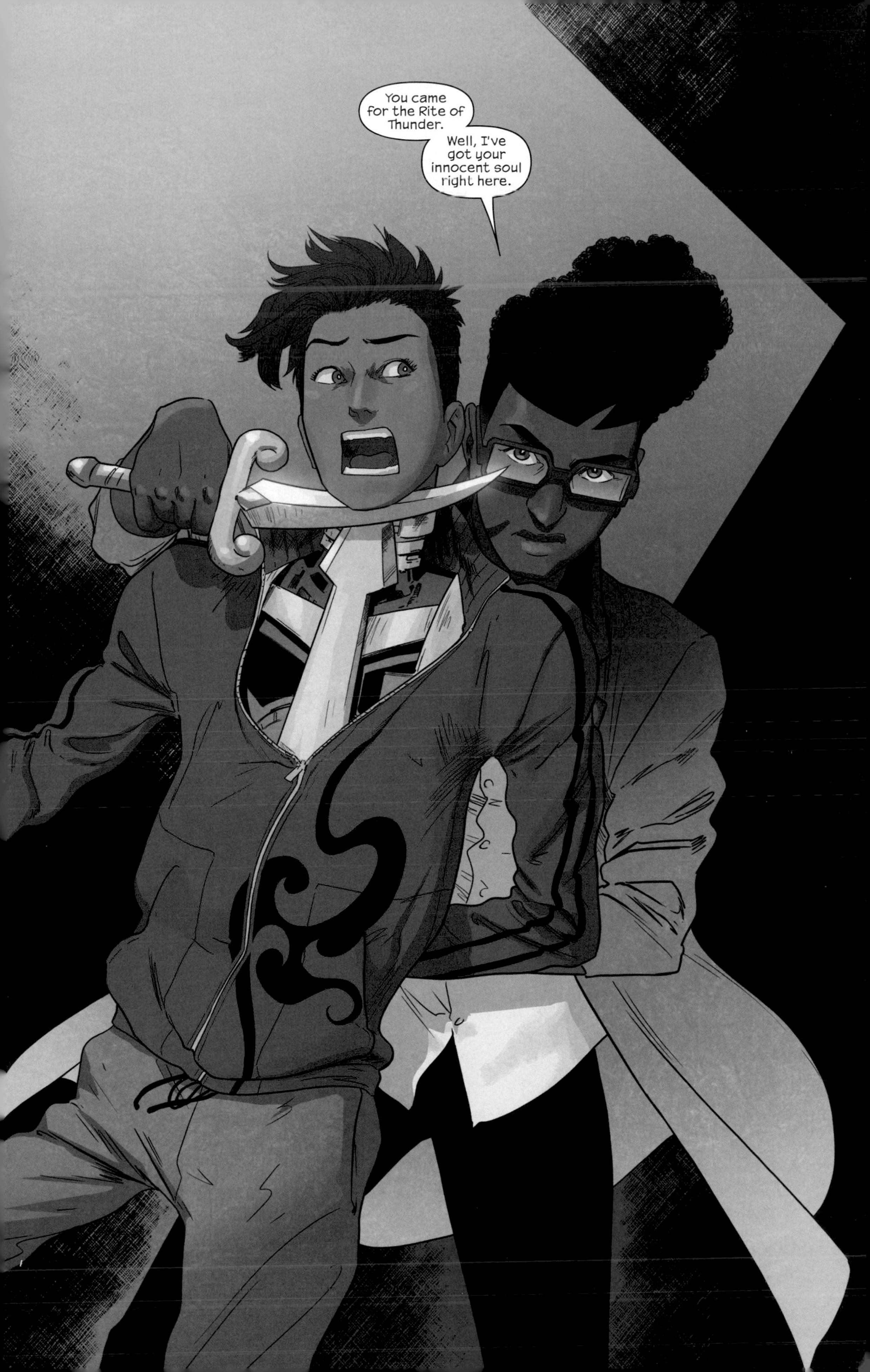
You came for the Rite of Thunder.
Well, I've got your innocent soul right here.

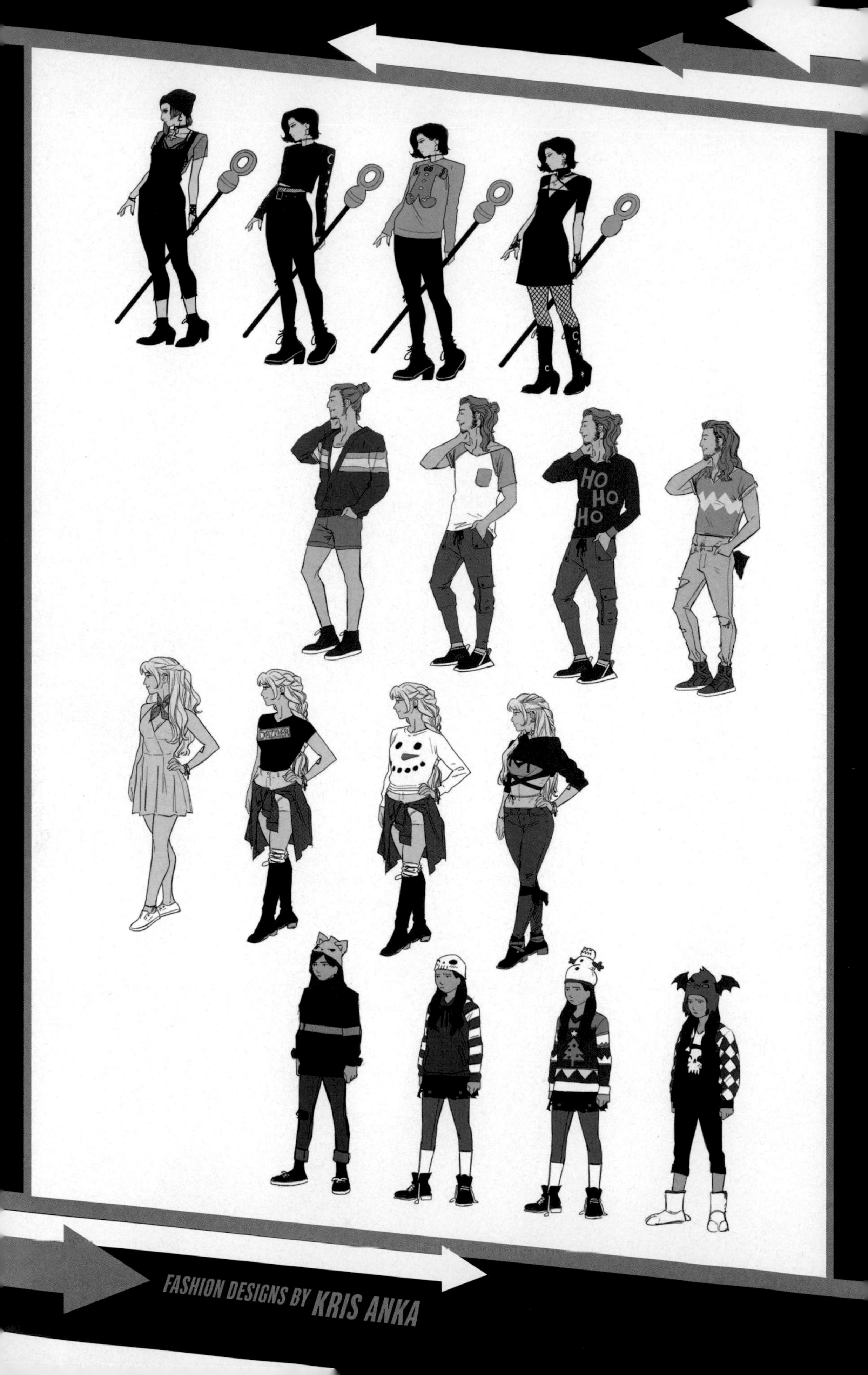
HO HO HO
DAZZLER

FASHION DESIGNS BY **KRIS ANKA**

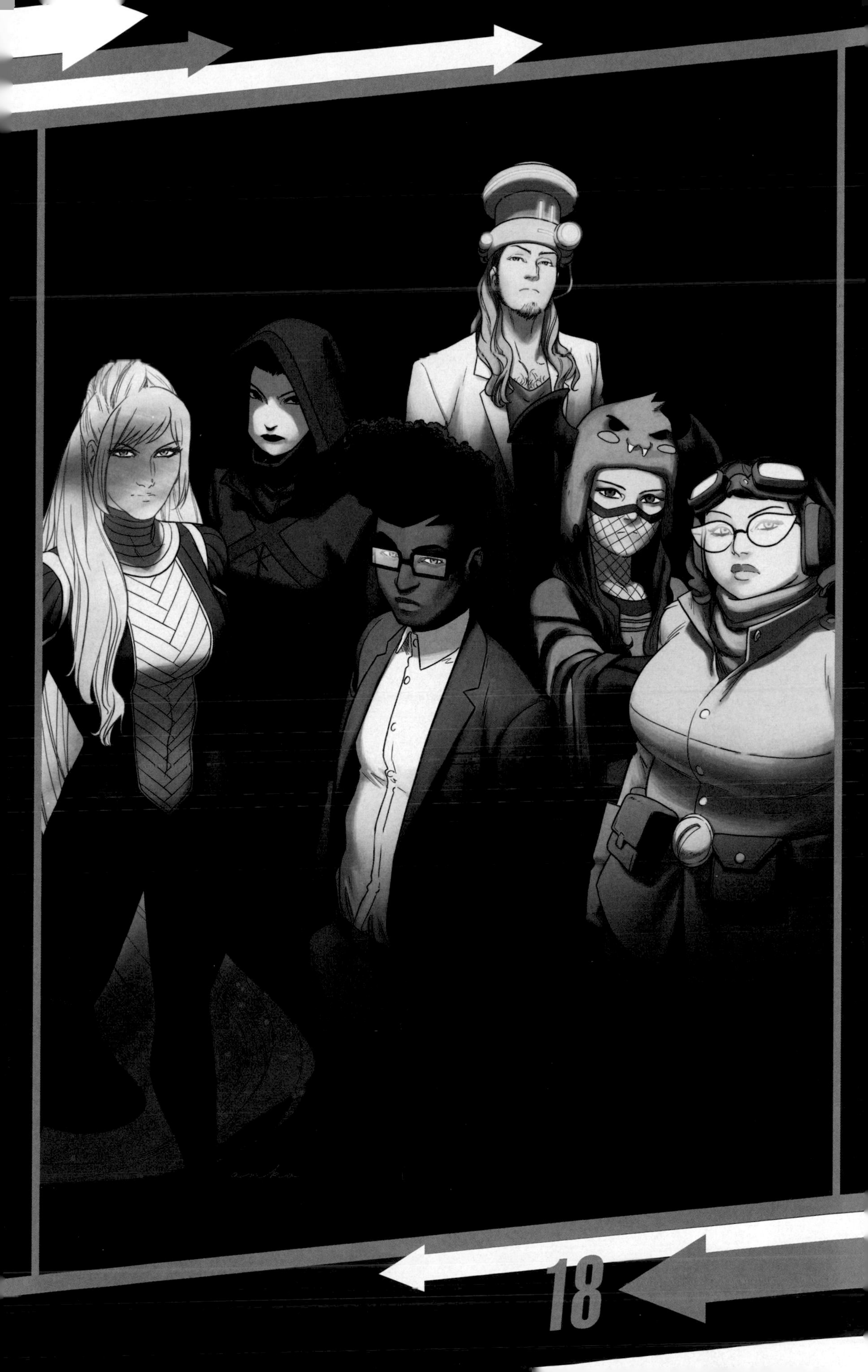

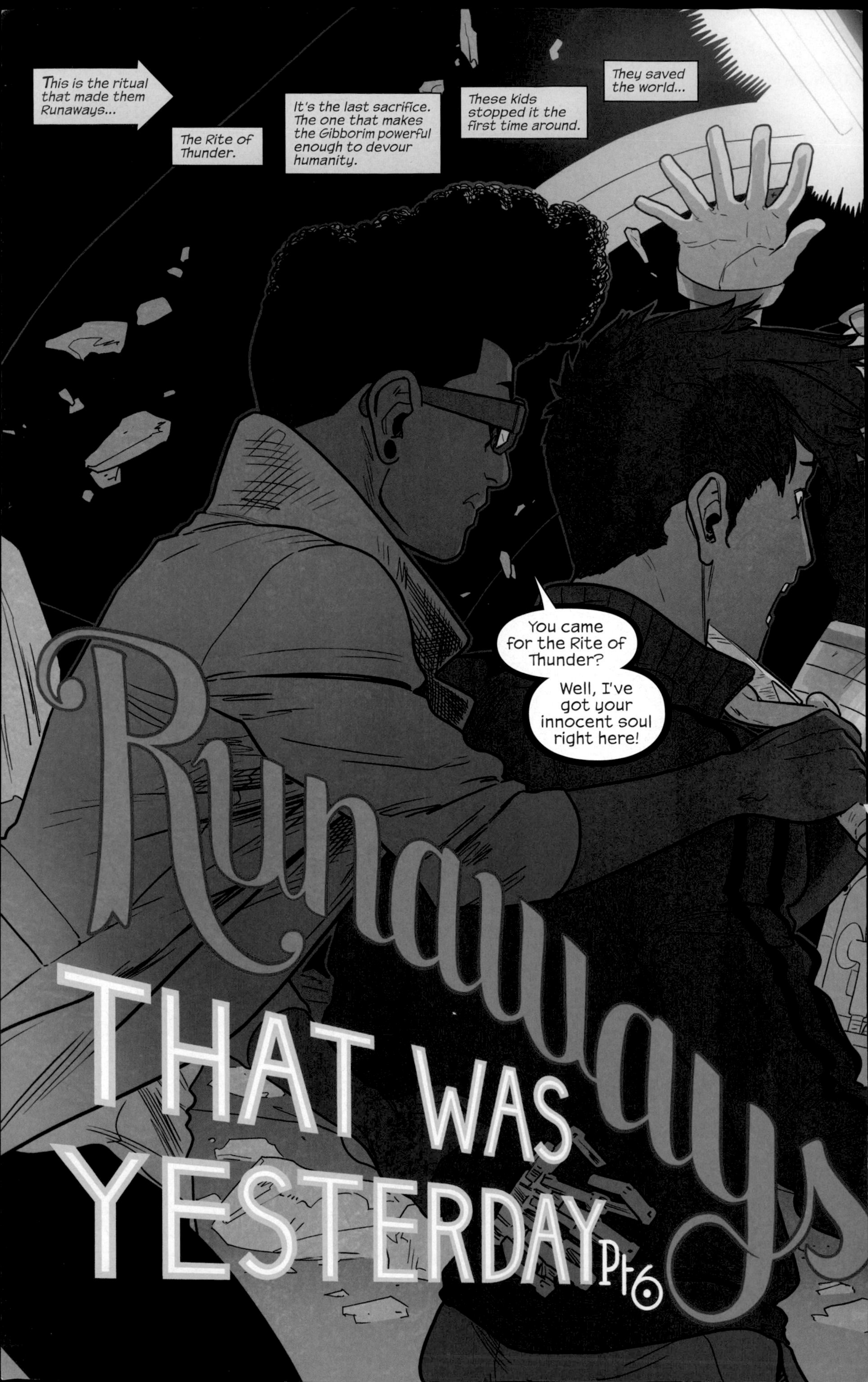

This is the ritual that made them Runaways...
The Rite of Thunder.
It's the last sacrifice. The one that makes the Gibborim powerful enough to devour humanity.
These kids stopped it the first time around.
They saved the world...
You came for the Rite of Thunder?
Well, I've got your innocent soul right here!
Runaways
THAT WAS YESTERDAY Pt 6

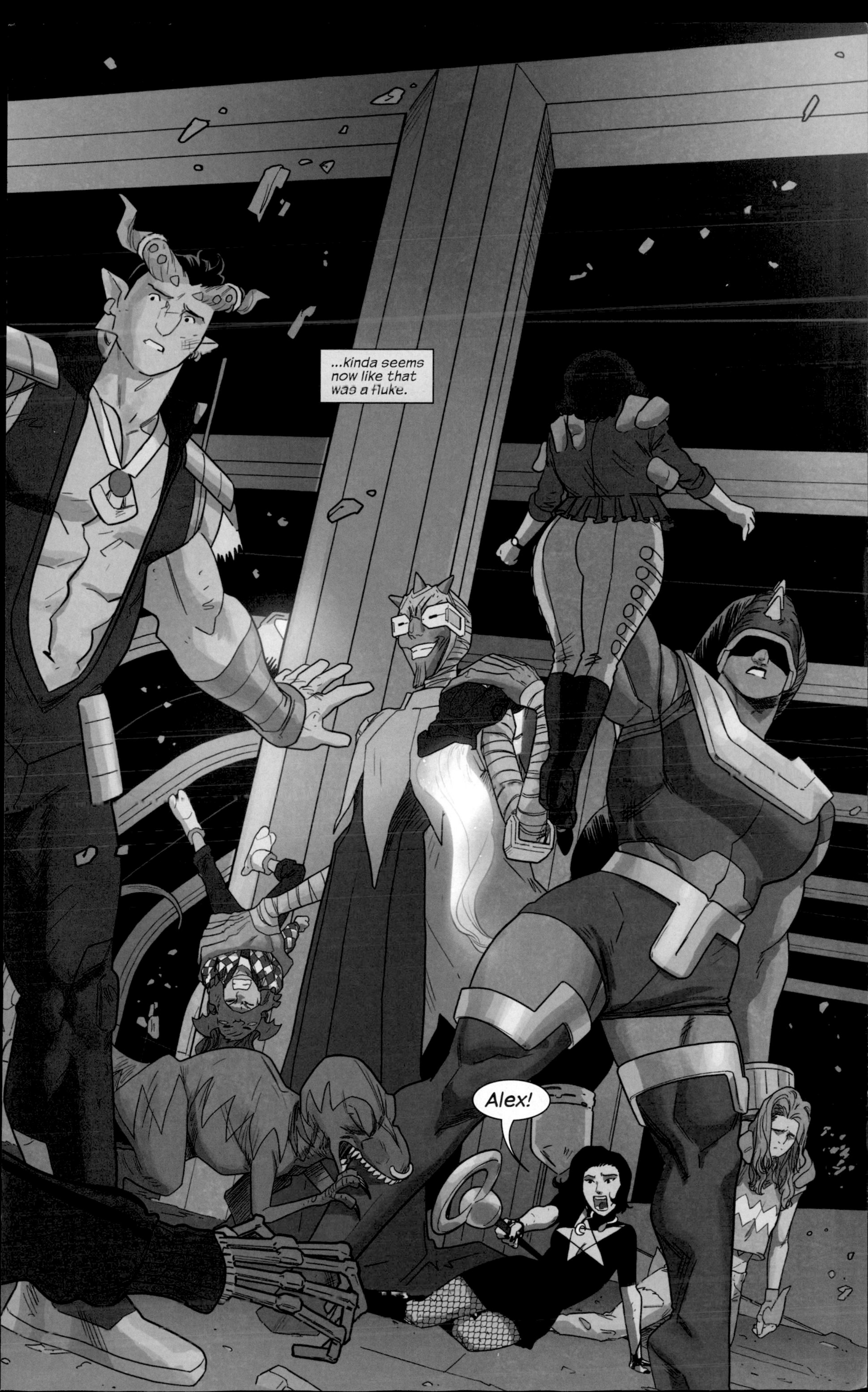
...kinda seems now like that was a fluke.
Alex!

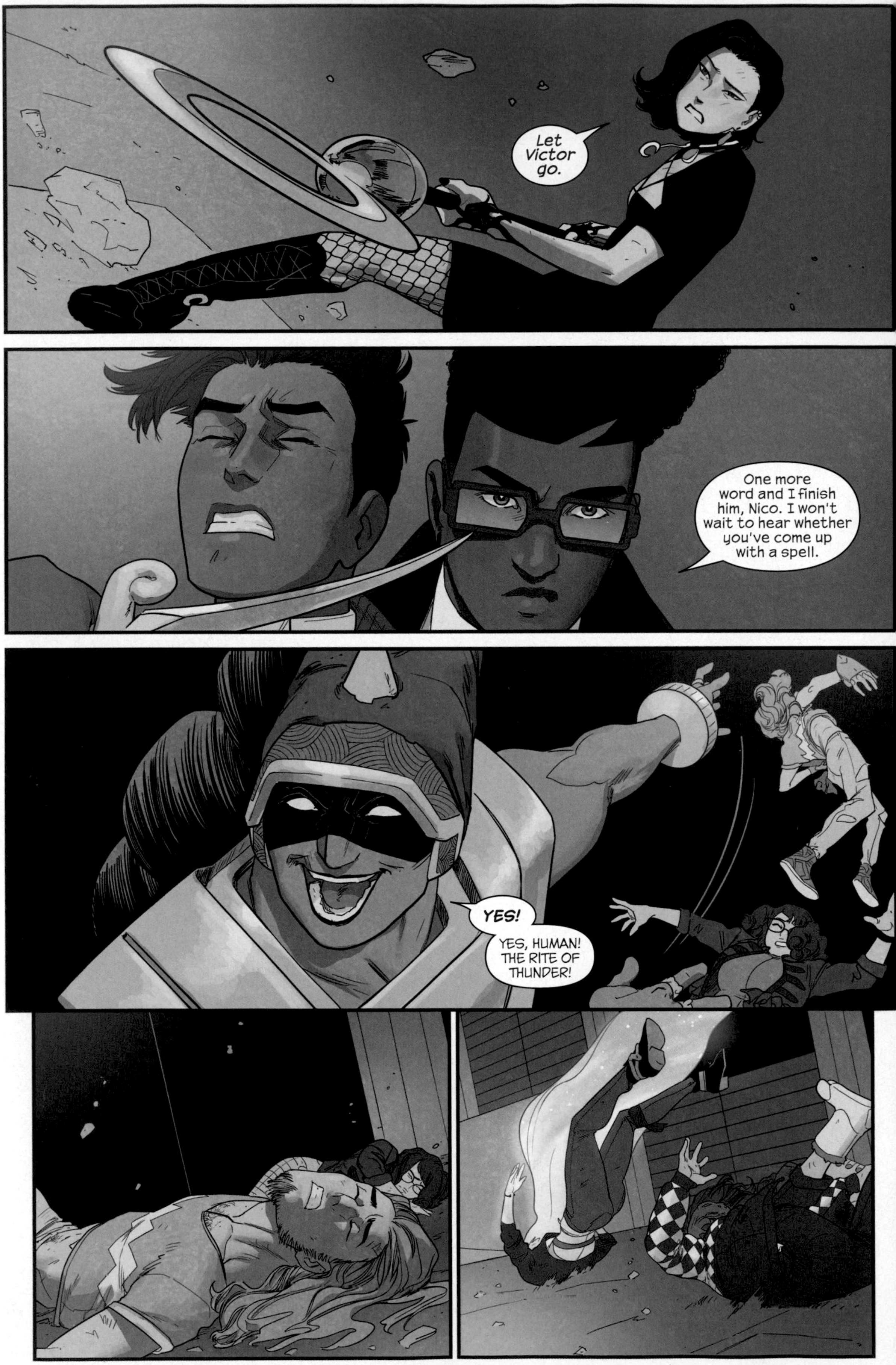
Let Victor go.
One more word and I finish him, Nico. I won't wait to hear whether you've come up with a spell.
YES!
YES, HUMAN! THE RITE OF THUNDER!

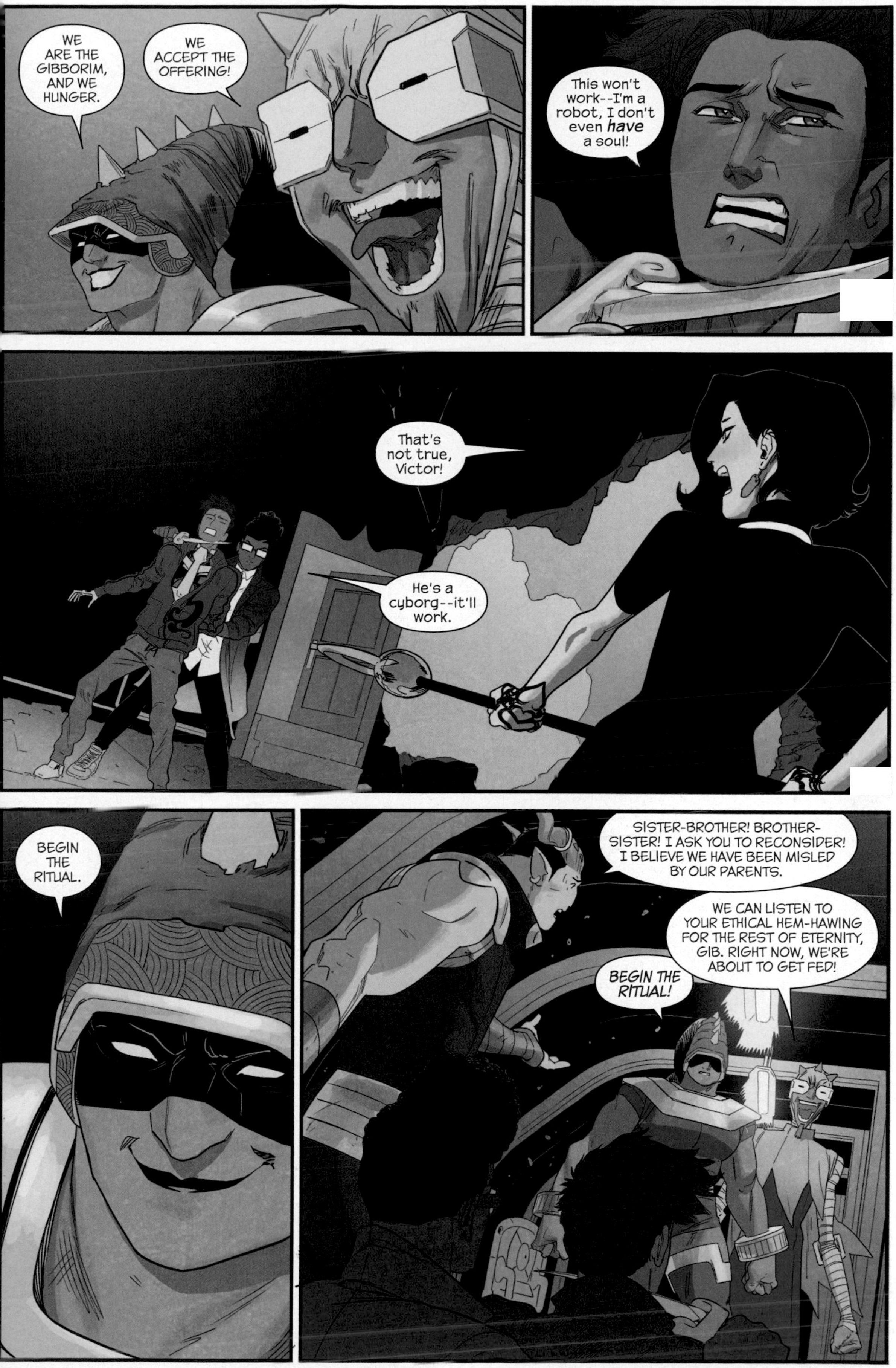
WE ARE THE GIBBORIM, AND WE HUNGER.
WE ACCEPT THE OFFERING!
This won't work--I'm a robot, I don't even **have** a soul!
That's not true, Victor!
He's a cyborg--it'll work.
BEGIN THE RITUAL.
SISTER-BROTHER! BROTHER-SISTER! I ASK YOU TO RECONSIDER! I BELIEVE WE HAVE BEEN MISLED BY OUR PARENTS.
WE CAN LISTEN TO YOUR ETHICAL HEM-HAWING FOR THE REST OF ETERNITY, GIB. RIGHT NOW, WE'RE ABOUT TO GET FED!
BEGIN THE RITUAL!

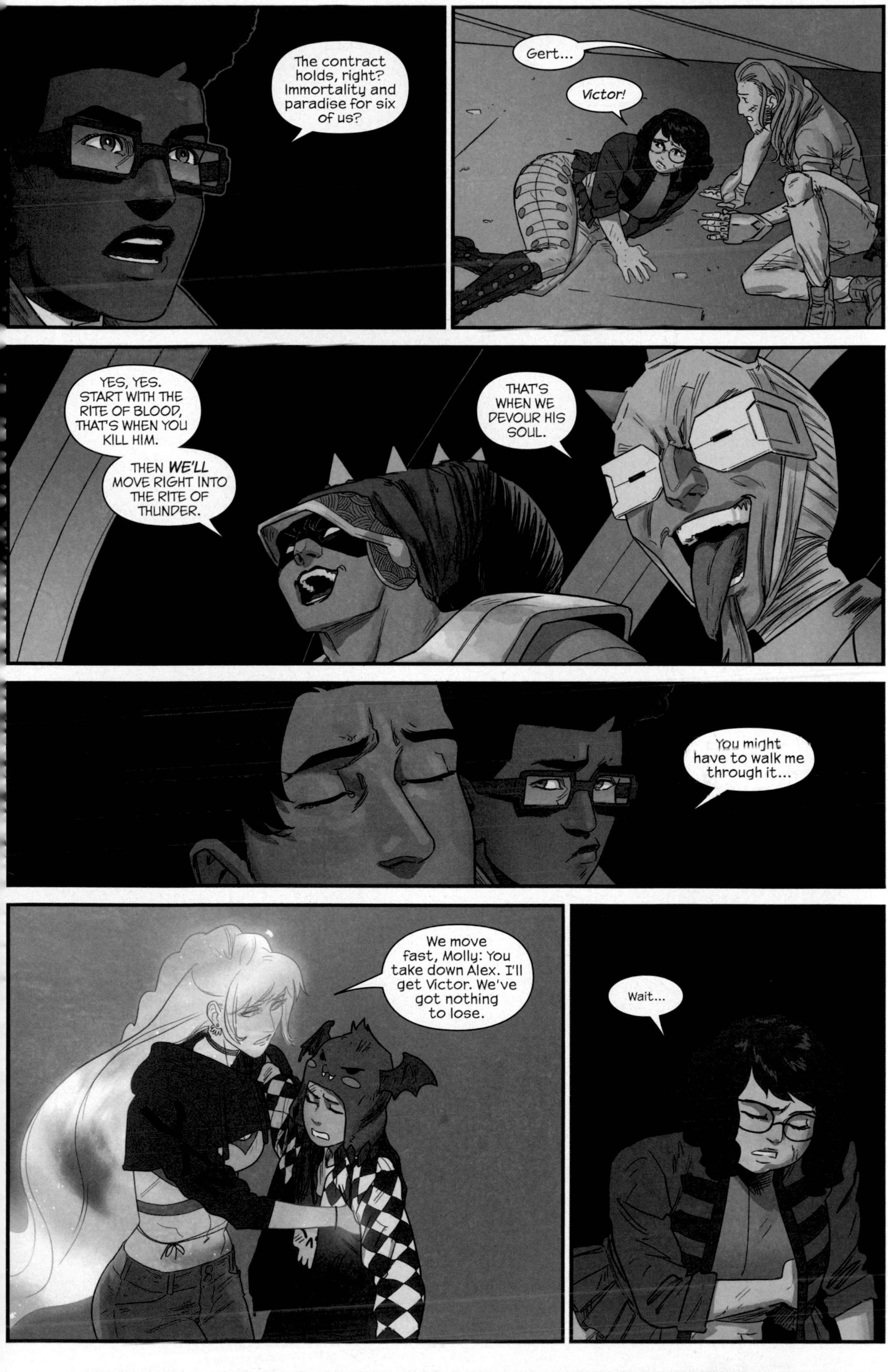
The contract holds, right? Immortality and paradise for six of us?
Gert...
Victor!
YES, YES. START WITH THE RITE OF BLOOD, THAT'S WHEN YOU KILL HIM.
THEN *WE'LL* MOVE RIGHT INTO THE RITE OF THUNDER.
THAT'S WHEN WE DEVOUR HIS SOUL.
You might have to walk me through it...
We move fast, Molly: You take down Alex. I'll get Victor. We've got nothing to lose.
Wait...

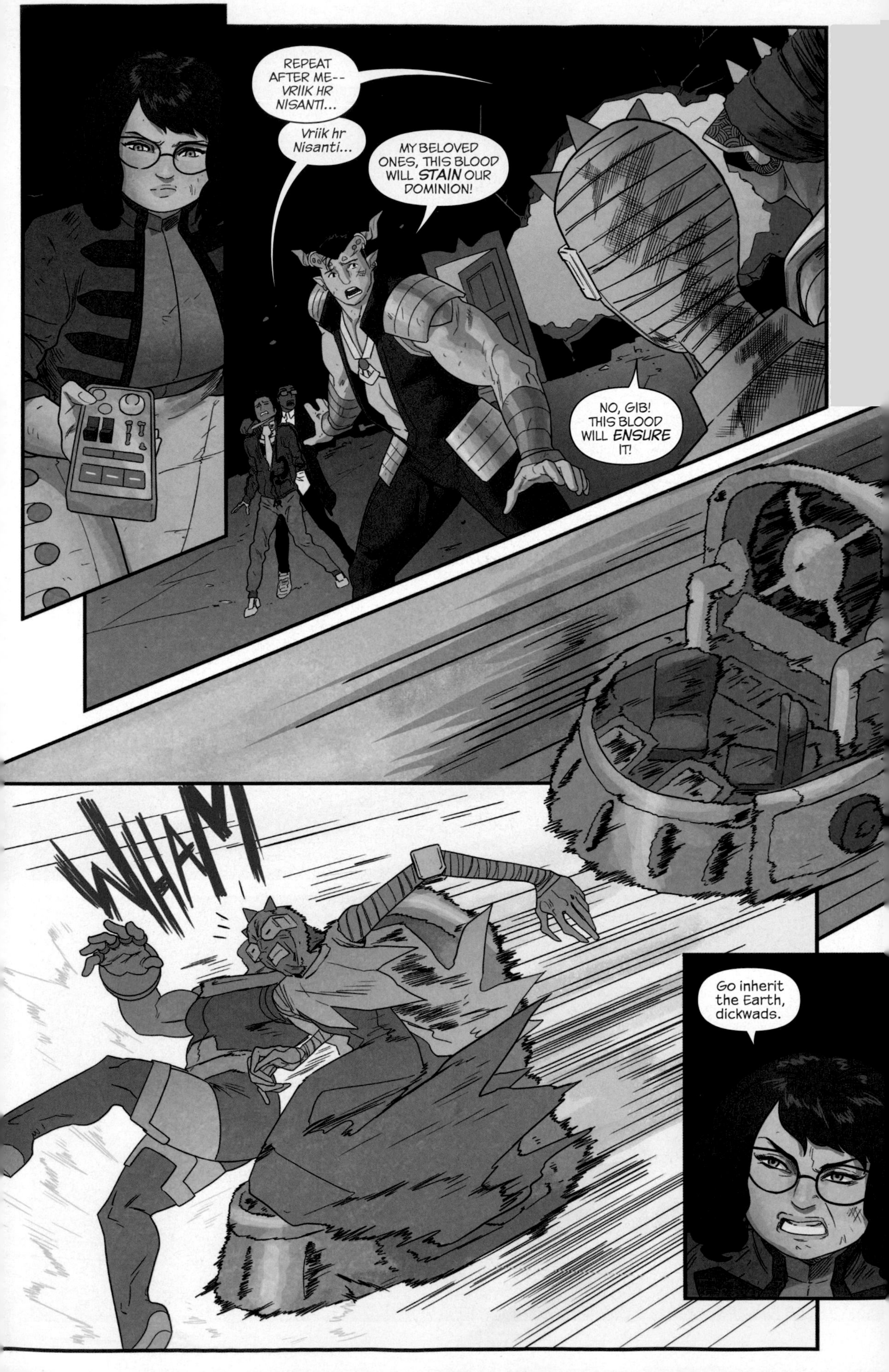
REPEAT AFTER ME-- VRIIK HR NISANTI...
Vriik hr Nisanti...
MY BELOVED ONES, THIS BLOOD WILL STAIN OUR DOMINION!
NO, GIB! THIS BLOOD WILL ENSURE IT!
WHAM
Go inherit the Earth, dickwads.

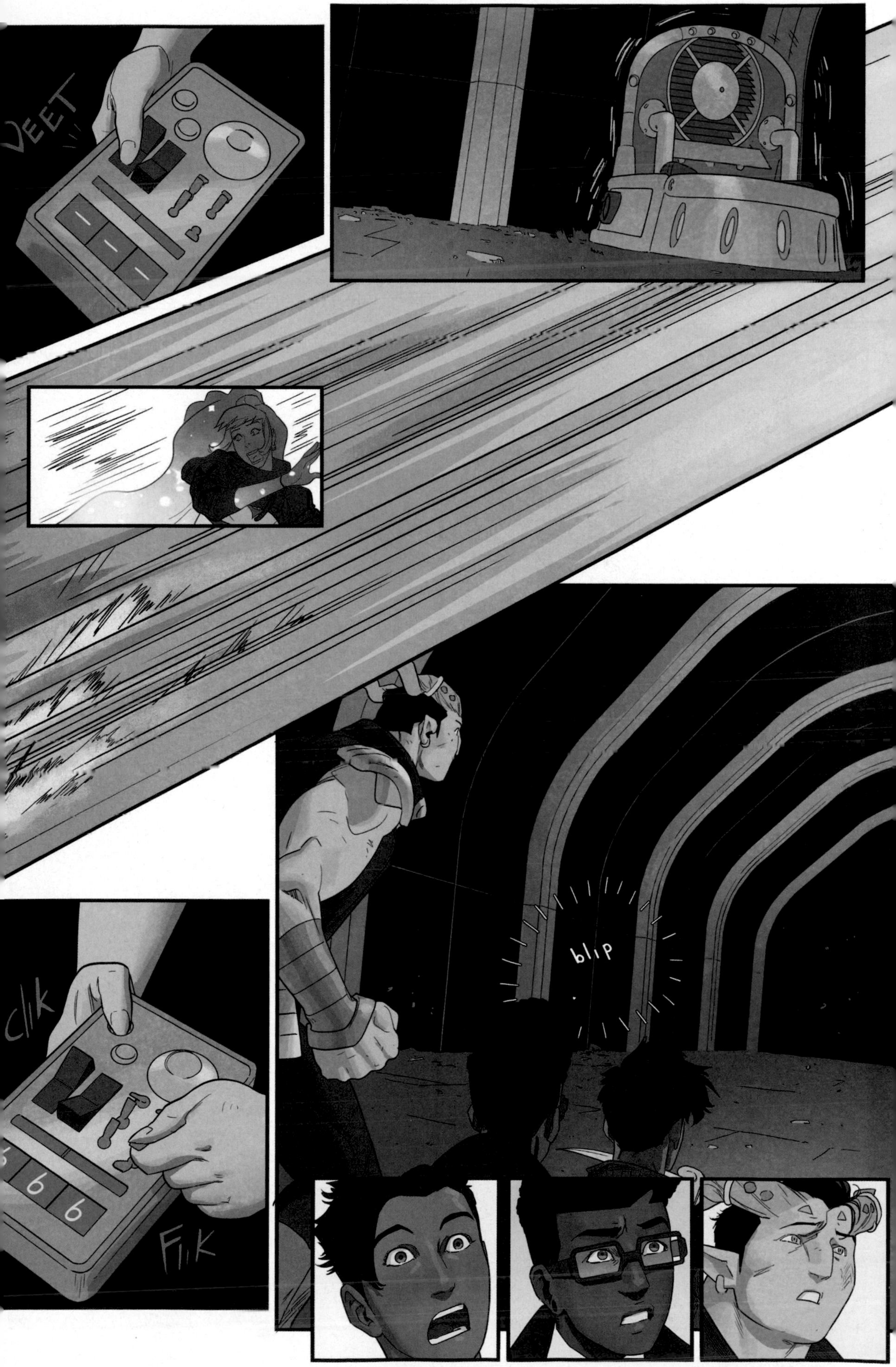
VEET
blip
clik
FLIK

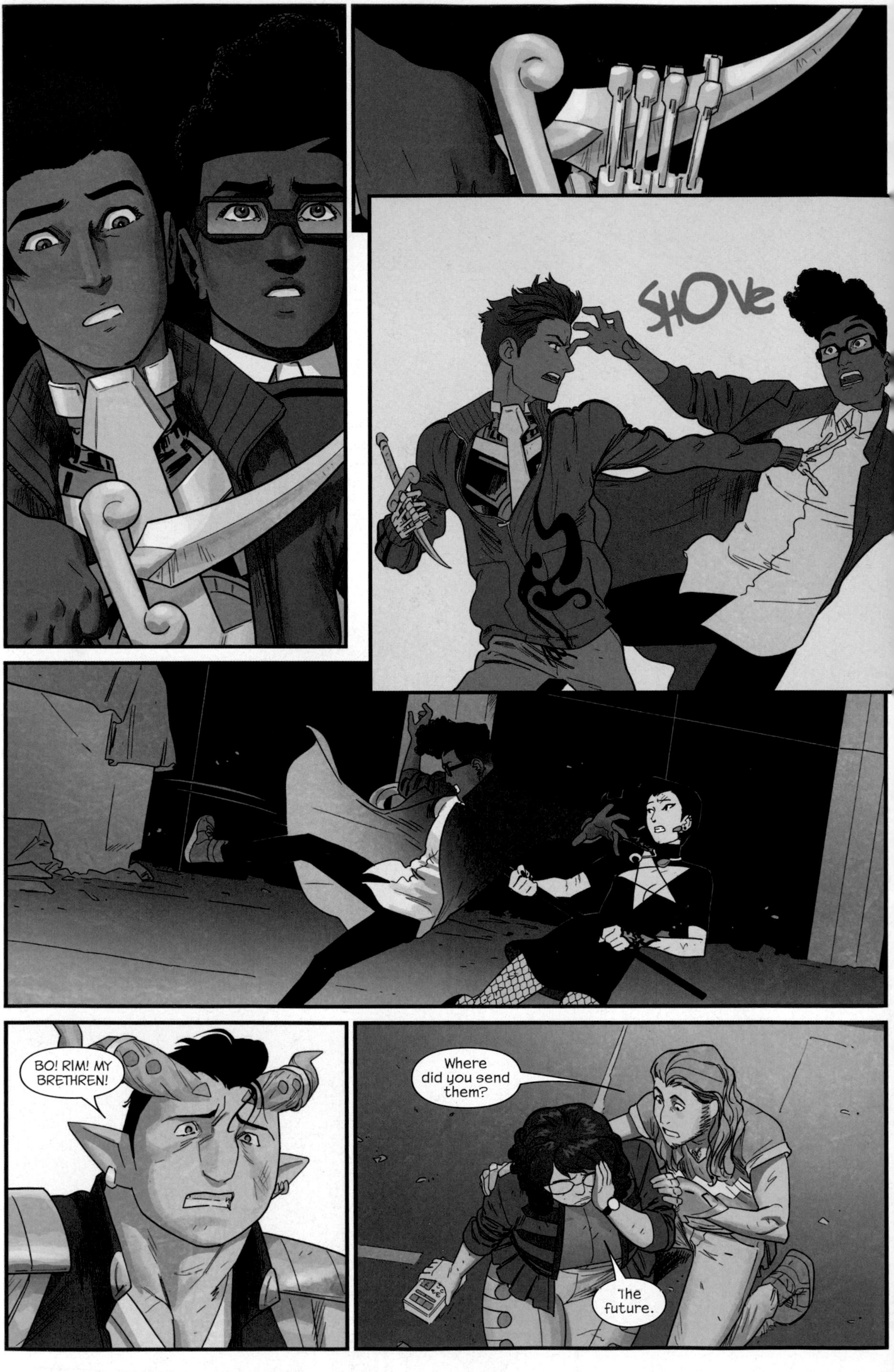
SHOVE
BO! RIM! MY BRETHREN!
Where did you send them?
The future.

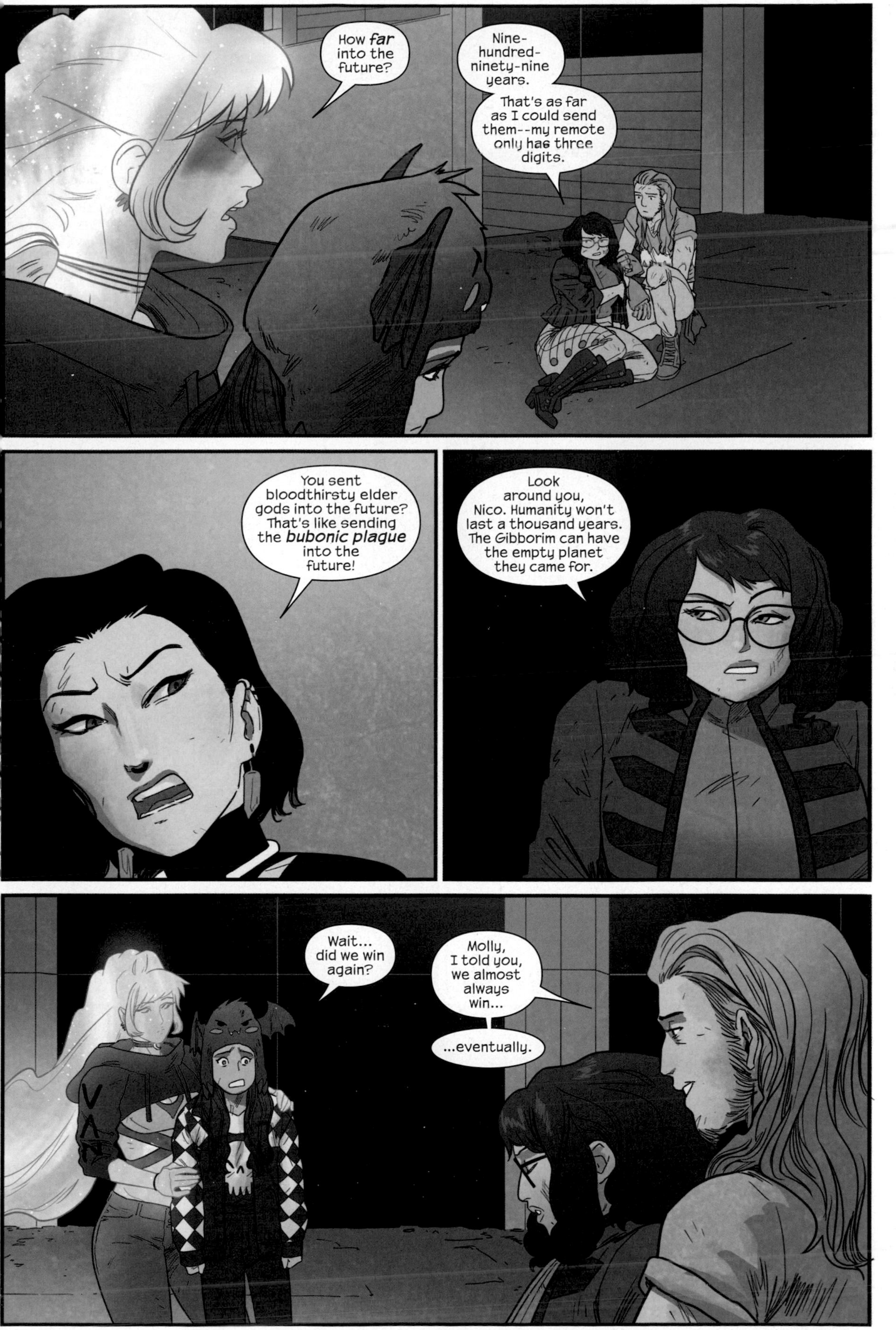
How *far* into the future?
Nine-hundred-ninety-nine years.
That's as far as I could send them--my remote only has three digits.
You sent bloodthirsty elder gods into the future? That's like sending the ***bubonic plague*** into the future!
Look around you, Nico. Humanity won't last a thousand years. The Gibborim can have the empty planet they came for.
Wait... did we win again?
Molly, I told you, we almost always win...
...eventually.

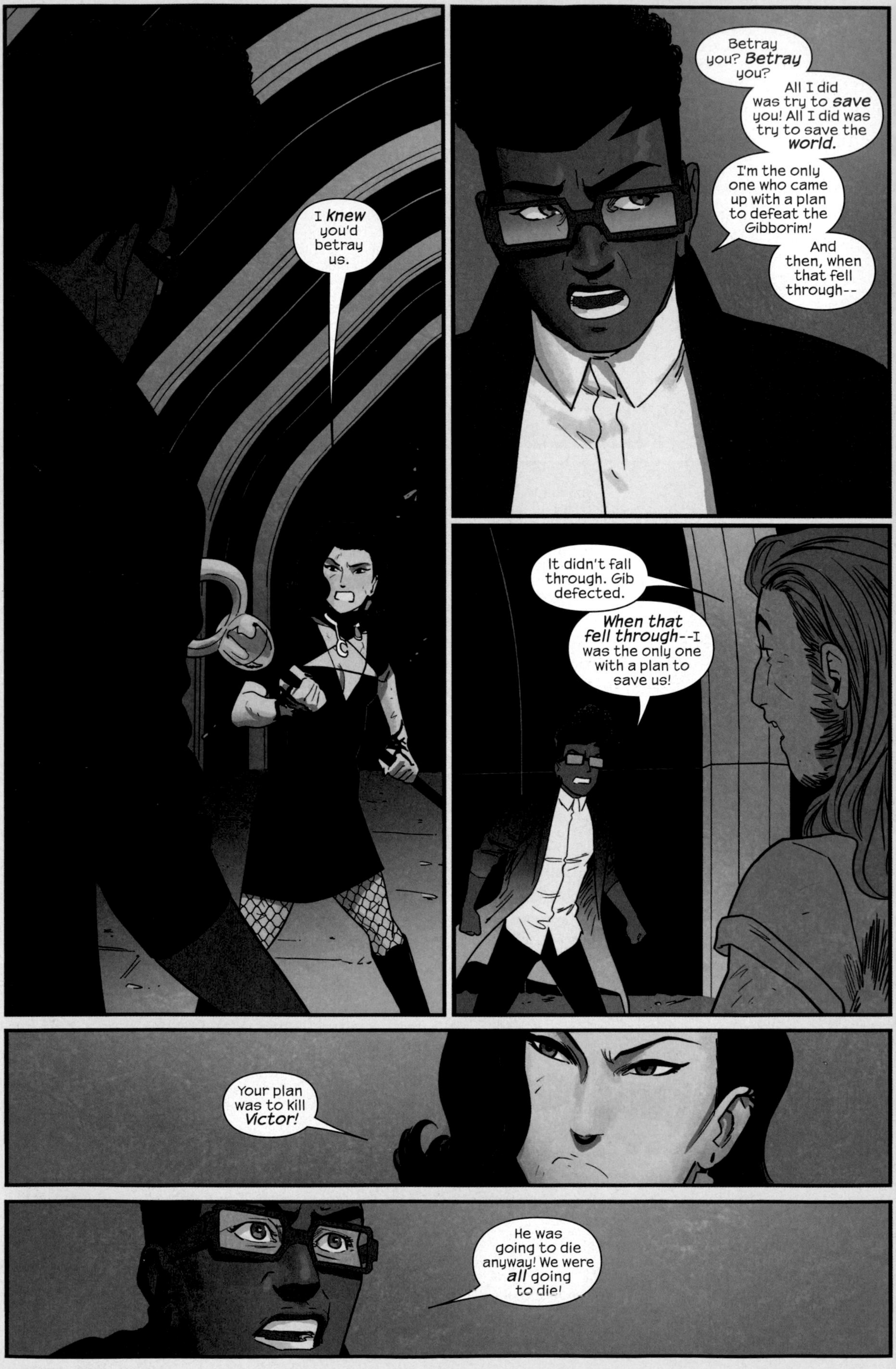
I knew you'd betray us.
Betray you? Betray you?
All I did was try to save you! All I did was try to save the world.
I'm the only one who came up with a plan to defeat the Gibborim!
And then, when that fell through--
It didn't fall through. Gib defected.
When that fell through--I was the only one with a plan to save us!
Your plan was to kill Victor!
He was going to die anyway! We were all going to die!

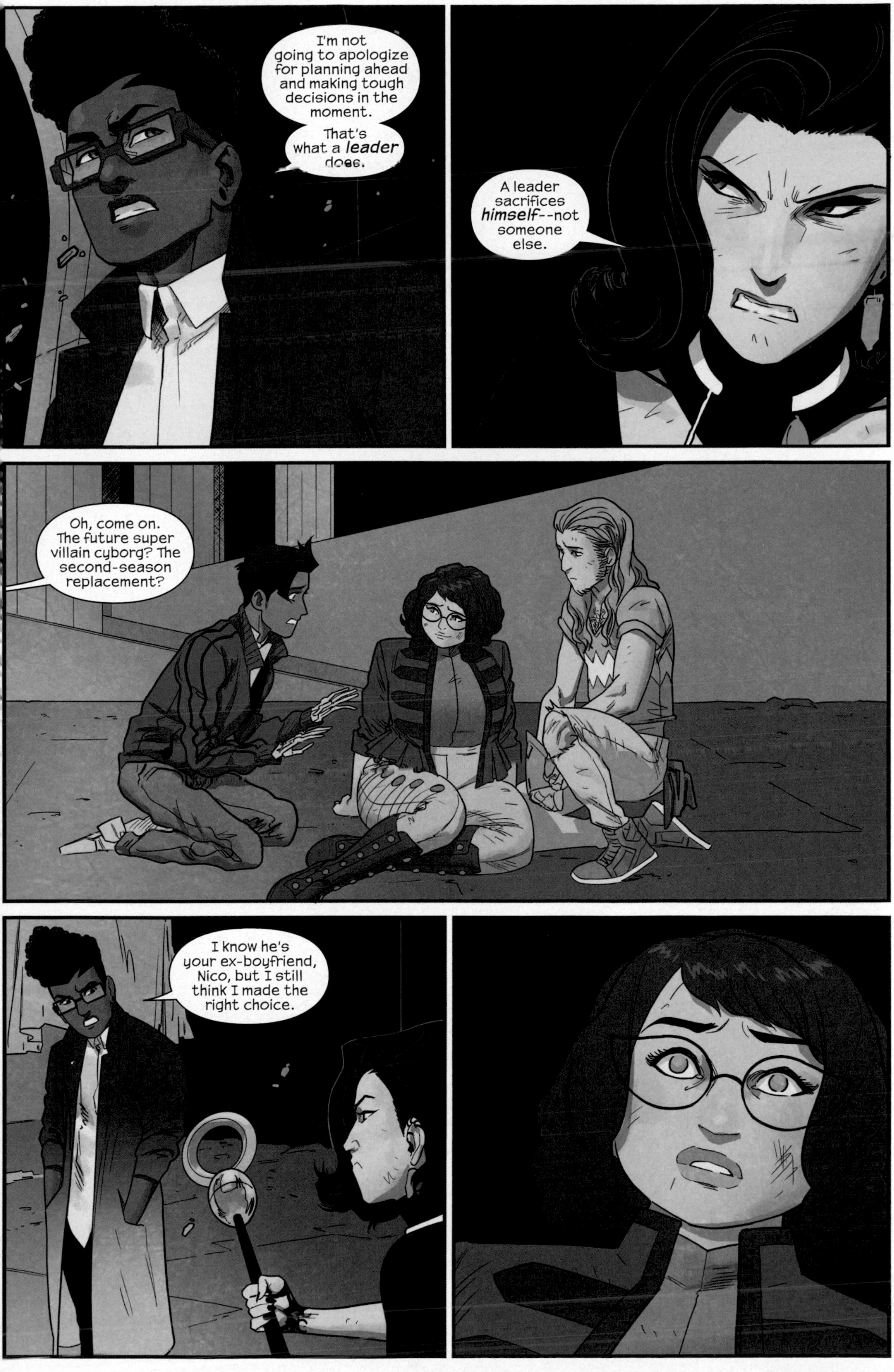
I'm not going to apologize for planning ahead and making tough decisions in the moment.
That's what a *leader* does.
A leader sacrifices *himself*--not someone else.
Oh, come on. The future super villain cyborg? The second-season replacement?
I know he's your ex-boyfriend, Nico, but I still think I made the right choice.

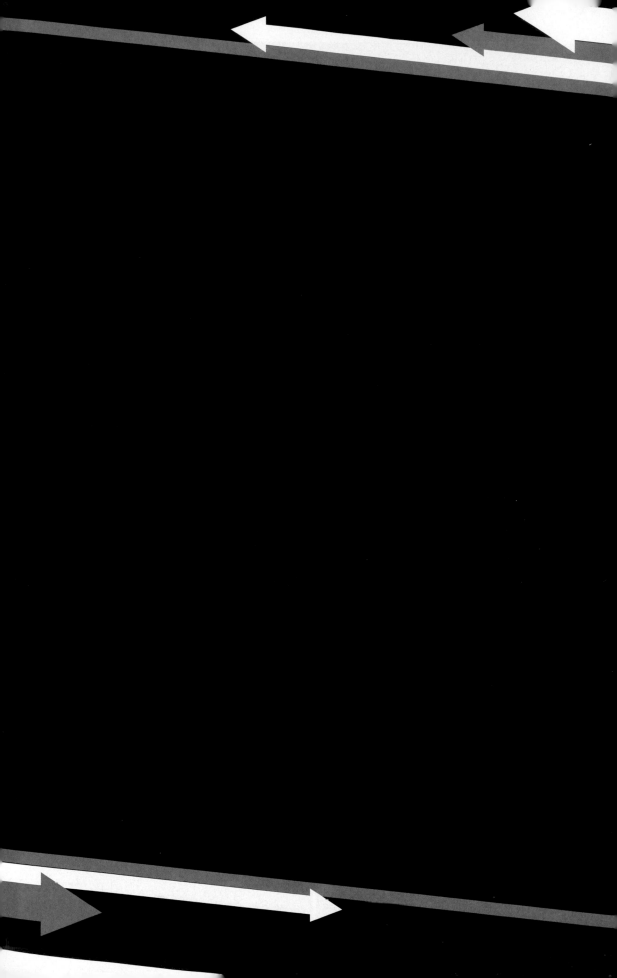

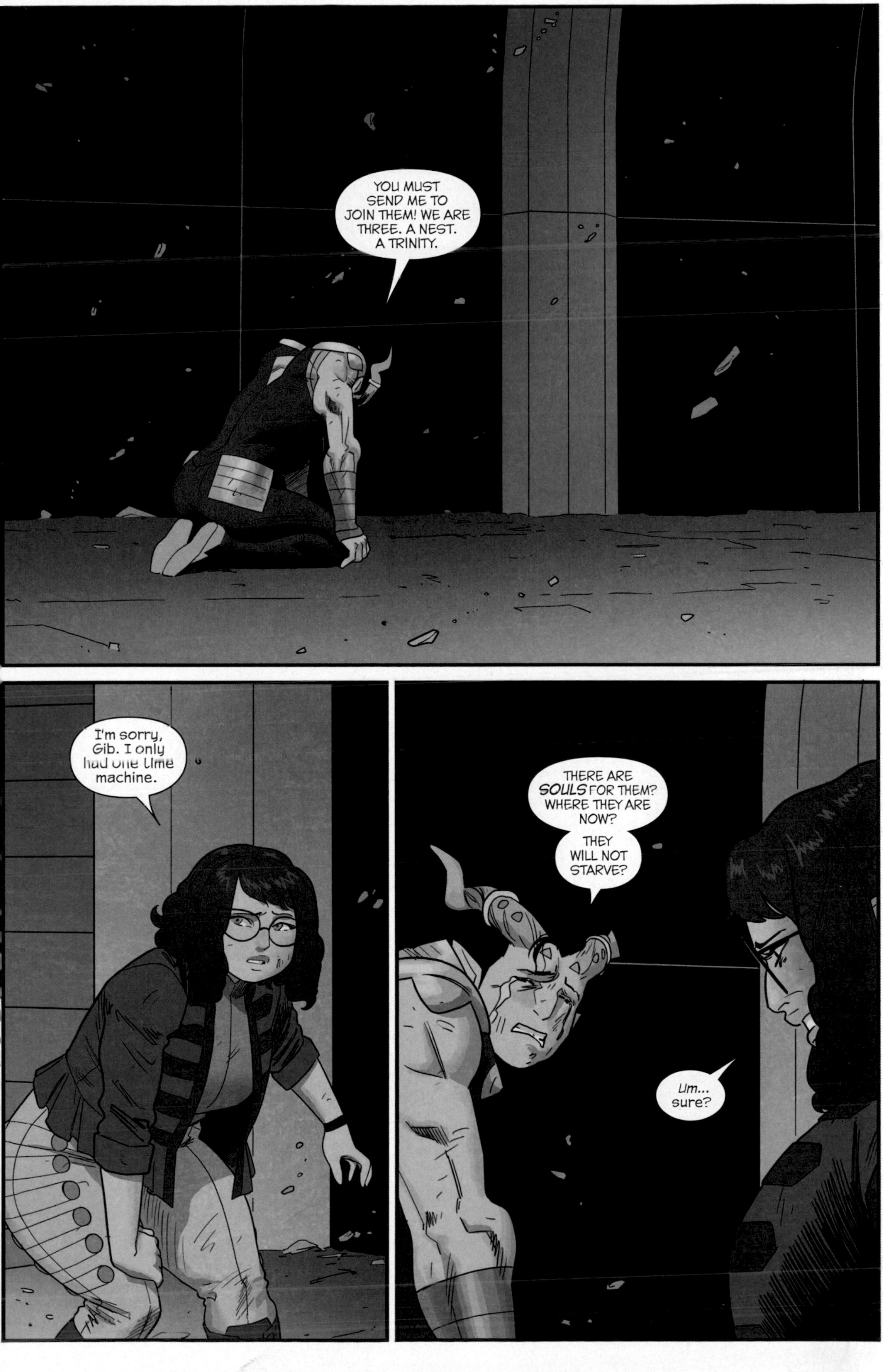
YOU MUST SEND ME TO JOIN THEM! WE ARE THREE. A NEST. A TRINITY.
I'm sorry, Gib. I only had one time machine.
THERE ARE SOULS FOR THEM? WHERE THEY ARE NOW?
THEY WILL NOT STARVE?
Um... sure?

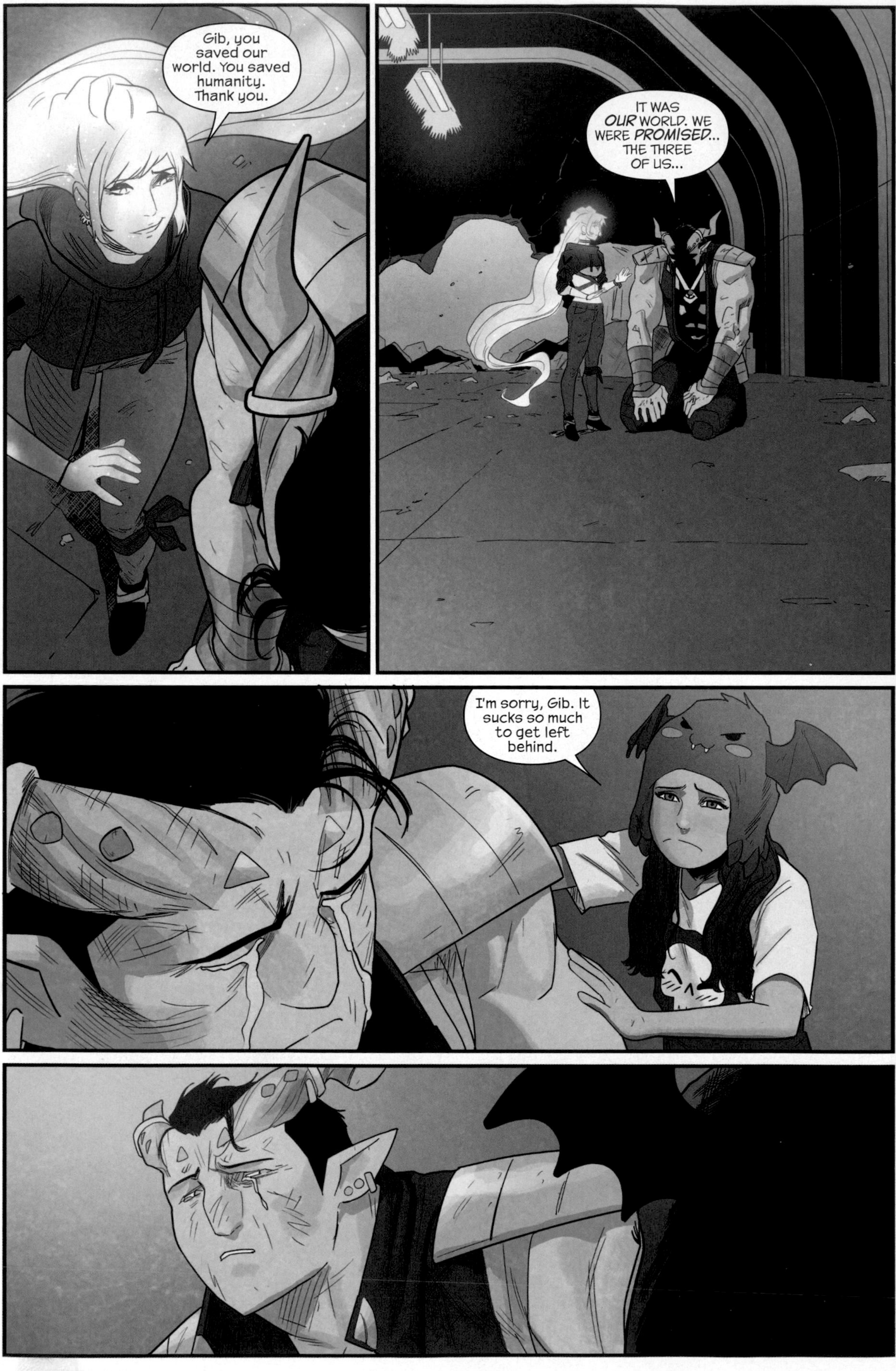
Gib, you saved our world. You saved humanity. Thank you.
IT WAS OUR WORLD. WE WERE PROMISED... THE THREE OF US...
I'm sorry, Gib. It sucks so much to get left behind.

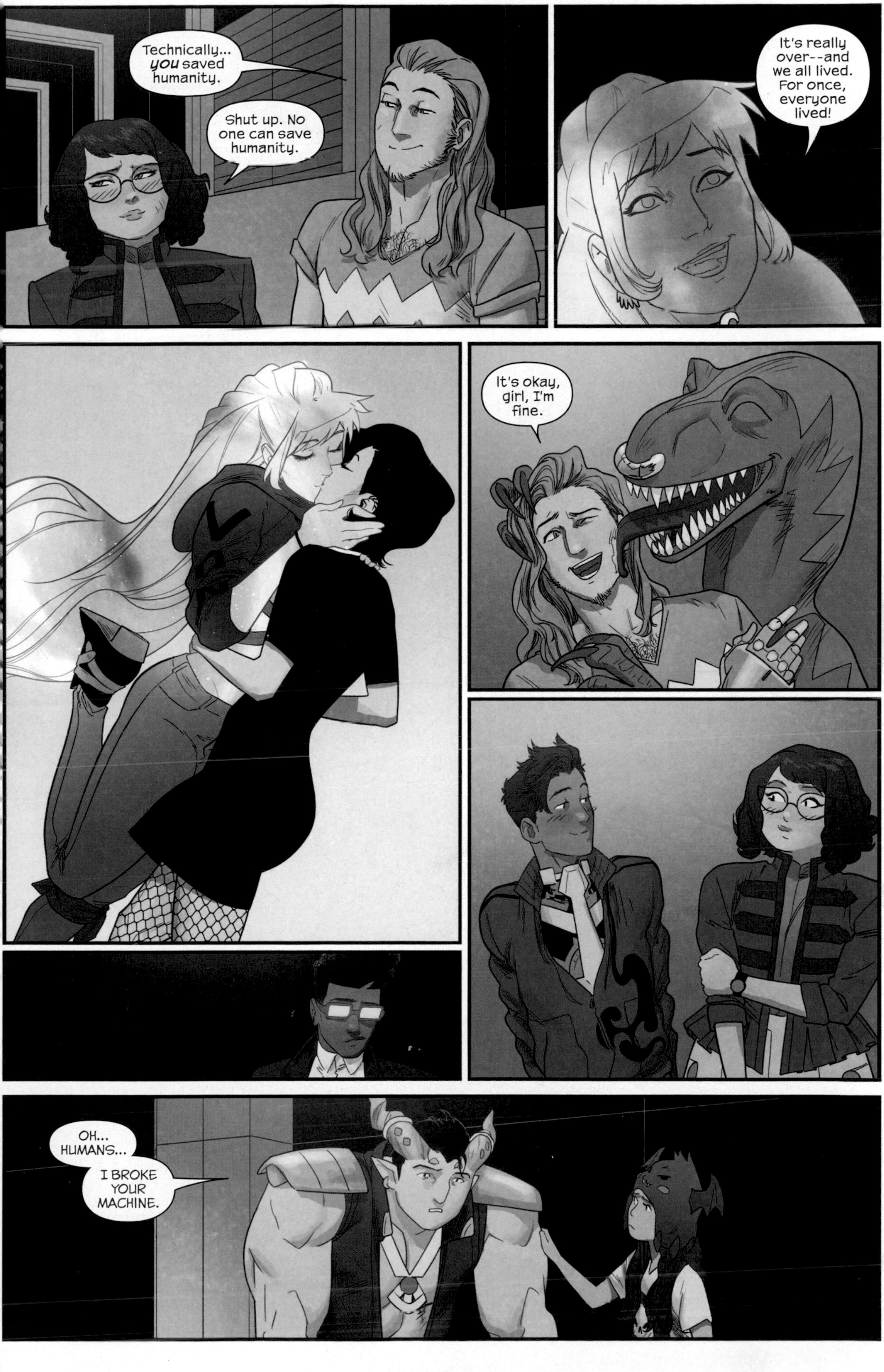
Technically... you saved humanity.
Shut up. No one can save humanity.
It's really over--and we all lived. For once, everyone lived!
It's okay, girl, I'm fine.
OH... HUMANS...
I BROKE YOUR MACHINE.

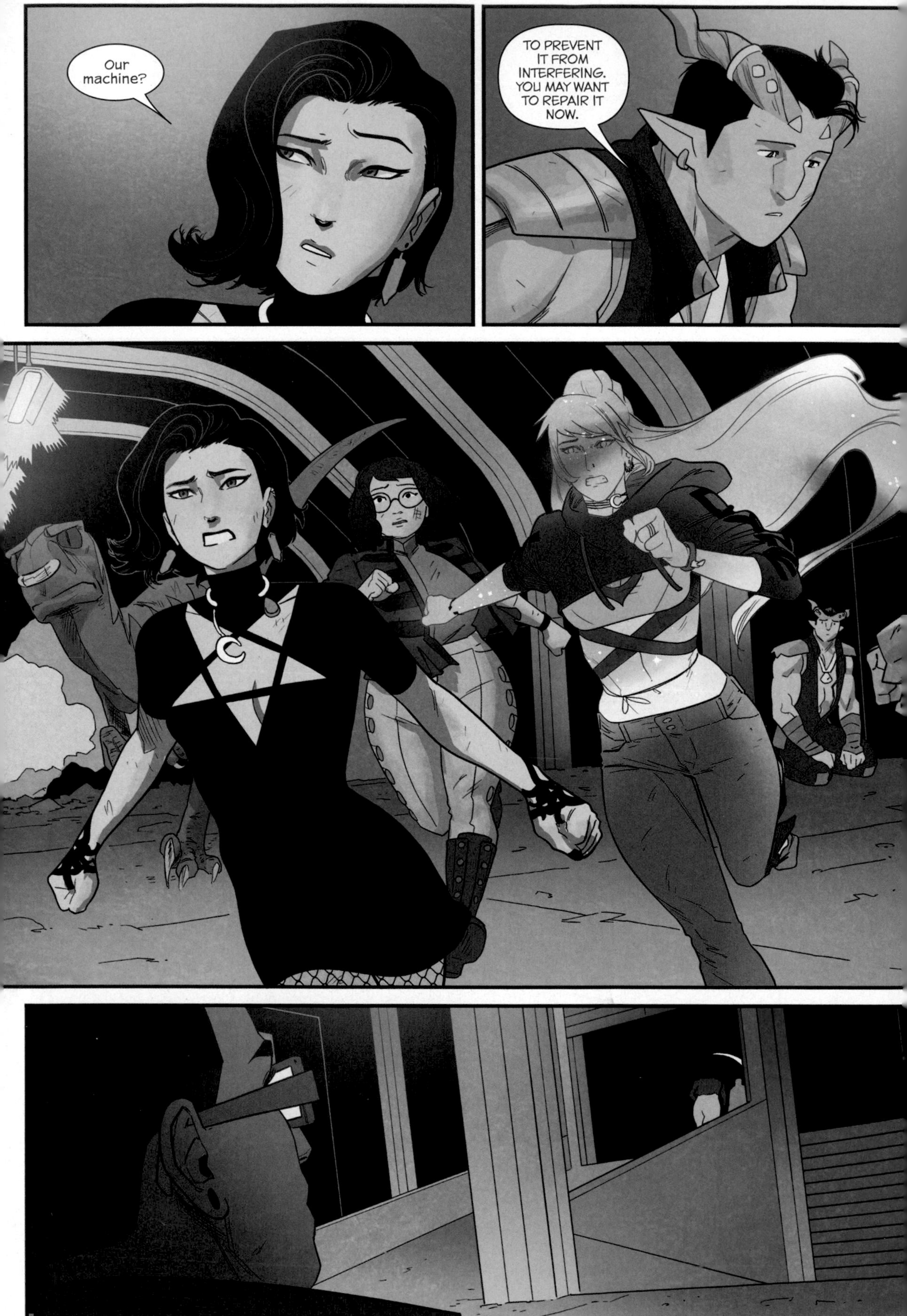
Our machine?
TO PREVENT IT FROM INTERFERING. YOU MAY WANT TO REPAIR IT NOW.

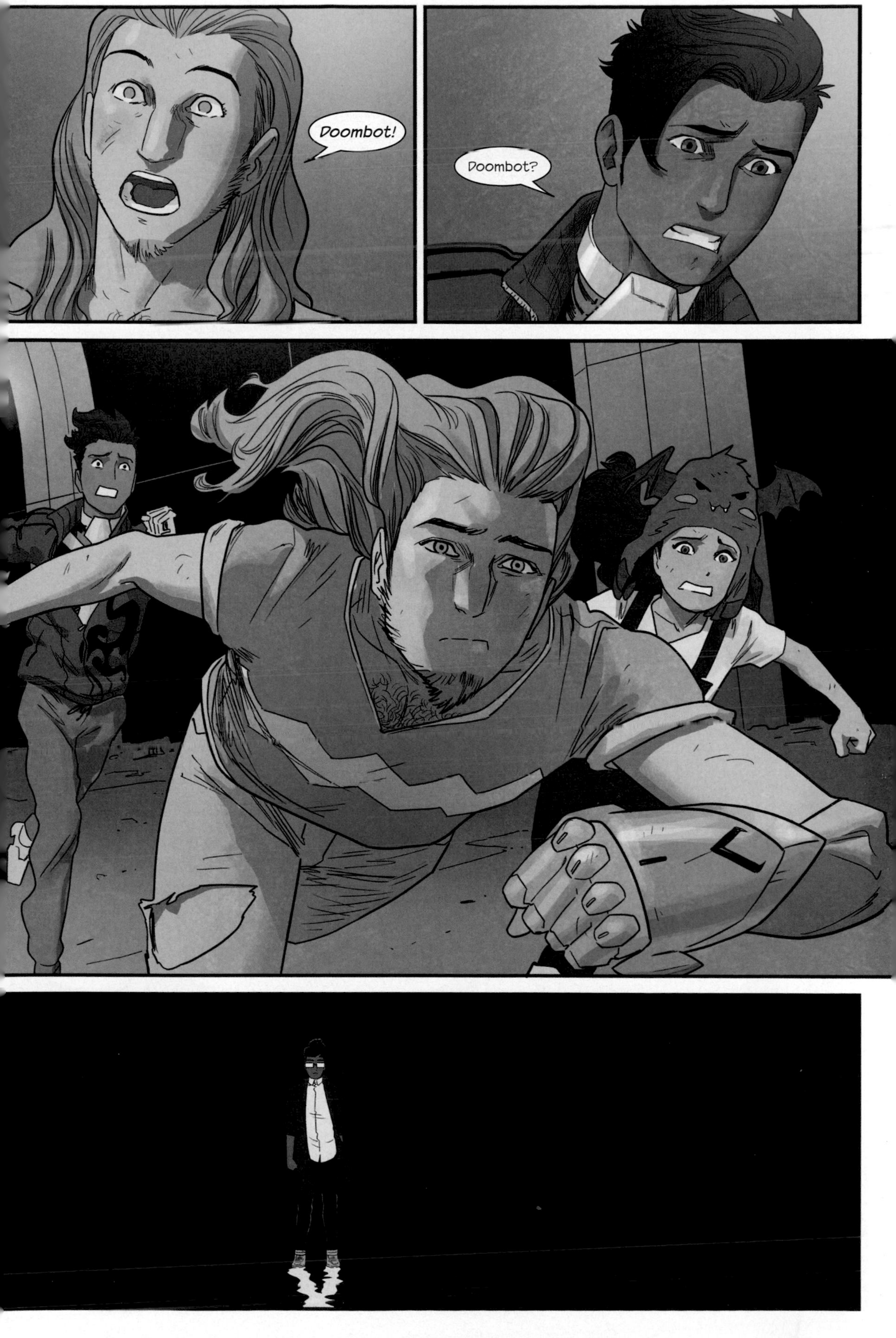
Doombot!
Doombot?

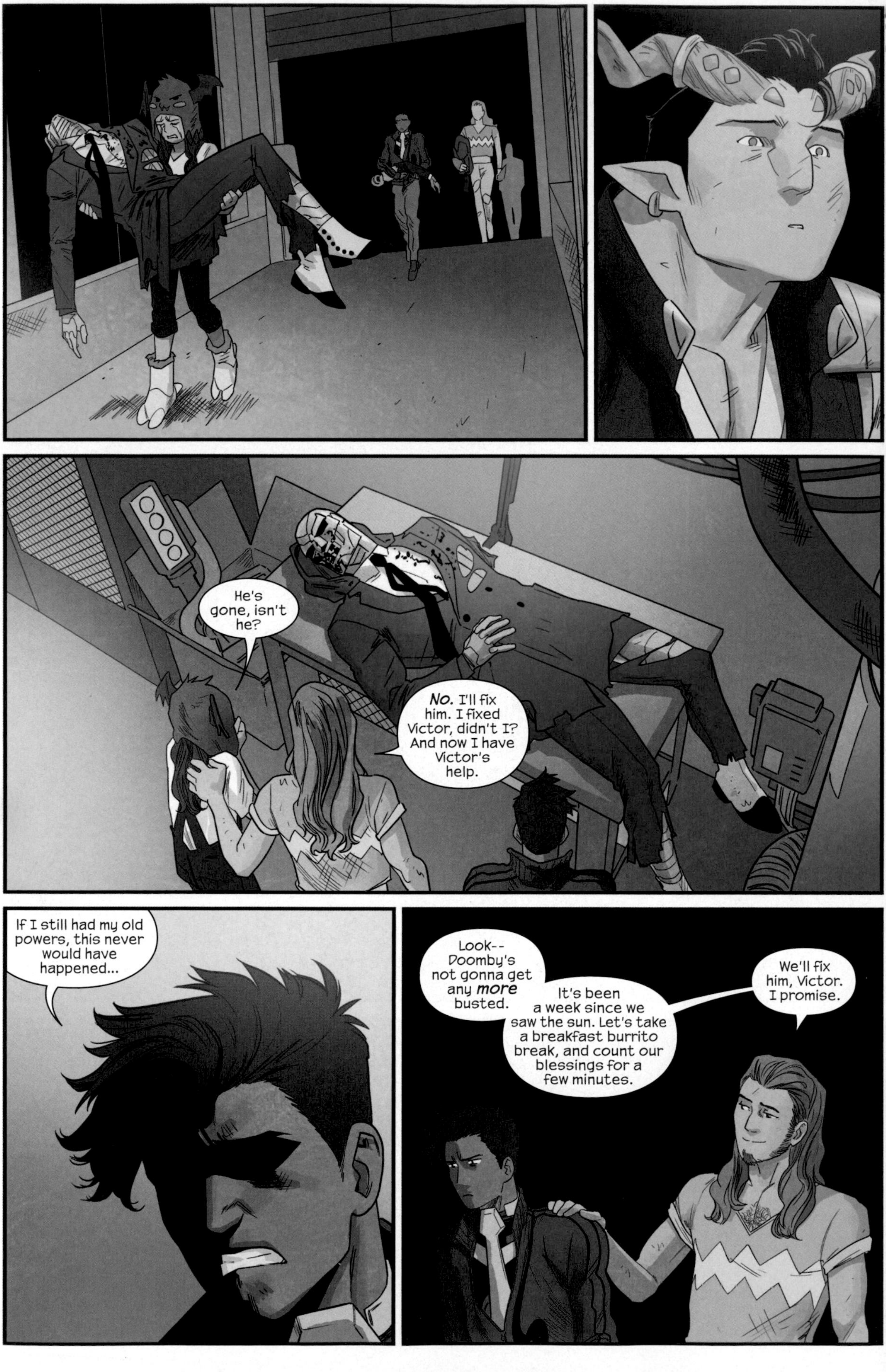
He's gone, isn't he?
NO. I'll fix him. I fixed Victor, didn't I? And now I have Victor's help.
If I still had my old powers, this never would have happened...
Look-- Doomby's not gonna get any more busted.
It's been a week since we saw the sun. Let's take a breakfast burrito break, and count our blessings for a few minutes.
We'll fix him, Victor. I promise.

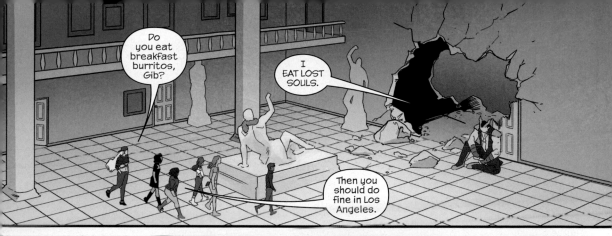

Do you eat breakfast burritos, Gib?

I EAT LOST SOULS.

Then you should do fine in Los Angeles.

Does that mean you have to kill people? Or *we* have to kill people? To keep you alive?

I DO NOT KNOW, PRIDELING.

Please don't call me that. I'm Karolina.

I'm going to see if Alex wants a breakfast burrito.

You're going to do *what?* Murderers don't get burritos!

Is that how it's going to be? Are we going to pretend we weren't *all* ready to kill Gib?

No offense, Gib. It's been a topsy-turvy half hour.

Yeah, but then Alex turned on us--because Alex *always* turns on us--he was ready to kill *Victor!*

Look, I'm not Team Alex or anything, but in the scenario you're referring to, we were *all* going to die. All of us, including Victor, and everybody else on Earth.

So...

I'm gonna go see if Alex wants a burrito...

Well, he's not staying.

"Team Alex"? There is no Team Alex...

I think Alex is gone.

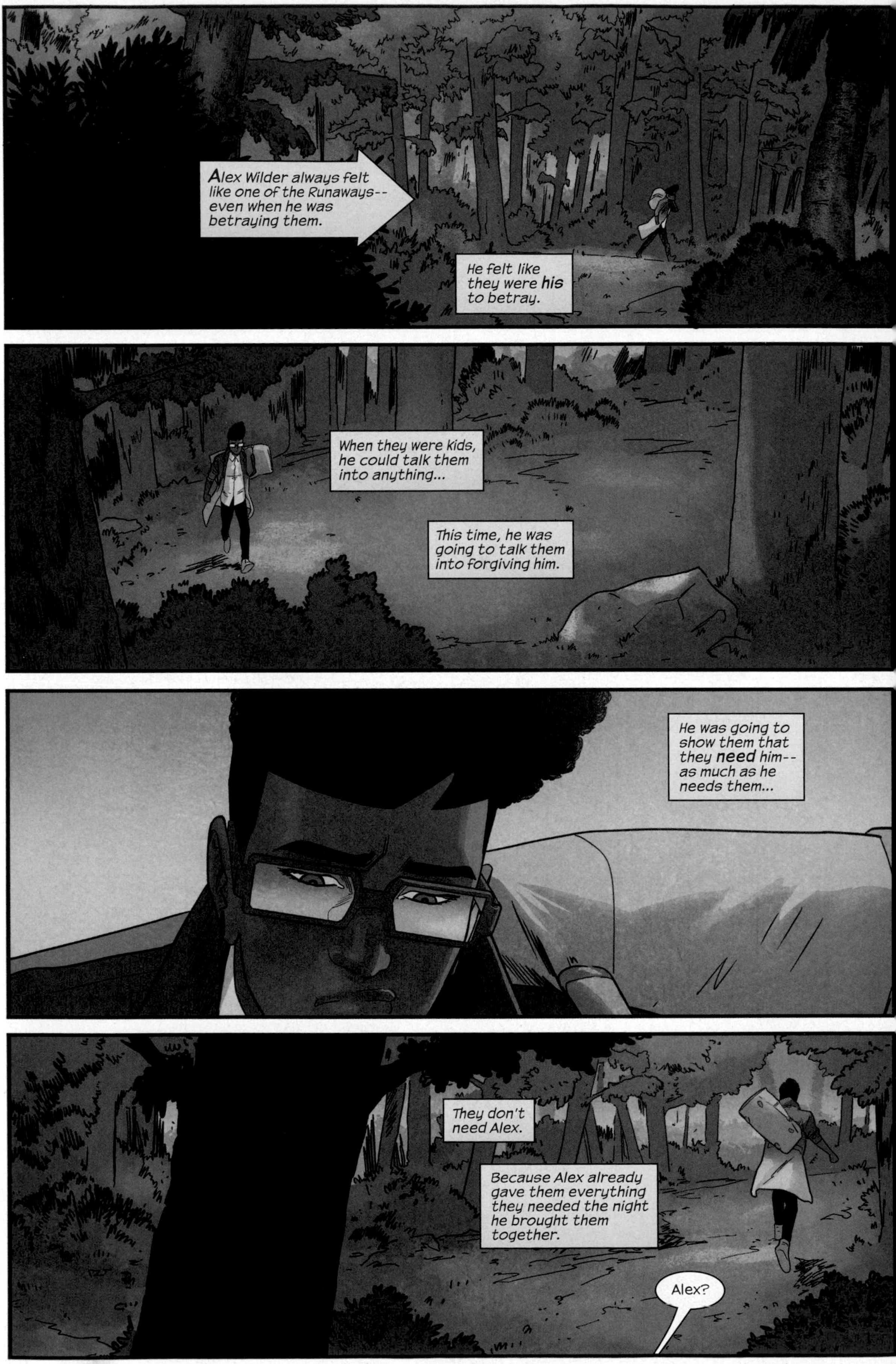
Alex Wilder always felt like one of the Runaways-- even when he was betraying them.
He felt like they were **his** to betray.
When they were kids, he could talk them into anything...
This time, he was going to talk them into forgiving him.
He was going to show them that they **need** him-- as much as he needs them...
They don't need Alex.
Because Alex already gave them everything they needed the night he brought them together.
Alex?

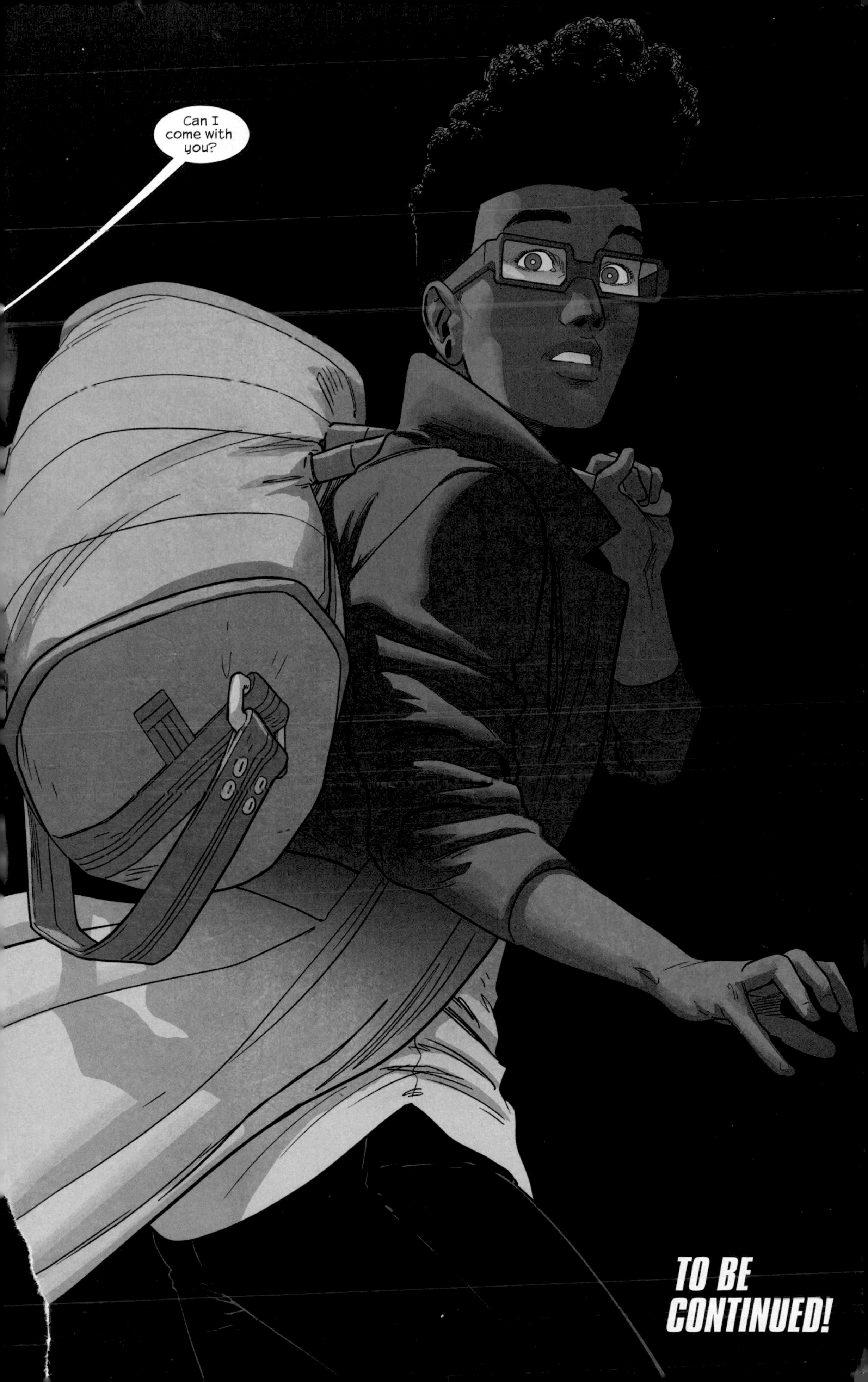
Can I come with you?
TO BE CONTINUED!

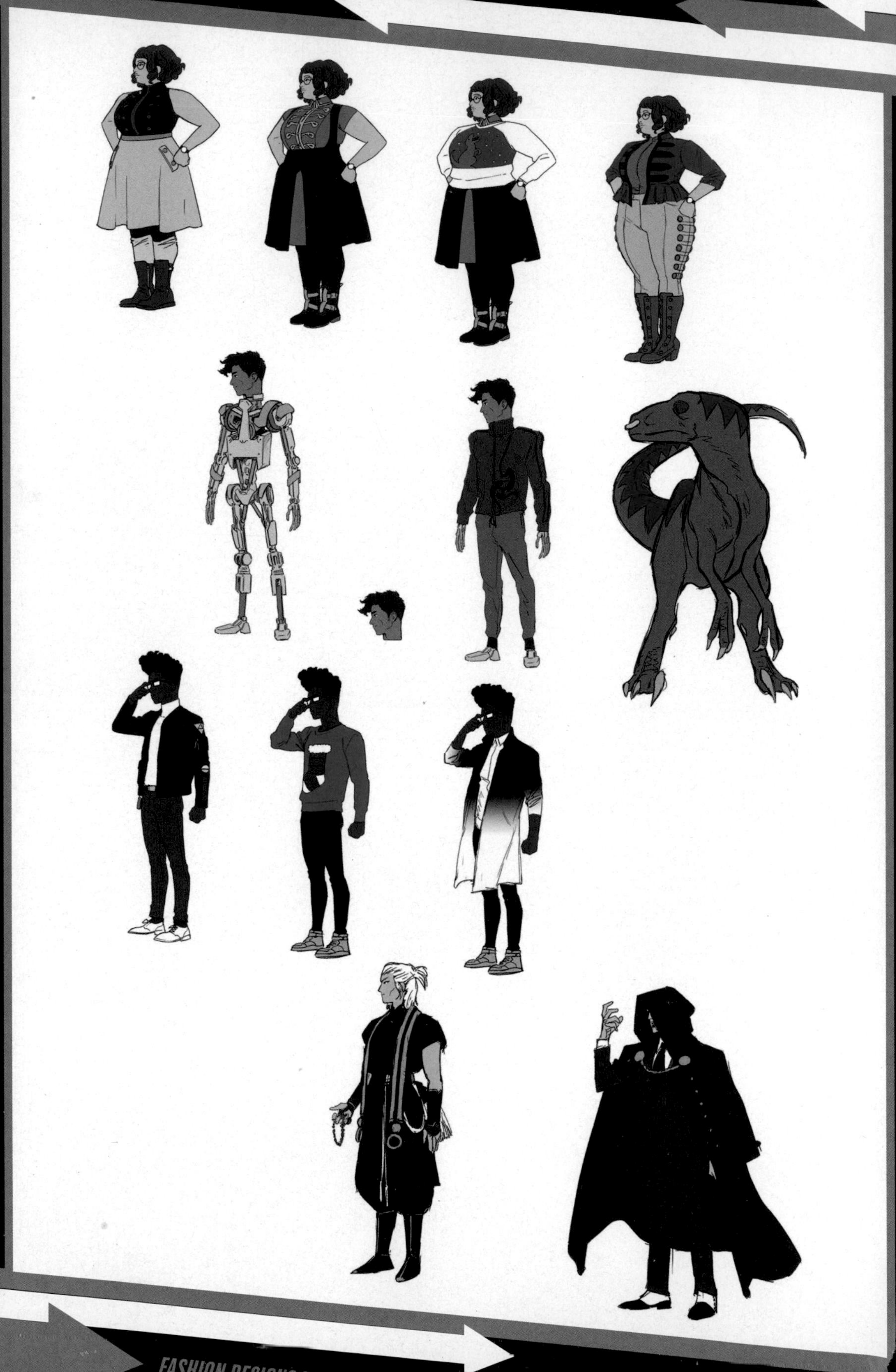

FASHION DESIGNS BY KRIS ANKA